DIE
HAPPY

DIE
HAPPY

499 THINGS EVERY GUY'S GOTTA DO
WHILE HE STILL CAN

TIM BURKE *and* MICHAEL BURKE

 ST. MARTIN'S GRIFFIN ⚟ NEW YORK

www.stmartins.com

Book design by Jonathan Bennett

Illustrations by Mark Matcho

Library of Congress Cataloging-in-Publication Data

Burke, Tim, 1972–
    Die happy : 499 things every guy's gotta do while he still can / Tim
Burke and Michael Burke.
        p. cm.
    ISBN-10: 0-312-35620-X (pbk.)
    ISBN-13: 978-0-312-35620-0
    1. Travel—Guidebooks.   2. Men—Travel—Guidebooks.
I. Title: 499 things every guy's gotta do while he still can.
II. Title: Four hundred ninety-nine things every guy's gotta do while he still
can.   III. Burke, Michael, 1975–   IV. Title.

G153.4.B85 2006
910.81—dc22

                                                              2006040026

First Edition: May 2006

10 9 8 7 6 5 4 3 2 1

CONTENTS

7. LOST WEEKENDS
- Pub Crawls. Poker Tournament. Grunk Dolf. Paintball. Parties. Impersonation Weekend. Rent a Porsche. Destination Unknown. Crash a Wedding.

8. DON'T WAIT. PLAN IT. DO IT
- Motivational Scare Tactics. Top Ten Lists. Your Own Top 25 List. Year 1. Year 2. Year 3. Year 4. Your "Check It Off" Accomplishments.

ACKNOWLEDGMENTS

We'd like to thank Tim's wife, Jennifer, for her support, tolerance, and sense of humor. Dan Lazar, our dutiful agent. Ben Sevier, our helpful editor. Every guy who said, "Oh yeah, I've got a story for you." Our brother, Brian. And, of course, our parents, who hopefully will find this book amusing, not appalling.

NOTE FROM THE AUTHORS

All stories are used here thanks to our friends and their own inter-
pretation of their lives. Sure, they may have embellished a little,
but they never let the truth get in the way of a good story. Some
names have also been changed on the off chance somebody runs
for president.

DIE

HAPPY

INTRODUCTION

Hey, let's face it, there are certain things in life that unfortunately come with an expiration date. Yes, it sucks. And most likely, you won't even realize this until it is way, way too late. It may hit you as you're standing with a pricing gun loosely gripped in your hand while your bride-to-be debates which bathroom towel she longs to put on the registry. Or it could come to you later when you're trying to put together one lousy poker night with the guys, only to be trumped by a "shower" of some kind at Mark and Betsy's new townhouse. Or it could creep up on you one evening as you're sitting down at the kitchen table perusing dozens of vacation brochures, only to notice that every single cover has a mascot on it. It might be an animal, a pirate, or a mermaid . . . it doesn't matter. Your life is no longer what it once was. For most of us, it's not a matter of **if** this scenario will happen; it's purely a matter of **when**.

Don't get us wrong, setting down is really not that bad. Marriage, kids, and the whole bit is a good thing. However, you have to trust us when we tell you that **the window for many unbelievable experiences is only open for a limited time**. *Just think about it.* You cannot (for reasons we all understand) experience Mardi Gras properly when you're forty-five years old—married or not. You cannot leave your wife and kids **(if you still want them to be there when you return)** at the last minute to road trip across Italy for three weeks with your best friends. And you cannot stroll through the Red Light District of Amsterdam toting a stroller. Plus, if you ever want to learn something, like how to rock climb, play serious poker, or make a French woman scream, "Oui, Oui!," this is the time to make it happen. You may not believe that your time is running out, but please trust us. Thumb through this book and think hard about what appeals to you. Let's say you read our description of the Exotic Erotic Ball in chapter 1 and decide you can't miss it (we wholeheartedly agree, by the way). Now imagine yourself standing half-naked in a room full of babes with their pretty little heads full of once-a-year dirty thoughts. Next to you is your wife, kids, aging parents, dog, and diaper bag. Sound appealing? Didn't think so.

As far as we go, Tim's time has passed. He's married, has a brand-new baby boy (future second baseman or outfielder, either is fine), and spends a lot of quality time in places like Babies "R" Us, Costco, and Home Depot. Tim's found himself biting his lip through conversations with once-normal guys as they go and on about "the benefits" of their kid's stroller, or how they "really can't wait to move to the suburbs to get away from the craziness of the city." These are dudes who once stayed out until four A.M. every Thursday, puked at work, and still showed up for

Friday happy hour. Tim has seen the demise in others, and can't deny his own movement toward a totally different world. But occasionally he fights the good fight with weekend golf/drinking outings, any friend's bachelor party, and a recent salmon-fishing/drinking expedition. Michael, on the other hand, is a free man. He's out making things happen and having good times at every opportunity. In the last year, he's reeled home a 180-pound marlin in Cabo, engaged in the renowned party boat scene of Lake Travis, and attended a heavyweight bout in Atlantic City.

Together, we've been kicking each other in various directions all our lives. From the time Tim threw his first high school party and Michael observed, learned, passed out on the kitchen floor, and threw a better party the next time around, to Tim's very own bachelor party, at which Tim got a bloody lip from an overly aggressive stage show and Michael quickly realized his natural gift for getting strippers to love his money. All along the way, Tim's given great big-brother advice like, "Michael, go kick that table with the guy dancing on it, watch him fall and spill his beer all over himself," and **"Yeah, you definitely need to do another shot."** One way or another we've been telling each other what to do, taking note of things done well, and not letting the other forget it when opportunities were missed. We're both very, very aware of the importance of the time you have before you get all married, responsible and shit.

Make this period a time of "Remember when . . ." and **"Oh yeah . . . I did that."** Not a "What if?" or an "I should've." The rest of this book is simply a collection of incredible things to do while you still can. We like to think of it as not only a "to-do" and a "how-to," but also an idea generator and a how-to-get-it-done-right.

We've created a **"Check It Off" system** to guide you through. So go ahead and dare yourself to see how many of the incredible, once-in-a-lifetime experiences you can **check off**.

> **NOTE:**
>
> Some of the events and activities listed take place in the great city of New Orleans. We are still in major denial over the devastation that has occurred there, and we sincerely hope it quickly resurrects itself to the grand place it once was.

CHAPTER ONE

FESTS, HOLIDAYS, *and* OTHER MUST-ATTEND HAPPENINGS

Ever seen the look on someone's face when they tell you about their trip to **New Orleans for Mardi Gras**? Or enjoyed the bumbling banter of a couple of friends trying to piece together a memorable (and not-so-memorable) night from **St. Patty's Day in Dublin**? Well, here's a compilation of incredible festivals, holidays, and other annual happenings certain to spawn many unforgettable stories for years and years to come. Yes, you'll still be spewing these tales when you're eighty-five, senile, and crapping in your trousers. That's assuming you remembered to put them on.

NEW YEAR'S EVE

It's midnight. You're seeing double. She's seeing triple. And somehow, despite all the rum-induced blurriness, you still manage to find each other's lips and maul one another among two hundred people doing the same frickin' thing. It's so unbelievably romantic that Meg Ryan should star in a movie about it. Ah, you gotta love New Year's Eve. If it's amateur hour, we don't want to be professionals. This is a time to forget last year and all the ladies that said you smelled funny. It's a time to start new and fresh. It's time for personal rebirth. But first, it's time to get stupid.

Las Vegas

Like peanut butter and jelly, chips and salsa, Paris Hilton and a night vision camera, **some things are just meant for each other**. Vegas and New Year's Eve are no exception. You've got two major options when traveling to Sin City for this momentous holiday. You can hit The Strip, where each hotel offers a different party and at midnight people pack the street for fireworks. Or you can head downtown (where the crowd is a little bit older) for an enclosed block party. We suggest you go to The Strip, **where you and a mere three hundred thousand peeps will get drunk together**.

Booking a flight and hotel should be done early for this popular event. When it comes to the hotel, either go big, with hipster places like **the Hard Rock** and **Mandalay Bay**, or just find the **cheapest internet deal** you can get on The Strip. There's no rule against spending all your waking hours at another hotel. Dinner reservations will be brutal for this holiday . . . so forget it, eat wherever, and **spend your money on booze, blackjack, and a *yo-ladies-get-in-my* limo**. Before you come here, perform some quality due diligence. Find out where the best parties are happening. Call ahead to put your name on any club lists. And get everyone on the same agenda. You'll no doubt lose buddies along the way. "Hey, anyone see Sully since that girl put her hand down his pants?" Have a place to meet up, even if it's the

Spearmint Rhino for lap dances at four A.M. Also, make sure to **place all your college bowl game bets the day before**. Who knows where you'll end up New Year's Day morning and how banged up you may be when you surface. At some point get to the Sports Book and exploit those amateur athletes by winning big on their talent. Like Ralph Macchio in *The Karate Kid,* this year will kick the silly stool out of any New Year's you've ever rang in.

WARNING: Stay away from that woman with the dazzling gold tooth who's really, really interested in seeing your hotel room.

Jost Van Dyke, British Virgin Islands

Accessible only by boat or inner tube, and boasting a permanent population of a mere hundred and fifty souls, this beautiful, hammock-swaying, unspoiled treasure of an island has become an incredible New Year's Eve destination. It all began when **Mick Jagger and a couple of the Beatles** rang in 1970-something here. Before long the secret was out. Today, more than eight thousand people schooner their way here to experience a one-of-a-kind place and event. **Foxy's is *the* bar** here and possibly the **most famous watering hole in all of the Caribbean**. Foxy himself is legendary, and the self-proclaimed "laziest man in the world." Be sure to get a taste of his impromptu comedic calypso sessions. Beyond Foxy's bar, you've got Ali Baba's, Happy Laury's, Soggy Dollar Bar, and Sidney's Peace & Love—great names, great places to enjoy a drink or ten.

For New Year's Eve, this four-square-mile island becomes one big, fun-loving beach fest. **Tropical cocktails, fresh fish, a pig roast and reggae music** all combine to make the perfect island party. Up and down the beach, everyone is jamming and having a good time. You can sleep wherever. Campgrounds are most likely your best option.

Getting here should be done from St. Thomas, Tortola, or another nearby island. Beautiful people abound, and the vibe is friendly, open, and free-spirited. It's not a huge singles scene, but you'll still have options. And you could always journey here with the "right" group of girls. When you're not sporting a pleasurable rum buzz, you can go diving, fishing, kayaking, or just boating with a dinghy rental. Pure paradise, Jost Van Dyke is the **last true Virgin of these islands**, and New Year's Eve makes for a wonderful night to sleep with her.

LINK IT UP: Happy New Year! Now carry on to more water-friendly activities. (See chapter 2 under "Diving, Sailing.")

New Orleans

With absolutely zero off-season, there is no bad time to hit New Orleans . . . only some times better than others. New Year's Eve is most definitely one of those times. You factor in the hopefully warm weather, bars that never close, streets that beg you to wander with open containers and the Sugar Bowl just around the bend—this is one sick place. The party begins on **Bourbon Street**, flows into the **French Quarter**, and around midnight finds itself in **Jackson Square** for the big old Ball Drop. What happens along the way and how you manage the chaos is totally in your court.

For this special day, you should probably find one all-you-can-everything party to attend, as bars will be packed and lines will be mind-boggling. Pat O'Briens, The Cat's Meow, Razzoo, and Bourbon Street Blues all are worthy of investigation. You can always go someplace less crazy early, then make your way to the madness of Bourbon Street. But hell, you're in New Orleans—do as you're supposed to do. If you really want to check something special off your list, **get**

tickets to a Bourbon Street Balcony and hover above the masses like the king you are. Also, obtain any and all beads ahead of time. You will discover that getting girls to flash their boobies never gets old, running out is a problem, and prices on Bourbon Street are retarded. For added shenanigans, bring along a voodoo doll, tell the ladies to pleasure him and then you. **Strip clubs are omnipresent** and fall into several categories, ranging from "pretty sweet" to "do not touch me, sleazy." **Casinos** are here to take your money. And lastly, bring a camera, because at some point you'll be running on blank tape and this will be the best way to remember what a great time you had and what a depraved human being you truly are. Upon waking up the next day, head out for a world-famous New Orleans Bloody Mary and start all over again.

WARNING: If you find yourself being smothered by the breasts of a large forty-something divorcee from Mississippi, use the straw from your Hurricane to breathe.

Prague

While everyone else is jammed in an overcrowded bar where a hundred bucks gets you an endless, but not easy-to-obtain supply of booze until midnight and second-hand nibbles from a nasty cheese-and-fruit spread, **you are halfway across the world toasting Budvar with aspiring Czechoslovakian models**, taking a drag of some fine Eastern European wacky weed, and witnessing a fireworks display that you'll have no choice but to describe with a drunken, "Dude— that is *awesome!!*"

Prague is far away, but it is a huge New Year's Eve destination. They refer to the celebration as "Silvestri," as it's the feast day of Pope

Silvestri. If he only knew how people were commemorating his big day. Anyhow, **plan to take at least a week off** to come here. Before or after New Year's, you can easily pop over to other European spots to maximize your time. In Prague, you can find hostels, cheap hotels, and even rental apartments—whatever fits your cash flow situation. The night of New Year's Eve, you can easily and aimlessly wander your way from bar to bar getting to know all your fellow celebrants. Or you can attend one of the bigger venues, like the Palak Akropolis, that are filled with DJs, bands, and a whole lot of hoopla. Wherever you are, at midnight tag along with the friends you've made to **Old Town Square or Charles Bridge for the huge fireworks display**. It's cold here, so grab a helping of whiskey for the road, find a cutie to cuddle up with, and when the moment is right, tell her you'll be happy to warm her hands in your pants. If she balks, blame your depravity on the language barrier—always a reasonable excuse. Clubs will be noisy into the wee hours. New Year's lap dances are available at a variety of welcoming places; and, overall, the party runs citywide, so no matter where you find yourself, you'll probably be having a totally *awesome* time.

JANUARY TO MARCH

San Sebastian Festival—Puerto Rico

As the Doobie Brothers once said, "Taking it to the streets . . . taking it to the streets . . . taking it to the streets." Well, you get the idea. The **third week of every January in Old San Juan**, people spill out into the streets for several days of fun and celebration. Technically, it's a cultural and religious celebration, but so is St. Patrick's Day, right?

Happening in the official "freeze-your-nads-off" month of January, this fest brings with it the sunny, warm weather you've probably been jonesing for. When you hit the fest, do it later in the day when the younger folks are there and plan to be out way past your bedtime. **They party till the sun rises and then some.** While roaming through the festival be sure keep yourself cool with **pina coladas the size of J.Lo's ass**. Plus, they say Old San Juan is the birthplace of this oh-so tasty coconut drink. Also, try some of the delicious Puerto Rican street vendor food offerings—at your own risk, of course.

While you're here, you should take a trip to the **Bacardi Rum distillery**. They won't give away the recipe, but free samples are a part of the tour. Make sure you test your luck at one of Puerto Rico's **seventeen casinos**. Learn the art of salsa dancing or the Lambada with a beautiful Latin woman (it's forbidden, you know), then return the favor by teaching her how to do the "Sprinkler." Also, although it may be cruel and the animal rights types might be all over us after this suggestion, you should definitely **check out a cockfight**. No, it's not some gay club where your cousin Patrick hangs out, we're talking about the sport where roosters peck the bloody bejesus out of each other in the name of gambling. It's legal in Puerto Rico, and it'll probably be your only chance to ever take one in. For fun in the sun all doused in rum, late night partying with Latin goddesses shaking their stuff all over the dance floor, and a lot of other good shit, this is the place to go.

WHEN TO GO: Mid-January

LINK IT UP: With water all around you, a trip to Puerto Rico presents the perfect opportunity to add on some scuba, sailing, and fishing adventures. Or puddle jump to the Caymans. (See chapter 2: Diving)

CHECK IT OFF
Your "while I'm still in control of my own money" list

☐ Put a large amount down on a sporting event.

☐ Put an even larger amount down at the blackjack or roulette table.

☐ Spend a Friday night at the best steak house in town—eat, drink, and be gluttonous.

☐ Get front-row tickets to a sporting event or concert.

☐ Rent a limo or stretch Hummer for a huge night on the town.

☐ Bid on and win the best item at an auction.

☐ Spend so much in one night that your credit card company has to call you to verify the charges.

☐ Invest in a really risky stock.

☐ Get bottle service at a club.

☐ Walk into a strip club while it's dark and walk out into daylight.

☐ Buy a totally impractical car, like an old caddy convertible or an Aston Martin.

☐ Rent a summer beach house even if you can't afford to.

☐ Take a vacation so ridiculous everyone will think your trust fund just got liquidated.

☐ Purchase one kick-ass, only-me-and-MJ-wear-this-particular-thread suit.

☐ Put those spinning hubcaps on your car. So what if you drive a Toyota—you're still dope.

☐ Even if it means no furniture, buy a sweet-ass television and sound system.

☐ Do *not* buy any expensive housewares—you'll get all the shit come wedding time.

Quebec Winter Carnival (Carnaval de Quebec)—
Quebec, Canada

The football season is now over, March Madness is still weeks away, and baseball is nowhere in sight. Life can be pretty boring this time of year. So, if you're looking for something to **give your February a Pele-like kick in the pants**, this is a good place to begin. It's Carnival in the Cold; a weird concept, but nonetheless an unbelievable time. It's hosted by Quebec City, one of the oldest towns in North America. **Most of the partygoers congregate in Old Quebec City**, a section so remarkable that you'll quickly realize that Canada has much more to offer than Wayne Gretzky, maple syrup, and the brilliance of *Strange Brew*—"eh, you hoser."

Despite the twenty-five-degree temperature, people here are not afraid to take the party outside. All day long you'll have the opportunity to participate in hilarious events. Try to get entered in the **Golf Tournament** (on groomed snow), the **dogsled race**, and the **canoe trek** across the frozen St. Lawrence River. There is also the snow bath where one hundred nut jobs strip down to their panties and speedos and roll around in the snow. Join in. After some healthy activity, it's time to plow into the streets, pick up one of the **hollow canes** they sell, and fill it with **warm Caribou**. No, not the gamey-tasting meat, Caribou is a local concoction that will help keep you tingly on the inside and will make the freezing cold pleasantly tolerable. There are also plenty of bars to warm you up from that frigid Canadian air. **Pub St. Alexander**, with hundreds of different beers and live music, is always a favorite.

You'll have many hotels to choose from, but one place that you can't leave without witnessing is the **Ice Hotel**. Living up to its name, The Ice Hotel is a hotel made completely of ice. To keep their guests nice and toasty, the hotel keeps 'em good and buzzed with a fully stocked Absolut Vodka Bar. Other amenities include **a bed of ice, an ice nightstand, and ice floors.** Needless to say, it can be brutal to sleep in. Don't spend your entire trip here. However, this place begs for a contest between you and your buddies. Whoever gets laid in a hotel made of ice wins. And with an Ice Chapel on location, who knows? Maybe you and your lovely participant can get married there one day.

WHEN TO GO: End of January to mid-February

CAN'T GET THERE? Make your own Caribou (Brandy, Vodka, Sherry, and Port), build an igloo in your backyard and have a party. The contest becomes getting laid in the igloo.

Mardi Gras—New Orleans, Louisiana

Oh Mardi Gras, **what can we say about Mardi Gras?** Boobs, beads, tits, beads, hurricanes, jugs, Bourbon Street, beers, knockers, zydeco, *show me your—I'll show you mine*—**get me the hell out of here**. If you've never been, take everything you think you know about Mardi Gras and multiply it by ten. The number of beers, the amount of booze, the sets of boobs, and the quantity of beads will exceed any estimation you formulate. Yes, despite the 50 percent chance of ending up on the Internet, girls still continue to flash on command—making dads everywhere so very, very proud.

Mardi Gras is the party of all parties and New Orleans is the perfect stage for it. With the drinking age still eighteen, thousands of bars, a main strip on Bourbon Street full of horny southern belles, no town is better equipped to host this celebration each year. Within the French Quarter, there are plenty of hotels, but the **prime real estate**

is a room with a balcony overlooking Bourbon Street. Try the Royal Sonesta. You'll have a bird's-eye view of the decadence, you'll be able to entice worthy girls to come on up and you won't have to go far when you can no longer function. Or you can hit Arnoud's restaurant, where dinner for six or more gets you balcony access. Costumes are highly encouraged. Riding on a float is a possibility—just call parade headquarters, pay some cash, and hop on. And after six P.M., it's not worth being on the street, so head to Uptown or Frenchman Street.

Chances are you'll have a lot of buddies along with you. So, before the party starts, set up guidelines for the week. **Establish some contests early:** Who can sleep in a different hotel every night? Who can make out with the most girls? And, of course, who gets serviced in the most public area? Also, as you migrate through the streets, put on shows and play games: one guy starts doing push-ups while the others cheer on, **have a narcoleptic in the group** who passes out on any unsuspecting girl's tits or ask a coed to take pictures of your group and when you get into a pose tell them you don't have a camera. If the teasing boobies are getting you all riled up, fortunately New Orleans offers some of the best strip clubs and sex shows in the country. If you're really twisted, you can actually pay money to wash a naked stripper. *Oh, you're so dirty.* Any which way you look at it, Mardi Gras is unlike anything you'll ever experience.

WHEN TO GO: Best time is the week leading up to and including Fat Tuesday.

WARNING: If you find yourself receiving a lap dance from an oversized forty-something divorcee from Mississippi, quickly hand her five bucks and guide her to your nearest friend.

MAXIMUM EFFORT IN MINIMAL TIME
Jeff, 34, Indiana, married with daughter

The clock was ticking. I was about to turn thirty and my girlfriend of six years and I were starting to talk wedding. Well, she had been talking about it for some time, but now I was joining the conversation. To make every last minute count, my best friend and I came up with a plan to hit the two biggest places in America for sin, boobs, and booze in the same week—Mardi Gras and Vegas.

Our week began on Fat Tuesday. We caught a morning flight to New Orleans, and we were soon in the heart of the action. I have to tell you, all the stories are true. The street was lined with drunken men and women stuck in the largest street party in the world. Boobs were being flashed and beads were being tossed. It was a sight to behold. The most popular balcony for obvious reasons was the Playboy balcony. My buddy had the idea that he was going to get up there. We all laughed as he approached the guards to try the old "I loaned my pass to some chicks" routine. Much to my drunken dismay it worked. The bouncer said, "Yeah, I remember you," and next thing you know he was up there tossing beads. He stayed for a while and caught up with us later in the night.

It was now time to head back on the bus to the airport, but first we wisely stopped to have a drink called a Hand Grenade. Let's just say, the next thing I remember I was being helped off the bus and onto the plane. Stay away from this drink.

Our flight returned to Indy where we then connected to Vegas. When we arrived at our destination, The Hard Rock Hotel, the place was abuzz with excitement. We had booked it way in advance and unbeknownst to us the hotel was hosting the Playboy Rock 'n' Roll party. Oh, what a happy surprise. All week we drank, gambled, and drank some more—getting about an hour sleep a night. When Friday finally came, the place was filled wall-to-wall with talent. You see, not only were all the Playboy girls there; but every girl who wanted to be "discovered" was there, too. Yes, it was rock stars, celebrities, hot girls, and us. Even Hugh Hefner with three hot blondes on each arm made an appearance. So this is what it's like to be a Saudi royal? We didn't want the night to end, but alcohol and fatigue dictated otherwise. We all stumbled back to the room one at a time. One guy in our group actually left three hundred dollars at the blackjack table. Idiot.

The next morning, we woke up with fuzzy memories and flew back. My girlfriend picked me up (I was still too drunk to drive) and took me to her place where I slept for twenty-four hours straight. I dreamt about all I had done, drank, and seen. And I still do.

Carnival—Rio de Janeiro, Brazil

"Samba!" Say it again louder: *"Samba!!"* That's what you'll be screaming as you dance, drink, and party nonstop during *Carnaval* (the Portuguese spelling) in Rio. Samba is a type of dancing, but in Rio it's more like a religion. Here's a quick tip: Learn how to Samba before you go, then ask a lovely Brazilian to teach you. Start slow, then impress her with how quickly you learn.

Simply put, Carnaval is a **Latin version of Mardi Gras**. It's a celebration, a party, and something everyone should experience. Carnaval is different in that, well, it's not in the United States. The people you'll meet, the things you'll see, and the memories you'll keep are simply not possible in the fifty states. Everything runs until Fat Tuesday, beginning as early as the Wednesday before. It's recommended to get there between Wednesday and Friday. The Samba Parade is the main event and takes place in the **Sambodrome**. Rio used to just line the streets, but in order to accommodate the hordes of people enjoying the fest, they decided to build a permanent stadium for the parade. Tickets are required, and seating is as expected: the more you spend, the better your seat. Definitely get tickets for at least one night, Sunday or Monday, so you can experience it.

Otherwise, enjoy the street fests and the Balls (not your balls, *the* Balls). You can get tickets for these during the day, and you'll want to reserve a table. Ask street vendors, hotel employees, and cab drivers which Balls are going on each night. Generally, there are three types of Balls, Gala (Gisele), Single (Shakira), and Gay (Enrique Iglesias).

During the day hit the beach. If you're familiar with the term "Brazilian" you should know to maybe wax your back before you go. There are four main neighborhoods in Rio, two of the most popular are **Ipanema** and **Copacabana**, both with beaches. After you party until eight A.M., pass out on the beach, wake up to a Cerveja Fria, and start your day again.

WHEN TO GO: The week leading up to Fat Tuesday

ST. PATTY'S DAY

"Everybody's Irish on St. Patrick's Day." This is a tried-and-true statement that welcomes all able participants to celebrate St. Patrick's infamous dare—**how much fun can you get away with and still go to heaven?** It's green, it's messy, and it's loud. But to many people and cities, St. Patty's Day is the single greatest day of the year. It is on this day that the Holy Trinity is represented by bagpipes, massive amounts of beer, and pasty, freckly, drunk Irish girls. Throw on your "Kiss Me I'm Irish" boxers and hit the town in search of the girl in the KISS ME I'M IRISH T-shirt. If you find one that is still out after ten P.M., there is probably a reason she's still out and in need of that kiss. Steer clear, you're drunk.

Chicago, Illinois

In the Windy City, they call it St. Patrick's Day Season, which means it's time to dye the river green, decorate the streets with PortaPotties (a.k.a., Lepre-Cans), and stomp your feet to the pipes of the Shannon Rovers. The "Season" always kicks off on the **Saturday before March 17** with the Chicago Parade. Get started early on Saturday by finding your way to any Irish pub between Madison Avenue and Irving Park. Some of the favorites that will cover you with shamrock tchotchkes, fill you with green Jell-O shots, and feed you delicious corned beef are **Chief O'Neills, Brehon Pub, and Glascott's Grogery**.

For Day Two, 'tis the season and time to stumble your way to the other end of the city for a repeat performance at **the Southside Parade**. Hop on the shuttle buses departing from one of the Northside Bars—McGee's or Glascott's—and make sure your Irish sweater isn't completely covered in beer sludge from the day before. You'll find thousands of Chicagoans drinking in the streets and swaggering from pub to pub along Western Avenue. Whatever you do, don't mention the Chicago Cubs on this side of town unless it's followed by, "suck donkey balls." As the week goes on, some of you will wish Chicago didn't extend St. Patty's Day as it does, but sure enough, you have one more celebration left. That's right, **March 17 is still to come**. Don't let us down, you're Irish (or at least you think you are).

Manhattan, New York

The second oldest St. Patrick's Day Parade in the country (first marched by **a few crazy Irishmen in 1766**, following Boston's lead) runs up and down Fifth Avenue, and it is held every year on March 17. If you're into parades, check it out, the cops and firefighters are pretty badass. If not, **start early, as the competition to be the drunkest guy in New York is fierce**. Manhattan is home to many Irish pubs that you could only find in New York. **McSorley's**, which was founded in 1854, wouldn't serve women until the 1970s. Today they serve anyone, but only two kinds of beer—light and dark. For a snack, crackers, cheese, and spicy mustard will tide you over. Be warned, if you don't drink fast enough, the old Irish barkeeps will not hesitate to toss you out on the street. On the other side of the city, you'll be greeted at the Dublin House, where on any given day you'll find people drinking before nine A.M. On St. Patrick's Day it's a real marathon. If you're coming in on the train to Penn Station, stop at Twin's, it's known to pour one of the best pints of Guinness in town. After you take in the nostalgia, head to the east side and start up **a Second Avenue Pub Crawl**. Begin around Twenty-fifth Street and head straight uptown; try to make it to the '80s. If you can, you have earned your shamrock.

Savannah, Georgia

Boasting the spirit of St. Patrick's Day and the insanity of the South, Savannah pulls together a day that feels something like **"McMardi O'Gras."** With over a half-million people flocking the streets, Savannah claims to throw the largest St. Patrick's Day celebration in the country. Just like Chicago, they set the atmosphere right and dye the Savannah River green. The place to be during the madness of March 17 is **River Street**. There are countless bars here, and for five dollars you can get a wrist band that warrants you the right to consume in the streets. With temperatures in the seventies, Savannah is the only warm destination that still knows what St. Patrick's Day is all about. Bands, dancers, and street exhibitions will be flourishing on the banks of the river. The people of Savannah are superfriendly and extremely proud. You may hear natives brag about their town's cameo in *Forrest Gump* (that's where Forrest meets little Forrest). But, if you want to fit in, avoid "stupid is as stupid does" comments and **tell everyone "how awesome Savannah is"** and that you want to move there. They'll love you. This is your opportunity to use lines like, "You girls are so great here, I bet you'll even show me your tits." Keep some beads and extra beers handy, and you'll be all set.

LINK IT UP: The Masters is three weeks away. Road trip it to a spring break locale in Florida, then make it back up to Augusta in time to watch Tiger drive on the first tee. (See chapter 3 under "Golf.")

Dublin, Ireland

"Do Asian massage parlors offer the same services in Asia?" **"Is St. Patrick's Day as crazy in Ireland?"** Yes and Yes. Never celebrating St. Patty's Day in Ireland is like never getting a rub-and-tug in Thailand— you'll regret it for the rest of your long, long life.

Until the 1970s, pubs were closed on St. Patrick's Day, as it was considered a holy day in Ireland. Realizing the potential, and feeling the need to show up any other city attempting to outshine its most coveted day, Dublin decided to kick this gig into gear. Sure enough, by 1997, the government of Ireland dropped "Day" and officially made March 12 to the 17 **"St. Patrick's Festival."** Packages that set up a four-day event for you are easily found, and many will even take you from London to Dublin and back to London. However, make sure the package has some built-in flexibility, i.e., not too many agenda items. The best part of Ireland is being on your own schedule. Many hotels will have special deals, and as Dublin is on many travel routes, there are plenty of hostels to help save cash.

The Festival offers everything from a parade to live music to art fairs. *Wait, fer fuck's sake,* you're in Ireland on St. Patrick's Day!! Go to the **Temple Bar area**, enjoy the brogues, the culture, the fresh Guinness and **high-five every old Irishman you see**. A year later, as you commemorate in your local Irish pub and share your tales of Ireland, you'll be that much more of a legend as you raise a pint, declare *Erin Go Bragh* and finish with a solid *slainte*.

WARNING: Beware of the Guinness farts, they're some of the deadliest known to man (or animal).

ROMPER ROOM AND SWEET PEA
Sean, 33, Illinois, now married

It was approximately two A.M. on March 18 in Dublin, Ireland. After a day of parades, Guinness, Jameson, Harp, Baileys, and other good spirits, my buddy Dave and I found ourselves looking for some late-night eats at a fast-food joint. While in line deciding between the Fish and Chips and the Double Beefburger, Dave and I were approached by a couple of surprisingly attractive ladies. The first line out of Girl #1's mouth was, "Where are WE staying tonight?" Caught off guard, Dave replied truthfully, "The International Hostel?" Yes, we were staying in the adult version of a romper room, complete with bunk beds and ten other roommates. Either she didn't hear him or didn't care, but she and her friend were happy to join us. Everything seemed perfect . . . until we got to the hostel. We quietly snuck them in, trying our best not to wake the eight other horny guys slumbering away, only to have Girl #1 flip on the lights and tell our roomies to wake up. She then paraded around, pulling off covers and calling everybody, "Sweetpea." After some time, Girl #2 was able to round her up, everyone else went back to sleep, and we were all going to get naked. Dave was with Girl #1 on the bottom bunk. I was with Girl #2 on top. The lights were off and Girl #2 and I were making out like high school seniors. I was touching her boobies . . . life was good. Then, I heard from below, "I'm not that type of girl." Followed by, "Well then get out." Followed by, "What?" Followed by "Listen, you've been a pain in the ass all night, if you're not going to at least blow me . . . go." That Dave is a classy fellow. Girl #1 left the room. Meanwhile, I worried that these girls might be thieves or something, because so far my night had seemed just too good to be true, so I dropped my wallet down to Dave. Not understanding what I was doing, he yelled, "Sean, you dropped your wallet." I told him to just hang onto it. Girl #2 and I went back at it. Girl #1 returned ten minutes later and proceeded to not once, but twice give Dave just what he asked for. The next morning, we left early, wallets intact, and left the girls sleeping in our bunks, but not before taking a lovely parting picture—not that we'd need it to remember that night for the rest of our lives.

JULY TO OCTOBER

Running of the Bulls—Pamplona, Spain

Sometimes an idea is so stupid that it's actually genius, like sending a pack of crazy-ass bulls down a narrow street filled with people ready to run or be gored. Okay, maybe it's not brilliant, but it's certainly intriguing. The good thing is—for most of us who are normal, not particularly speedy, nor skilled at outmaneuvering giant animals—this event offers so **much more than just running and bulls**.

Taking place every July 6 through 14, **La Fiesta de San Fermín**

(the running of the bulls) is a week where wine, partying, and cele-
brations flow nonstop. It's a madhouse in so many ways. Spectators
come from all over and hotels book up easily six months to a year in
advance. So get yours early, or do like many visitors do and find
your pillow on a piece of grass in one of Pamplona's parks. It's particularly safe during the day, which, if you party all night, will work
out beautifully.

Now the big question: **To run or not to run?** We can't recommend
joining the masses of runners without our lawyers asking for seventeen pages of legal disclaimers. However, we can say this, if you go
all the frickin' way to Spain for the Running of the Bulls at least sort of,
kind of run . . . even if it's for 3.5 seconds and then you jump over the
fence. No one else needs to know the logistics of your jaunt. If you're
really hung over or using liquid courage as your motivator, you probably should just watch. Whatever you decide, **the running starts
every day at 8:00 A.M. sharp**. You need to get there as early as six
A.M. to claim your spot. If you're running, be sure to enter through the
official gates and listen for the sounding of the rockets. **The first rocket**
signals that the bulls are out. **The second** informs everyone the bulls
are now in the street. And **the third** means that they've made it to the
ring and you're not going to die. All in all, the running only lasts
about two minutes. Remember, people have been mauled, trampled,
and pummeled like there is no tomorrow, so be smart and stay the
(you-know-what) away from the bulls.

The nighttime is when the real pounding begins. People wander
the streets, particularly **Calle San Nicolas, Estafeta, and Calle de Ja-
rauta**, bouncing from bar to bar. They drink. They eat. They drink
some more. While you're here, enjoy some tapas, check out the
nightly fireworks, take in some live music, and make your way to
a disco for late-night drunken dancing. When mixing it up with the

ladies, don't be afraid to tell them how you are the **#1 bull fighter in the state of Rhode Island**. Also, if you happen to be here a day or two before the event starts, bring your camera to the **"Running of the Nudes,"** an annual naked race in protest of the actual Running of the Bulls. What a great way to begin a momentous experience.

WHEN TO GO: Early July

WARNING: If you happened to get hit by a bull, stay down and remain motionless; bulls respond to movement. Plus, you probably can't move anyway, so don't bother trying.

LINK IT UP: Didn't get gored? Looking for more fiesta? Trek to Ibiza for a party that kicks harder than a bull during castration. (See chapter 4, under "Ibiza.")

Nudes-a-Poppin Pageant, Ponderosa Sun Club—Roselawn, Indiana

All you have to do is glance at the contest lineup to realize that this is the **"Best in Show"** for naked people. You've got the Miss Nude Galaxy Pageant, Miss Nude Showstopper of the Year, Miss Nude Go-Go, Miss Nude Rising Star, Miss Hot Buns . . . and the list goes on. Don't worry, it won't be Aunt Betty from the local Wal*Mart shaking her stuff on stage, most of the contestants are strippers by trade. Nonetheless, we're not going to lie, it's pretty trashy. But it's hot, naked trashy, and it makes a really good story. You'll see porn stars make cameo appearances, washed-up acts like Vanilla Ice help MC the event, and lots of other not-so-everyday sights . . . like **nude erotic wrestling**. What a great way to spend a Saturday or Sunday.

This glorious event happens in Roselawn, Indiana (basically nowheresville) at a lovely nudist camp. Your best bet is to drive from Chicago, which is only an hour-long trek. You can stay the night in Lowell, Indiana (eight miles away) at the luxurious Motel 8, or just drive back to the Windy City. A limo always makes a nice way to travel, because you will want to indulge in adult beverages here. Heck, it's **BYOB, so bring a cooler with plenty to go around**. Get drunk, get the ladies around you drunk, and start your own contest with them. You're at a nudist camp, how hard can it be to get people naked? On your way back to Chicago, make a pit stop at any of the **casinos in Gary, Indiana**. If you're still in the mood for more boobies, well, you can top it off with a trip to one of the fine gentleman's clubs in that area as well. All in all, you won't forget your trip to Roselawn, Indiana.

WHEN TO GO: July

CAN'T GET THERE? It's time to throw the ever popular **"Nudes-a-Poppin-in-my-Apartment" Party**. Yeah, make arrangements with some strippers, bikini models, and naughty girls you know, and hold contests all night, with the winners receiving a free trip to see the posters in your room.

La Tomatina—Buñol, Spain

We haven't checked the official records, but this event has to be the **largest food fight** our world serves up. Happening on the last Wednesday of every August in the small town of **Buñol**, more than thirty thousand Roger Clemens wannabees gather to hurl approximately one hundred fifty thousand smushed up, smashed up tomatoes at everyone and everything around them. It's pure veggie madness . . . and precisely why you should participate.

Buñol is a teeny, tiny town. Thus, for this event, you should **make your home base in Valencia**—a larger city where accommodations and activities are aplenty. On the morning of the big brawl (or the night, before if you don't mind staying up all night), you can take a bus, train, or private "money is no object" car. Bring along your favorite beer or wine and start drinking early. **The more numb you are, the less pain you'll feel.** The tomatoes are held at bay until the masses first are able to climb up and cut down a ham (yes, a ham) tied to a greasy pole. Not an easy task, it takes a human ladder and some climbing proficiency to get that piece of pork down. During this time, be sure to take a look around and scope out potential targets worth pelting. After the ham has been conquered, everyone waits for the sound of **tomato-packed rockets whistling through the sky** to signal the battle's commencement. At that sound, trucks teeming with tomatoes come rolling in and **the fight is on**.

THE BATTLE DOESN'T HAVE MANY RULES, BUT HERE ARE A FEW:

- You must crush the tomatoes before chucking them.
- No tearing anyone's clothing (unless she asks).
- Tomatoes—and only tomatoes—can be thrown.
- As soon as the second shot is heard, the throwing must stop.

We recommend you **wear your nastiest clothes**, because they will be ruined, bring some **eye goggles** for protection against the stinging tomato juice, and afterward you'd best find a shower, hose, or local firefighter to clean you off. However, **be prepared to find tomato shrapnel** in every possible part of your body for at least three days following.

Why do they do this? Is it to honor the native Tomato God? Is it an act of gratefulness for a plentiful harvest? Nope. Folklore tells us that it began in 1945 when some rowdy locals got in a huge-ass fight. And yes, there happened to be a fruit stand nearby. The rest is history.

WHEN TO GO: Late August

LINK IT UP: From tomatoes to marinara, head to Italy and more of Europe by Rail. (See chapter 5 under "Europe by Rail.") Or continue the battling theme and make your way to a bullfight. (See chapter 3 under "Bullfight.")

CAN'T GET THERE? Create your own backyard food fight with grapes, hard-boiled eggs, or canned peaches (ouch!).

Burning Man—Black Rock Desert, Nevada

Burn baby, burn! Every year, the week before Labor Day, some thirty thousand half-naked people journey out into the middle of the desert to create the **universe's largest temporary city**. Better known as **Black Rock City**, this crazy town is made up of tents hosting a huge variety of sights, services, and freaky fun. Walk around and you'll find absinthe bars, body-painting artists, pole-dancing lessons, and full-blown raves. You'll discover there's **no buying or selling of anything**. It's a free exchange. The only mode of transportation is by bicycle or your own two feet. And no one is in charge . . . it's total anarchy. Amazingly though, this transient town runs rather efficiently and is equipped with radio stations, a pancake house, a courier service, and many other practical businesses.

When hitting the madness that this fest is sure to be, bring a ton of food, water, and alcohol. As we've said, **there's no 7-Eleven out here**. As many others do, you should invent a unique theme for your particular camp area. A few ideas would be: The "Free Advice" camp (where you can become the Dr. Phil of Burning Man), the "Breast Exam" camp (a noble cause, beneficial to both parties), and the family favorite, "Wet-and-Slippery Naked Twister" Camp.

While here, **expect the unexpected**—especially from the weather. You're in a goddamn desert! Super hot days, really cold nights, and blinding sand storms are all a part of the experience. Be prepared for the worst. Also, bring your rubbers—you'll have a good chance of getting some here, and you don't want your own version of the "burning man" three weeks later. To the delight of pyromaniacs everywhere, the festival wraps up with the impressive torching of the massive Burning Man structure. Days later the town completely vanishes without a trace . . . until next year.

WHEN TO GO: Late August

LINK IT UP: After you're done with the dry heat of the desert, cool off in one of Vegas's many fantastic pools. (See chapter 4 under "Vegas.")

CHECK IT OFF
Your . . . "I dared someone to do that" list

- ☐ Streak in a public place.
- ☐ Order a Zima at a Biker Bar.
- ☐ Ask out the hottest girl at a bar.
- ☐ Ask out the oldest woman at a bar.
- ☐ Ask out a girl while she is obviously on a first date.
- ☐ Run onto the playing field of a sporting event.

(continued)

- [ ] Jump into some off-limits body of water or fountain, with an audience.
- [ ] Sing Karaoke to Elton John's "I Guess That's Why They Call It the Blues."
- [ ] Get a lap dance from the most pimple-butted stripper.
- [ ] Chug a gallon of milk, followed by a loaf of bread.
- [ ] Wear a diaper (and only a diaper) to the beach.
- [ ] Pretend to have Tourette's Syndrome while hitting on a group of girls.
- [ ] Try to pick up chicks at a lesbian bar.
- [ ] Snort Tequila. (ouch)
- [ ] Get a lap dance wearing Umbros.
- [ ] Buy a random dude a drink at a bar and wink at him when he gets it.
- [ ] Start dancing in the middle of bar to the Billy Idol's "Dancing with Myself."
- [ ] High-five everyone in the bar while saying "High Five, High Five."

Oktoberfest—Munich, Germany

How do **five hundred million liters of beer** and **two hundred thousand pairs of sausage links** sound to you? Exactly. So now it's time to head to Munich, Germany, and celebrate the marriage of Prince Ludwig to Princess Therese, which took place in the year 1810. The Munich Oktoberfest is known to be the largest public festival in the world, and is held from mid-September to early October.

The partying takes place mostly in the dozen or more massive beer tents set up throughout the city. The **Hofbrau Festhalle** (counterpart to the well known Hofbräuhaus) is one of the more popular tents, and it's heavily attended by Americans. Also, make sure that you spend some time at the **Hippodrom**, where, if you have any ability, you'll be sucking face with some chick who speaks very little English (see Check It Off: "your hook-up" list) and has a striking resemblance to the St. Pauli Girl.

Huge steins of beer are everywhere. And each one seems to have this infectious power that incites friends and strangers alike to uncontrollably and continually raise their mugs to the sky, yell something incoherent, and chug. Plus, the more you drink, the more fun this ritual becomes. **Reservations can be made at the various tents** and are not a bad idea. This will ensure a solid starting point, where you can get some food and drink before journeying from tent to tent. Everyone is always competing over how many liters they've polished off, so be sure to keep count of your 7, 8, 9—holy shit that's a lot of—liters.

Full participation will only make your experience that much more enjoyable. So, we highly recommend that you give 110 percent in this area. We're talking **lederhosen**, **funny hats**, **big old German shoes**, and, if you're Irish or Scottish, put on a kilt. The ladies of Oktoberfest will appreciate your effort. Also learn a couple of German **"oom-pa"** dance moves. Munich is a big city, so hotels and other accommodations can be found on most travel sites, and travel guides are a plenty.

WHEN TO GO: Mid-September to early October

LINK IT UP: While you're all the way over here, be on the look out for a soccer, football that is, match. (See chapter 3 under "International Soccer Match.")

CAN'T GET THERE? Buy a keg of Warsteiner, Hofbrauhaus, or Beck's, cook a bunch of sausages and soft pretzels, hire a German brass-and-accordion band, and whoop it up at your place.

WHAT HOTEL?

Brad, 30, New York, still single, and in no hurry to change that status

It was my first vacation since college—not that the concept of vacation really applies during college—and I was on my way to Germany for Oktoberfest. This event meant nothing more (and nothing less) to me than Rusty touching boobs in *European Vacation*. It was my buddy Wolfe's idea and I was just along for the ride. He was the cruise director of this trip . . . or so I thought. After meeting up at the airport, I logically suggested we drop our stuff off at the hotel. Confused, Wolfe responded, "Why, did you get a hotel?" With that, we decided to go figure a few things out over beers. Another great plan. Stein after stein, I got more nervous. Where the hell were we sleeping? The next thing I knew, Wolfe was chatting it up and telling people that without a place to stay, I wouldn't be any fun. Somehow, his simple plan worked: some Belgian students offered to let us crash at their apartment. So we carried on, tackling a beer fest and then bong hits.

The next day, we got up early to find another place to stay—a near-impossible task, since it was the first day of Oktoberfest. Luckily, we found a spare bedroom in a family apartment. We paid about fifteen dollars per night for three nights. From there, we were off. We bought tickets to a tent, downed a couple of brew-ha-ha's and ate some sausage. We then jumped from tent to tent to tent. At one point, we were clanking steins and laughing for no good reason with a large German family—for several hours. The hysterical part was that we spoke zero German, and they knew no English. Everyone was trashed and things were getting a little odd. An older man kept squeezing me together with an attractive young German girl. He kept signaling to ask if I liked her. And of course, I tried gesturing back that I did. Amongst the signaling, she grabbed my balls and stuck her massive German tits in my face. And for some reason, I thought I better nibble her boob. I then got a slap in the face, followed by a sloppy wet kiss. It was at this moment that I realized Oktoberfest rules, and yes . . . we still had three glorious days to go.

Fantasy Fest—Key West, Florida

At first we weren't sure if this event should fall into the Halloween category or not. There are costumes and it happens in late October. *But,* it technically ends the day before Halloween. So after going to the booth for further review, we decided that although close, this is not an official Halloween festival. Consider it Halloween's ten-day-long spring training. Taking place in Key West—the Margarita capital of the universe—**this festival puts out more parties than Jimmy Buffet has songs about drinking**. You've got the DeadBanger's Ball, where guests dress like their favorite dead rocker, Party in Plaid at Captain Tony's Saloon, Sloppy Joe's Toga Party, the Red Party, Beach Party, an 'eighties party—and the list doesn't stop there. All attendees throw their inhibitions way the hell out the window and truly anything goes. Plan ahead so you'll have costumes to fit in. When in doubt, just throw on an eye patch, carry around a stuffed animal parrot, and say "arrrr" a lot.

Duval Street is where all the craziness goes down. Get a hotel within stumbling distance if you can. On this lovely street, you'll witness an **insane amount of women wearing nothing but body paint**. Be sure to critique the work and ask in depth about Picasso's influence on that left-breast smiley face. Bonus points if a girl lets you inspect the brush strokes up close and personal. You'll probably hit every single bar on the Duval strip, but even if your energy is flagging make sure to go to Fat Tuesday's for a highly potent frozen drink, and follow it with

Rum Runners, Margaritaville, and Sloppy Joe's. For something a little different, try **Garden of Eden—Key West's clothing-optional eatery**. Persuade one of your buddies to get naked and order a wine spritzer with a twist. To find professionally naked ladies, there's no better spot than Teasers. However, with plenty of nudity to be found free of charge, we recommend using your money to buy shots for whatever body-painted ladies catch your eye. When you're not totally shit-canned and busy admiring the lack of clothing, you could take a break and **hop on board a deep sea fishing charter**. Otherwise, drink up, parade around Duval Street, and incite as many indecent acts as you possibly can. You'll be amazed just how easy that can be at Fantasy Fest.

WHEN TO GO: The ten days before Halloween

WARNING: Swingers (not the movie) are abundant here; you don't want to be the meat in that sandwich . . . right?

LINK IT UP: Bag some more Halloween treats with a trip to Tampa for Gauvaween (See chapter 1 under "Halloween.")

Exotic Erotic Ball—San Francisco, California

We've all stayed up late watching HBO's *Real Sex*, episode 1 through—god knows how many there are. Well, once a year in San Francisco, anyone can feel like they've been transplanted **smack dab in the middle of their very own episode**. The Exotic Erotic Ball started as a way to raise money so the founder could run for President of the United States under the Nudist Party. Just think of the slogans for that campaign!!! Decades later, it's grown into a no-holds-barred sex fest. You'll see quiet, reserved librarians by day let themselves go and become dirty sexhibitionists by night. Thongs, dildos, and fetishes are encouraged. You don't have to be an active participant, but why wouldn't you be? In any case, an appreciation for all that is naughty is a necessity.

This is one party you don't skimp on, or you will be stuck among the throngs of dirtball guys looking to snap photos of fake DD's with their Motorola camera phones. Go VIP and go big. **VIP is about an extra $100, but well worth it**, as you'll have the chance to talk world politics with the girls of the Bunny Ranch, pay tribute to Ron Jeremy, and leave smelling like a stripper, without paying for a dance. Dress in costume. Some men will be wearing women's panties or leather chaps. Don't be those guys, but put together something tough like a gladiator costume, something funky that employs a huge pimp coat with medallions, or something classy—you can't really go wrong with a tuxedo. Also, the ball is actually just south of San Francisco, in Daly City. **Take a limo**, as this will only improve your chances of convincing those girls with the edible underwear to join you for a late-night snack. Speaking of which, there is usually an "after party" or two that go on until the next morning. Find them and carry on as long as you can.

WHEN TO GO: End of October

CAN'T GET THERE? Throw a Pimp-and-Ho Party, with the added fun of a hired dominatrix to spank your guests. (See chapter 7, under "Parties.")

HALLOWEEN

Boo! This is the one day of the year where dressing up like a total and complete idiot can actually be rewarded with love and attention. It's the one time where Spiderman can take home Wonder Woman, a Proctologist can bag a Naughty Nurse, and a Priest can have his way with a Catholic Schoolgirl—without any ramifications. Okay, we're going to hell for that last one, which reminds us that Satan always makes a decent costume, too. Our recommendation on costumes is to find a really good one and milk it for years and years. Be creative—make business cards for your costume and have props that go along with it. At any Halloween party, one of your main goals should be to find the ying to your yang, the Indian to your cowboy, the Miss Piggy to your Kermit the Frog, etc. If you can make the match, you've done well.

Fetish & Fantasy Ball—Las Vegas, Nevada

For years you've had that pair of ass-less chaps and spiked dog collar just hanging in your closet, well now is your chance to finally put them to work. Just kidding . . . sort of. This **bizarre Halloween bash** is exactly what you'd expect from Vegas. Scantily clad ladies abound. Fire performers, laser shows, and DJs entertain the crowd, and everyone competes to have the **freakiest, naughtiest, sexiest, and most creative costume** in the house. Now, you don't have to go completely balls out (and we mean that literally) to fit in, but you need to have some kind of funky costume. **They'll actually fine you if your costume is lame.** So go crazy—be a Ronald McDonald Pimp, a Caveman on Viagra, or a SpongeBob No-Pants. Or if you're up to the challenge, do something completely deviant and way the hell out there. The top prize can bring in over one thousand dollars. Just think of the damage you could do at the craps table with that.

The Travel Channel calls it one of the **top-ten party spots in the world.** And it's hard to disagree. Book yourself well in advance, as the event sells out. While sporting full costume, be sure to play some blackjack, get a lap dance, and take a ride on top of the Stratosphere Hotel. Trick or treating will never be the same after this. Also, take a look at our Vegas section in chapter 4 for more ideas.

WARNING: Stay away from that woman with the dazzling gold tooth who's just tickled your crotch with her five-inch, multicolored nails.

LINK IT UP: You just spent a long weekend in Vegas. There is absolutely no need to go anywhere but home.

NYC Halloween Parade—Greenwich Village, New York

Yeah, it's a parade. Yeah, parades can be pretty lame. And yeah, this book is not about doing lame stuff. But . . . this parade is pretty flippin' cool, and it's in New York, where if you can't have a good time, there's something wrong with you. The parade itself is open for any and all to join in, as long as you're in costume. It's **the nation's largest public Halloween celebration**, with over two million people attending. And it flaunts some of the wackiest, most hilarious, most creative get-ups you'll ever see.

All in one place, you'll witness puppets on steroids, little people with ginormous masks, jugglers, break-dancers, bands playing all kinds of music, and thousands of other acts of strangeness. It's a true spectacle. Be sure to dress in costume just for the shit of it. Bring a camera to capture all the oddities around you. And don't forget your flask—every good Halloween parade should be taken in with whiskey. Hey, the whole friggin' night's about spirits, right? After it's over, we recommend you **cruise the streets of the Village**, freak your way down Bleecker Street in search of a good place to drink, or head straight to Town Tavern and/or Automatic Slims. With New York already well known for its wild, weird, and crazy nightlife, just imagine it, come Halloween. This place is a guaranteed good time.

Guavaween—Tampa Bay, Florida

They say it's "Halloween meets Mardi Gras." We say, "Where do we sign up?" Every year, this huge Halloween celebration transforms Tampa's Latin District, **Ybor City**, into one massive, retarded party. To get things off to a good start, you can hit the **Guava Eve Masquerade Ball**. At the ball, you can indulge in cocktails, palm readings, a Dungeon of Delights, music, and of course a game of "is your face as nice as your boobs?" Party all night and sleep all day. It's a family-friendly event while the sun is out, so you won't miss anything.

The big day begins with the **Mama Guava Stumble Parade**. It's open to everyone, and as the name makes clear, intoxication is part of the theme. The rest of the night is up to you. The streets will be filled with seventy-five thousand-plus people to get to know. **Big name music acts** will be performing at various stages. There's a huge costume contest. And, as you can imagine, you'll bear witness to hilarious debauchery of all kinds. Be on the look out for something called The Pleasure Zone. Also, if you have any free time away from the celebration, find your way to one of Tampa's globally renowned ballets. Mons Venus would be a fantastic selection. And don't forget . . . wear your costume.

LINK IT UP: To give yourself a real post-Halloween scare, head to Fort Lauderdale for shark diving. (See chapter 2, under "Shark Diving.")

Festival of the Dead—Salem, Massachusetts

All things frightening journey to Salem this time of year for what becomes a total and complete scare-yourself-shitless fest. Unlike other

Halloween destinations, partying is not the big attraction. Instead, it's about delving into a world of eerie. You can learn the art of **ghost hunting** from experts in the field. You'll explore the latest technologies in capturing paranormal activities. Peruse actual galleries containing ghost photos. You'll hear chilling tales of true Salem hauntings. And to conclude things, you'll visit one of New England's most ghostly graveyards. Freaky crap all around.

You can also experience **the shocking world of serial killers**, bearing witness to all the gruesome details, reliving their vicious histories and even learning how to profile your friends and coworkers for similar murderous tendencies. Other activities here include: dining with the dead; participating in a full-blown séance (Uncle Louie, is that you?); and peeking into the future with a psychic reading. There are a couple of crazy Halloween Balls to attend. One is **the Official Salem Witches' Halloween Ball**, with food, music, a costume contest, and plenty to drink. The other is **the Vampires' Masquerade Ball**, which boasts gothic music, blood ceremonies, a voluptuous vixen, burlesque, and drinks. Both will have you feeling a little disturbed, but, hey, that's not always a bad thing. Overall, Salem will leave you freaked out and muttering the famous words of Haley Joel Osmond: "I see dead people." Bring several changes of underwear in case you tinkle yourself.

CAN'T GET THERE? Stay home and watch *The Ring, Manhunter*, and any of the *Omen* movies.

FESTIVALS YOU'D BEST STAY AWAY FROM:
- Garlic Fest—Gilroy, California
- The Moose-Dropping Festival—Talketna, Alaska
- Golden Shears, Sheep Shearing Festival—Masterton, New Zealand

- Frog Festival—Rayne, Louisiana
- Cooper's Hill Annual Cheese Rolling—Gloucester, England
- World Grits Festival—St. George, South Carolina
- Brotherhood of Goat-Meat Eaters Festival—France
- Sauna Bathing World Championships—Heinola, Finland

MUSIC FESTIVALS

Gathering around and listening to live music has been a staple of humanity for ages. But the modern day musical festival that leads you on journeys of peace, love, jam sessions, and plenty of substances was set in motion in 1969, thanks to Woodstock's "Three Days of Peace and Music." Even as music fests have evolved, there are several themes that have stayed constant: half-dressed woman, friendly folks, sketchy vendors, the desire to take your mind to a different place, and most importantly, great tunes. At the same time, there are also unwritten rules that exist only to ensure a better time: no fighting, sharing is cool, don't buy drugs from the shady guy in the tie-dye, drink gallons of water, P.D.A.-ing is encouraged, and always double-check girls for hairy armpits. Any fest has to really miss the mark to be disappointing, but here are a few that guarantee to deliver the goods and get you dancing.

Austin, Texas

They call it **the "Live Music Capital of the World"** for a reason. That's why we have not one, but two fests that are really worth checking out. They each have a unique vibe, so make your decision appropriately. If you can get to both and you don't live in Austin, go ahead and deem yourself "The Greatest Live Music Fan in the World."

SOUTH BY SOUTHWEST (SXSW)

For four, loud days and nights, this once modest, now renowned fest turns Austin into **the Mecca for recording industry pros**. It's a wet dream for small-venue music fans, and it's unlike anything else out there. Literally, you can find musicians performing their craft around the clock, not to mention daily panels and discussions about the industry. Over a thousand acts typically take stage. And the great thing is, almost every single one of them is trying to prove that they're **the Next Big Shit in the music world**.

Norah Jones, as well as the Strokes, have confirmed that **it's a great place to be discovered**. Just keep a list of everyone you see—you never know, you may have just heard and seen the next U2. There's no right or wrong way to approach this fest. To have unlimited access, simply buy a Music Badge that gets you in anywhere you wish to go. It's expensive, so if you're only interested in nightly music, get a wristband instead of a badge. Some venues do allow a pay-as-you-go policy, too. To find the good music, check the schedules and figure out which acts or types of music you want to hear, and then head on over—this is one fest where it pays to be organized. But there's plenty of **hooting, hollering, and drinking, too**. Indulge in all three as much as you can. If you want to take a break and hang with the record company and Hollywood crowd, try the Four Seasons Lobby Bar. If the thrill of seeking out new tunes and catching bands before they've made it big sounds cool to you, this is your festival. If bigger names, in a bigger setup is more to your liking, try Austin festival number two.

AUSTIN CITY LIMITS

This is definitely for the less hardcore music aficionado than SXSW, but the caliber of talent is still not of this planet. It's less about bands that are on the cusp of making it and more about those that already have. And the music industry won't be here prospecting; but never fear, they'll be replaced by really good-looking chicks. Anyhow, let's quit comparing it to SXSW and let's talk about why you need to get your ass there.

During late September in Zilker Park, "Austin City Limits" brings you **three days of incredible music**. Historically, they've had performances by artists like **Coldplay, The Black Crowes, Wilco, and Widespread Panic**. Plus, they bring in a ton of other well-known, but less-huge names to play on a variety of stages. At any given moment you could have three great acts playing at the same time; or two of your favorite musicians could go back-to-back. Map out which shows you really, really want to see. Chances are you'll probably just end up meeting some girls, following them around, and letting them decide what you actually see. Anyhow, it's all outdoors, so bring a beach ball, a hacky sack, and other forms of entertainment. Enjoy a few cold beers under the hot Texas sun, jam with a braless, free-loving young hippie girl, and at night get cozy with some cutie under the stars, showing her your knowledge of all the constellations (we like AndromAmadeus, Boba Fett, and Cletus.

Whichever Austin fest you decide to attend, there are some other Austin activities worth engaging in. Make certain you **feast on some BBQ**. Muscle your way to Sixth Avenue for **a shot of tequila off the belly of a University of Texas cheerleader**. And for something really bizarre, check out **the 1.5 million bats that take flight each day at sunset from the Congress Avenue Bridge**. Holy shoelaces, that is a huge quantity of bats, man. If you love music, make this town a priority—get here and soak it all in.

WHEN TO GO: SXSW is in March. "Austin City Limits" is in September.

Jazz Fest—New Orleans, Louisiana

Don't let the name fool you. **Jazz Fest is hardly just about jazz.** It's about New Orleans, tasty food, intoxicating drinks, boob-friendly beads, and crazy visitors. Plus, the music is truly a little bit of everything: jazz, blues, R & B, folk, Latin, rock, rap, country, Cajun, and plenty of stuff they don't have a name for. Jimmy Buffet has sung to drunken Parrotheads here. Bob Dylan has crooned his magical lyrics here. Dave Matthews has been here. Jack Johnson, the Neville Brothers, Lenny Kravitz, and even Nelly (it's getting hot in here) have been here. With **ten days of festivities, twelve stages jamming and over a half million visitors**, this event is monstrous. Thus, it makes the perfect venue for you and your friends to have some ridiculous fun.

It happens in late April, early May—just enough time for Mardi Gras revelers to shake off their hangovers, gather up their beads, and get there. Hotels book early, so plan wisely. The weather can be hot as a mother, so bring a floppy hat and hit the AC in the Grandstands. And the drinking can quickly get out of hand, so pace yourself to survive the long haul. With so much music, you need to check the schedule and figure where you want to be and when. Bouncing around can get exhausting, so have a general plan. Food is a huge part of the fest; stuff your face with some **tasty gumbo, po'boy sandwiches, and coconut macaroons**. Down it all with mind-erasing Hurricanes and refreshing Abitas (the local brew). After you're fested out, it's time to hit Bourbon Street for drunken good times. Or try Tipitina's, an old-school music hall worth a gander. As with any trip to New Orleans, probably your best bet is just to hit the bars and see what kind of interesting things you can stir up. Break things up with a trip to a strip club. And be sure to dance like a silly, drunken schmo with a woman twice your age. It's all fair and game while you're here.

WHEN TO GO: Late April, early May

WARNING: If you find yourself in the hotel room of supersized forty-something divorcee from Mississippi, tell her to close her eyes and wait for a big surprise, then run like the wind.

Telluride Bluegrass Fest—Telluride, Colorado

This fest is pure Colorado. It's laid-back, mellow, serene, but full of energy. Telluride, in its own right, is one of the most beautiful towns around. Hidden in the San Juan Valley, it's not easy to get to, and consequently hasn't fallen prey to the glitz that has hit other ski areas. It's **exactly what you picture when you think of an authentic "Old West" town**. Walking down the main street will bring visions of Doc Holiday and Wyatt Earp. They say Butch Cassidy made his first bank heist here. Anyhow, it's now home to one impressive display of music. Don't be turned off if bluegrass isn't your thing. The lineup has really expanded to include jazz, rock, folk, pop, Celtic, alternative country, and more. Artists like Wilco, Bruce Hornsby, Béla Fleck, and Bobby McFerrin have all played here.

The fest goes for four days, usually ten A.M. until midnight, in mid-June. Getting there can become a *Planes, Trains, and Automobiles* affair, so spend some time figuring what's best. Also, forget the luxury of lodging and **plan to camp out**. It's much cheaper, and the town offers several decent options, with shuttles for getting around.

Camping will only add to the non-artificial vibe this fest embodies. Plus, between the mountains, the booze, the drugs, and the girls, your tent will quickly become a slice of heaven. While here, **indulge in many micro-brews**, especially the local favorite, Fat Tire. If you like to smoke pot, dude, light up—this fest is ripe for being stoned. And take advantage of the outdoors: go hiking, mountain-bike to Bridal Veil Falls, or kayak the Gunnison Gorge. Bring tons of water, tons of beer, frisbee, hacky sack, portable cd player, water gun, plenty of clothes (it'll get cold at night), tent, sleeping bag, guitar to serenade the ladies, and rain gear. This fest has its share of hippie veterans, but the young still rule. It's easy to meet people, as most are down-to-earth, good-times kind of folk. With the Grateful Dead permanently retired, Telluride brings you the best chance to capture that fun, free-spirited feeling. It's Woodstock in the mountains. Metallica and Marilyn Manson fans probably best stay at home on this one, though.

WHEN TO GO: Middle of June

Summerfest—Milwaukee, Wisconsin

Beer, brats, and some the **best music you'll ever see in one place**. Each summer for approximately ten days, Milwaukee churns out a musical mixture that rivals anybody, anywhere. Rock, country, reggae, jazz, polka—you name it, you'll hear it blasting loud and clear here. They have a huge amphitheatre where big names like **John Mellencamp, the BoDeans** and **Tom Petty** have played. They also have five or six smaller stages (each usually sponsored by a different tasty cold beverage). These stages are free with standard admission, and they've put forth some really fun talent such as **Survivor, Rusted Root, Kool & the Gang, Better than Ezra** and **the Violent Femmes**. You'll also stumble upon comedy acts, carnival-type games, small roller coasters, contests of all kinds, and other good stuff.

While you're here, don't be afraid to put on a cheese head and tell the ladies that you're Brett Favre's cousin. Outside the fest you can explore some of Milwaukee's finer activities, such as taking a **tour of the Miller Brewery**, enjoying brats and beers at a **Brewer's Game**, and drinking beer on board a great **booze cruise on Lake Michigan**. Do you sense a theme here? Just remember, "Say no to Bud products," you're in Miller country. There are plenty of places to stay around Milwaukee and transportation to and from the fest is easy to set up. There's also a free shuttle to Potawatomi Bingo and Casino from the fest—go play a few rounds of craps and come back. When it's all finished, you'll wake up hung over from too many incredible tunes and way too many Millers and Leinenkugel's.

WHEN TO GO: Late June, early July

World's Largest Block Party—Chicago, Illinois

Legend has it that this is **the place** to meet your future spouse—that year after year, lucky ladies come here and discover Mr. Right. Now, before you get scared and stop reading, just think about it for five seconds and you'll quickly realize that this translates only into good things. Women—ready, willing, and anxious—journey far and wide for this event. They wear their most eye-popping getups. And they will no doubt come close to outnumbering you and your fellow man, which according to the supply and demand table we recall from Econ 101, equates to a greater likelihood of profitable returns for you.

The fest takes place **every July in downtown Chicago**. Historically, The Block Party brings in **some really top-level bands**, like Counting Crows, Blues Traveler, and Rusted Root. Other bands also play on a smaller stage. The music certainly adds to the overall fun and vibe. Beer flows like Gatorade at a marathon. And it's **all in the name of a good cause**. The proceeds go to St. Pat's Church and its charitable programs. Don't you feel good already? To add the festivities of this weekend be sure to maximize your time in Chicago. Greektown is right next door to the fest, so go have some flaming cheese and throw some plates. Hit the beach for volleyball, a Cubs game, if they're in town, and any other fests that are happening that same weekend. Because of their ass-chilling winters, Chicago is one town that really comes to life in the summer, and this event is proof.

WHEN TO GO: July

Big Valley Jamboree—Camrose, Alberta Canada

Have you ever watched The Great Outdoor Games on ESPN and wondered, "What the hell do these people do for fun?" **The Big Valley Jamboree** is a good start, when in search of that answer. If you're not road-tripping there, your best bet is to fly into Calgary or Edmonton, rent an RV or van, and then cruise straight to the Camrose Exhibition Center. In order to make sure you don't stand out, **pack a ten-gallon hat and a pair of cowboy boots**. Before you know it, you're blending right in at this country music festival. With Clint Black buzzing in the background, there is no better time to cheer on two guys fiercely competing to saw a log faster than the other. Each morning, as you pour maple syrup on your flapjacks, don't miss **"Breakfast with the Bulls."** While you may think you can ride bull, just eat your pancakes and remain a spectator. This, however, doesn't mean you can't walk with a slight limp and tell girls that you "took a nasty fall off Smoky this morning."

The festival and camping grounds are huge and hold over seven hundred thousand people each year. **A kick-ass camper will get you the necessary attention**, and you can play host to a party each night. During the day, enjoy both types of music, Country and Western, walk the grounds and drink your face off. If you are fan of country music and lumberjacks, then you know why the Jamboree is the place to be. If this experience is foreign to you, then take this opportunity to learn why RV's are so popular and Nashville is renowned for its music.

WHEN TO GO: End of July

LINK IT UP: Enjoy an encore by biking south into the states and Glacier National Park. (See chapter 2, under "Road Biking.")

FILM FESTS

If you think film fests are all about hanging out with Roger Ebert clones, sitting around dark theaters and eating Goobers, well, you're way, way off. These are usually more than a week long, and while they are certainly about checking out some new movies, more importantly they bring in a huge spread of Hollywood talent, and along with them the truly unrealistic lifestyles they lead. At these fests, happenstance can have you flinging back shots with Jack Black, dancing with the leading actresses of Cinemax's late-night offerings and, if you play your cards right, playing the part of lead lap dancee in the remake of *Showgirls*.

Sundance Film Festival—Park City, Utah

Ski, watch some movies, party with celebrities . . . ski, watch some more movies, make out with Jennifer Aniston. . . . A trip to Sundance brings so many opportunities for fun it's surprising the Mormons of Utah allow such festivities. **Taking place for ten days every January**, this film fest triggers a massive pilgrimage from Hollywood. Everyone from A list directors to "look at my lips, I'm the next Angelina Jolie" actresses to the assistant boom guy in a fifteen-minute short, come here to mix it up, make connections, and have a ludicrously good time.

Movies like *Reservoir Dogs*, *The Brothers McMullen*, and *Memento* have been catapulted to fame through this fest. So listen for the buzz about which movies are supposed to be breakthrough. When they become hits, you can tell everyone, "Yeah, I caught that at Sundance . . . really top-notch." And, if you feel compelled, you can embellish and add "Yeah, I shared a long gondola ride with that actress . . . if you know what I'm saying." Beyond the films, you can ski or snowboard at three nearby resorts: **Deer Valley**, **Park City** and **Canyons**. There's also Soldier's Hollow tubing park . . . where nothing is more fun than flying down a hill on a tube while you're butt-wasted. There are a ton of parties being thrown every night. It's just a matter of finding out where they are and what they're for. Talk to people, find out the lowdown, and glom on to anyone who can get your nobody ass in. Parties are given by everyone from the totally obscure filmmaker to the big names—obviously, the larger the venue the better, so work your magic. Hopefully, after a few days here, **you'll be inspired to write a screenplay about it**, called *I Banged a Mormon, a Celebrity, and a Naughty Assistant Key Grip.*

WHEN TO GO: January

Cannes Film Festival—Cannes, France

This is **one tough mother of a festival to crack**. Unless you're in the film business, a lucky member of the press sent to cover what's going on, or a local yokel who's been thrown a bone to shut up and be happy, access to screenings and other related activities are very, very difficult to obtain. If you can finagle or are given the rare opportunity to have red carpet access, seize it. Otherwise, consider it a dare to come here and do your best to beat the system and the *man* (French *man*, that is) at his exclusivity game. If you lose, don't worry—you're still in the South of France.

There's a reason the film industry is willing to journey from all over to get there. Cannes is a beautiful beach town where beautiful people come to **take off their tops, show off their yachts, and get loopy on champagne**. Money is helpful to make the most of this place, but if you're running low on funds, fuck it, you can still have a good time. It's the perfect setting to **pull out your best fake personality**. Are you "Agamemnon," the heir to a Greek shipping conglomerate? Are you "Bo Luke Duke," the race car driver? Or how about "Vortex," the award-winning cinematographer? Whoever you are, be sure to hit the main promenade La Croisette for quality people watching, roll the dice at the Carlton Casino Club in the Hotel Carlton, or in the Casino Croisette, and make it a mission to get invited onto a yacht. French kissing a French girl should certainly be on your to-do list as well. All in all, Cannes brings you sun, celebrities, crazy money, and a boat-load of unbelievable potential. If you've got the savvy to mix it up with the rich and famous and you can put forth A-game effort, **this fest can be an experience for the ages**.

WHEN TO GO: Mid-May

Toronto Film Festival—Toronto, Canada

Leave it to the Canadians to find a way to create **a huge, star-studded festival that's actually very accessible**. This event certainly sees its share of Hollywood types, but it's also a huge destination for your average nobody film fan. And there's no theme to the films they show. Blockbusters looking for a jump start come here. Low-budget flicks about lesbian mimes can be found here. It's a cornucopia of movies, and it's been a launch pad for movies like *Life is Beautiful, Leaving Las Vegas,* and *American Beauty.*

The great thing is, you can totally overdose on movies, which, if you're a fan, can be pure nirvana. However, if you want to mix it up, Toronto is one town that holds its own in the nightlife arena. Hell, it's a pretty big-ass city. You'll want to **stay near Queens Street**, where the majority of the action is. On this street you'll find bars for all occasions. The Horseshoe is a good old dive with live music. Irish pubs are as plentiful as Starbucks. And if you want something funkier, clubs and lounges will be hopping all night. For celebrity sightings, try **the bar at the Four Seasons**. Adult entertainment can be found all too easily. And if you love beer, make your way **the Esplanade Bier Market** for an unrivaled selection to choose from. Also, **bring your barrel**—Niagara Falls is only an hour and half away. Between the films, the celebrities, the Canadian hospitality, and the unending onslaught of drinking establishments, this festival has all the makings of something Oscar worthy.

WHEN TO GO: September

International Erotic Film Festival—Barcelona, Spain

Why not? You don't have to be a porn afficionado to join in on the hilarity certain to ensue at this festival. More than just movies, this is **the** trade show for the international adult entertainment world. Names we've all heard and maybe accidentally seen while surfing The Spice Channel late at night are here promoting their latest cinematic masterpieces. And yes, **the public is more than welcome**. You'll have the opportunity to see live shows from renowned striptease artists, attend a sex product fair, and everywhere you go you'll be surrounded by more silicon than a semiconductor factory worker.

While you're not watching two women engage in a game of "who can moan louder," Barcelona is equipped with an arsenal of ways to have a different brand of fun. Take a trip down **Las Ramblas**, where you can watch whacked-out street performers as you sip a refreshing sangria cocktail. This is also the area where you should find accommodations; hostels and pensions are bountiful here. Off Las Ramblas is an area called **Placa Real**, where you can stumble upon mucho bars and clubs. For late-night good times, head to **Puerto Olympico**, a huge harbor where you can freely bounce from club to club. Also, to feel better about all the tasteless porn you watched, take in **the interesting architecture of Gaudi**, especially the Sagrada Familia. This way, you won't feel so wrong and dirty. Barcelona and porn stars— what a truly beautiful marriage.

WHEN TO GO: Early October

LINK IT UP: You're in Spain, rent a car, drive around, and find your way to Ibiza. (See chapter 4, under "Ibiza.")

OTHER GREAT HAPPENINGS

Full Moon Party—Koh Phangan, Thailand

Thailand is known for beautiful beaches, hot girls, cheap liquor, and an insane nightlife. Every twenty-eight days, when the moon is full and a month's worth of pent-up party aggression threatens to explode, you can find all of the above on the spectacular **Haad Rin Beach on Koh Phangan**. The island is small and accommodations are tight, so get there a few days before the full moon to secure a spot. You can easily get around on **tuk-tuks**, which are the local version of taxis. Make friends with these guys, they are your access key to all that Koh Phangan has to offer. Another option is to stay on nearby Koh Samui or Koh Toa and take water taxis to and from the party. The last and possibly best option is to party until you drop, and sleep where you fall. You won't be alone, as thousands lose consciousness on the beach every month.

The festivities begin at first sight of the full moon and go until morning. Most people here are travelers with little responsibility, so the partying is as intense as you can imagine. Your only concern is making it out alive. You can consume just about anything you want, but the favorite seems to be **Thai Whiskey and Red Bull**. This will make for a wicked hangover, but it's nothing a plunge into the Gulf of Thailand can't cure. Drugs are plentiful, but so are undercover police. Be smart, use the friends you've made, like the tuk-tuk guys; and if anything seems sketchy, bail. We've all seen those movies—so don't end up in a Thai jail. You can stay legal with the local blends of alcohol and still get pleasantly wacked. The loud music and spinning DJ's will keep you dancing, and the ladies love to get freaky under the moonlight. If you can't find a home for your hang-low here, you should quit girls altogether. As the sun starts to rise and you still have your party on, stumble to **The Backyard**. Chances are, at some point in the night you'll make plans for the next day with newfound friends. To make the most of your time, just go along with whomever offers the best "next day."

WHEN TO GO: Anytime there is a full moon. Schedules are on the Web.

LINK IT UP: You're all the way over there, so keep the exotic Far East thing going. (See chapter 5, under "The Far East.")

Full Moon Party—Bomba's Beach Shack, Tortola, British Virgin Islands

He makes mushroom tea, a rum punch love elixir, and invites every girl to take off her clothes. To some he's just a dirty old man, to us . . . **Bomba is a hero**. His shack is made of driftwood, aluminum siding, old water skis, and license plates. It was once destroyed by a hurricane, but its simple structure allowed for easy rebuilding. Nestled right on the beach overlooking Little Apple Bay, the beach shack is the perfect backdrop to host **the best full moon party in the Caribbean**. Every month Tortola becomes a destination for partygoers from all over the Virgin Islands; and they all come to Bomba's. There are plenty of places to stay on the island, all depending on your budget. You can definitely sleep on the beach, but you won't find as many joining you in this endeavor, so a hotel makes more sense here.

Mushrooms (the funny kind) are actually harvested locally in Tortola. Thus, they are a legal crop. You'll find people selling them throughout the island. The mushrooms are legal, but selling them is not. So, be careful of whom you buy them from. At Bomba's, **you buy the cup and the special mushroom tea is free**. Talk about beating the system. The sounds of **steel drums and reggae music** will carry you through the night. The effects of the psychedelic fungi and booze navigate the evening for you. And the women will be loosened up by Bomba, as he serves them his rum punch while encouraging them to pin their intimates above the bar. Leave panty sniffing to the old man, though. Once again, you'll find yourself on a picturesque island, with beautiful people—and there is no doubt you'll be feeling good. It's all about a good mood and continuous partying as the full moon shines over this side of the Atlantic Ocean.

WHEN TO GO: Any time there is a full moon. Schedules are on the Web.

Anytime, Any way, anyhow Playboy Mansion—Los Angeles

In a guy's world of constant "my schlong is bigger than yours," "my job is better than yours," and "my girlfriend is more bendable than yours," the **first one of your friends to get invited to the Playboy Mansion wins all wars**. Girls do walk around naked, guys do get head in The Grotto, and Hef does have three girlfriends. Access to the Mansion is limited, and the security there is tight. So, to the average guy, this sucks. But for those blessed enough to get by the gates, you will quickly understand why this sanctuary is protected like the Olsen Twins on a college campus. And this exclusivity is definitely a benefit. As soon as you walk in you are instantaneously elevated to a status level capable of landing you on top of a playmate or a B-level actress.

No matter how you got there, while you are there your story is that you are **"independently wealthy and working on some interesting projects."** No matter how geeked out you may be or how badly you want to giggle and call your friends, do not do it. This is just a normal Saturday night for the mover and shaker that you are. Getting to the mansion is an every-man-for-himself crusade. So don't be afraid to enter contests on the Internet, call Howard Stern, or write letters to those who might get you in. If and when it becomes a reality, make sure you don't bring a bunch of dudes with you. This is one move that will get you kicked out. The mansion has a strict limit on the amount of sausage it wants in the pool. Work hard and follow the rules. It's worth it. While all your buddies are at home playing Madden football and drinking from a pony keg, you'll be pitching a tent while receiving a massage from Miss August.

WHEN TO GO: Whenever you can. If you get invited and do not go, please turn in your penis.

CAN'T GET THERE? Throw your own Playboy Mansion Party. Start with the obvious amounts of booze, beer, champagne, and blended drinks. Throw invites out to Fred Durst and Pauly Shore. Put up a strippers pole, strobe lights, and The Playboy Channel on the flat screen. Pull together a shitload of comfy pillows and throw them everywhere. Have a soft room in the house with pillows and a bong, and something similar outside. A pool and hot tub are a plus, but, even if you don't have those, set up a minipool and christen it "The Grotto." Create a theme with a time-tested and worthy objective of getting as many girls as possible lubed up and barely dressed. "Pajama Party," "Playmate of the Year Party," or "Will You be my Sugar Daddy Party?" will all turn you into the Godfather of Sex (at least for a night).

CHAPTER TWO

ADVENTURES *in* ADVENTURE

Now that you've read chapter 1, it's apparent that you could, if you wanted, travel the world hitting up different events and festivals for the remainder of your existence. And while this certainly would be a great time, we fear it could mess with the overall state of your sanity. So, in order to round things off, you should set up a list of adventures to tackle. As you sit in a kayak one hundred yards from a seventy-five-thousand-pound whale, captain a ship to Santorini, or spend a week with Sherpas in Nepal, there is no doubt that you will have **seen indescribable views, achieved unimaginable feats and had life-changing experiences**. We all have shitloads of fun at our local tavern, so it can be tough to muster up the motivation to set out on some of the conquests we've highlighted. But guess what? Your bartender will still buy your sixth beer when you return. You may have dropped in your golden tee rankings, but you'll also have chipped one in at the real St. Andrews. Plus, the guy who stole your ranking still hasn't been laid in two years.

It's imperative on several levels that you take on these events while you still can. **First**, as you get old, your body won't be able to take the abuse it used to. The physical requirements alone require you to be the strapping stud that you are now. **Secondly**, soon enough, things like sleeping in your rental car, showering in a waterfall, and eating dinner directly from your fishing line will no longer be an option, due to your wife's veto. **Third**, these adventures will introduce you to and teach you the skills that just might make you an interesting guy for the rest of your life. **And lastly**, these trips you do while you're single just might give you an automatic hall pass when you're married. For example, Michael has been going on an annual fishing trip with his buddies since 1993. While several of his friends are now married (even some with kids), they still make every one of these annual jaunts. "Honey, we've been doing this forever. *You* knew this when we got married, why are you pulling this now?" Get it? It can actually work. Trust us, you'll thank yourself later.

SCUBA DIVING

Take a trip underwater and discover a sight unlike any you've ever seen. Diving vacations offer the best of many worlds. You'll enjoy warmth, water, and beautiful scenery. Not to mention resorts with swim-up bars, casinos, and ladies looking to let loose while they're on vacation. You'll also hone your aquatic skills while mastering the art of using a Self Contained Underwater Breathing Apparatus. And after a day of mingling with the ocean's finest creatures, you'll have plenty of fabrications to spin that night at the local disco about sharks and barracudas—so much so that you'll understand why Jacques Cousteau probably got laid a lot. Continuing on that theme, you'll be able to carry those very stories home with you— embellishing them at every step. Here are some top places to get your scuba on.

Belize, Central America

Cry me a reefer! Located just south of Mexico, Belize owns the longest coral reef in all of the Caribbean. For scuba adventures, the best place to hold down the fort is **Ambergris Caye**. There, you can swim alongside nurse sharks and stingrays in **Shark Ray Alley**, take stunning underwater photos, and still make it back to the beach bar by noon to toast tequila shooters. One spot you absolutely must hit is the infamous **Blue Hole**. No, we're not talking about Smurf porn here, but rather a giant, 412-foot-deep limestone sinkhole in the Belize Reef. Also, be sure to **freak yourself out with a night dive**.

While not diving, you'll have amazing rain forests and outrageous wildlife to take in. On Ambergris Caye, you can **rent golf carts** to get your lazy ass around. You won't find the nightlife to be too crazy, but it has its share of bars, clubs, and even a casino. Don't miss the world-famous (slight exaggeration) **Chicken Drop Game**. This gambling game, best compared to roulette or bingo, consists of dropping a chicken on a huge board with numbered squares and if the chicken craps on your square, you are the lucky winner. Of course, part of the deal is that the winner cleans up the mess.

WHEN TO GO: November through May (Wet season starts in June.)

WARNING: If offered the popular dish of gibnut, politely say "Sorry, but I'm on a strict no-rodent diet."

LINK IT UP: Now head to Cancun where the tequila goes in and the boobies come out. (See chapter 4, under "Spring Break.") Or for further outdoor adventures Costa Rica is right next door. (See chapter 2, under "Kayaking.")

Cayman Islands, Caribbean

More than just a place to launder your money, the Caymans shell out some of the best diving in the world. Divided into three islands, Grand Cayman, Little Cayman, and Cayman Brac, this destination offers a little something-something for everybody. For you, the most logical place to settle in is **Grand Cayman and its seven-mile beach**. There you'll have the ammunition to stay where you want and dive as you please. Not to mention, this island has the most nightlife. From pulsating clubs to calypso playing pubs, it'll be way too easy to tie one on.

For diving, Grand Cayman alone has 159 sites. The most popular is **Sting Ray Alley**, where you'll mingle with tons of these floppy creatures. Be careful: they're called "sting" rays for a reason, and their sucking/grinding method of eating can give you one nasty hickey. You can take side trips to Little Cayman's Bloody Bay Wall (named for its color, not dead divers) and Cayman Brac's sunken Russian warship. Also, around Easter the Caymans throw a huge party, called **Batabano**, as their answer to Carnival. Come for that, and plan on doing less diving and more drinking. While you're here, don't forget to check on that $1.5 million you had wired to your account.

WHEN TO GO: November through August—avoid hurricane season

Great Barrier Reef—Queensland, Australia

It's over 500,000 years old, has 2,800 species of fish, 500 kinds of seaweed, and is the only living organism that can be viewed from outer space (Kirstie Alley's ass not included). Yet, all they could come up with is "Great?" How about the "Fucking Awesome" Barrier Reef? Or the "Most Snizzlest, Dizzlest, Dazzlest" Barrier Reef? Anyhow, go see this worldly wonder.

Choosing dives is about as easy as selecting the five women you'd most like to find yourself naked in the back of a Chevy with. Some favorites are **Hastings, Saxon, Norman, the Ribbon Reefs and Cod Hole**. During the right season, you can hit **Fraser Island for humpback whale sightings**. And for serious sea creatures, there's **the wreck of the Yongala**. The place to stay is Cairns, where you'll have a fleet of diving boats and a nearby rain forest. At night you can gamble, drink stubbies (bottled beer), and sing your favorite Men at Work tunes at a karaoke bar. Make trips to Port Douglas for more diving and the Whitsundays for escapades on your rented dinghy. Hit the outback at some point. **Sleep on the reef.** And pick up some quality lingo like, "G'day there ladies, whaddy say we throw some tasty bugs on the barbie, get blotto on some slabs of amber fluid, and then have wild and crazy root." Translation: *Let's eat, drink, and have some sex.*

WHEN TO GO: October through April

Phuket, Thailand

What's with the names of places in Thailand? You've got Bang Kok and Phuk Et. Coincidence? Or marketing genius? We don't know. Either way . . . they rock. Yeah, it's pronounced Foo Ket but hey "phuck it." This place brings you pristine beaches, amazing islands, and world-class scuba. It's a total 180 from your normal existence. Head west to the Andaman Sea and shack up (literally) in **the beach town of Patong**. There you'll enjoy your nondiving time by frequenting Bangla Road, and its many beer bars. Side lanes lead to naughtier spots.

Strangely, you'll find many young girls who really dig you. Not all are all-female, so pay attention.

From Patong, you can embark to many a great site. **The Similan Islands are a must-see**, and best accomplished with a night on the boat. Your overnight amenities will be directly related to how much you pay—much like that back-alley massage. Other worthy trips are **Shark Point, Anemone Reef, and the Phi Phi Islands**. Hopefully, you'll see leopard sharks, lionfish, manta rays and whale sharks. While here, dare your friends to eat the strangest food. Check out a snake show and ride an elephant. When your job sucks, life is lame, and you just want to say, "Fuck it," well . . . this is the place.

WHEN TO GO: November through May for calm seas and little rain

WARNING: Thai culture is very antifeet and antitouching of the head—so whatever you do, don't pat someone on the head with your foot.

OTHER SCUBA DESTINATIONS RECEIVING VOTES
- Bonaire, Netherlands Antilles
- Florida Keys, Florida
- Red Sea, Egypt
- Bali
- Jules Undersea Lodge (underwater hotel off Key Largo)

MOVIES NOT TO WATCH BEFORE YOU GO

Jaws

Jaws II

Jaws 3-D

Jaws IV

Open Water
Piranha
Deep Blue Sea (actually, don't watch that at all)

SWIMMING WITH SHARKS

"Anyone seen my leg?" If the thrill of mingling with pretty little fishies doesn't quite do it for you, take it to the next level and take on the fiercest creature in the ocean. There are several destinations that bring you face-to-face with these jaw-dropping, body-amputating friends of the sea. It's certainly a thrill on the same level as skydiving, only you'll be screaming on the inside as you try not to suck in your entire oxygen supply. Have fun, bring an underwater camera, and just don't cut yourself shaving the morning of your dive.

South Africa

Forget *Jaws*, the nightmares you'll be haunted by after this adventure will be on a par with the first time you saw Hannibal Lecter say, "Hello Claaarice . . ." If you ever happen to be visiting South Africa—you know, on a random weekend, or whatever—you must grow a pair of balls and take on this challenge. It's relatively safe, only two or three limbs are lost a year. Or is that a month? Whatever—the cage will protect you.

Here you'll see **the MacDaddy of all sharks**, the Great White. These bad boys can weigh up to five thousand pounds. Their teeth are sharper than your Mom's best Ginsu. And they can sprint up to fifteen miles per hour. But don't worry, they're not huge fans of the way we taste . . . we're not fatty enough. On this trip, you'll head out to **Shark Alley**, where you'll be put in a galvanized-steel cage and sent underwater to immediately wet yourself. **Just hope the other divers don't feel the warm spot.** From the boat, you'll also see the fins circling, and even a shark's head breach the water in *Jaws*-like fashion. In the end, you'll someday be able to go to the aquarium with your kids and say, "That shark is nothing. Your Dad has done battle with much bigger." Just leave out the part about peeing in your rented wetsuit.

WHEN TO GO: Best times are from October to April, but you can go anytime.

Point Judith, Rhode Island

Who would have thought that you'd utter "sharks" and "Rhode Island" in the same sentence? But it's true. If you live on the East Coast or are visiting the area, you can easily scoot over to our nation's tiniest state and venture out to see the ocean's biggest killer. Out here, you'll come nose-to-nose (not including the huge-ass cage that separates you) with **migratory blue sharks**.

You'll need a charter boat for this adventure. They'll take you out, hurl some tasty chum to the sharks, and then send you down in a cage for your viewing pleasure. It's like that 3-D Imax movie, without the little kid kicking the back of your chair. The water is scrotum-chilling cold, so you'll need a wet suit. As soon as you're done, make way to a nearby bar to warm up and **begin spinning your tale of how the cage door unexpectedly opened** and a shark came flying in to eat you and Oprah Winfrey, who just happened to be in there with you, only to have his snout pummeled by your wicked left-right combo. Hey, you're a hero, you saved Oprah.

WHEN TO GO: Summertime

Nassau, Bahamas

You aren't menstruating today, are you? Because the sharks can pick up on that, you know. Just kidding, you're safe—sharks don't care if you're on the rag. Here in the Bahamas, shark diving is really catching on, and thus, dive operators are willing to oblige with trips specific to that intention. You'll have a range of options. Choose the one you think will be the coolest, yet the least likely to get you chomped into tiny pieces.

On this excursion, you and other fearless folks will travel to a known shark area; the operators will toss out the yummy chum and then toss you out to watch the sharks rip apart their free meal. You'll see mainly **black and white reef sharks**. You could be daring and swim out to get extra close, but that's up to you. We say go for it. If you survive, you can carry on with many other great dives in the area. You can go sailing, fishing, or just engage in the Bahamian tradition of **drinking rum until you actually start resembling a piña colada**. Also, take a trip to Atlantis on Paradise Island for super water slides, golf, and a little Caribbean poker.

WHEN TO GO: Anytime but hurricane season

Tenneco Towers—Fort Lauderdale, Florida

For the more advanced scuba dude, this site gives you the combo of a wreck and sharks. The Tenneco Towers are named after a bunch of sunken oil platforms that have developed into quite a reef of underwater wildlife. You'll have to go pretty deep here . . . 75 to 190 feet. So, if you consider the front-crawl something you do to get to the swim-up bar, or the breast stroke something you do before moving on to third base, this is not the trip for you. If, however, you're up to the challenge, you'll have one helluva meet 'n' greet with **the big bull sharks** that swim in these waters.

Beyond this wreck and its sharks, Fort Lauderdale has many other great dives. There's one called the **Mercedes 1**, which, as you can guess, is not your traditional wreck. **Sadly, Fort Lauderdale is no longer the wet T-shirt capital of the world**, but you'll still find a good time. **(Or head to South Beach, where it's guaranteed.)** Either way, when you go out, dare one of your buddies to tuck his right arm into his shirt and dramatically tell all the ladies about his unfortunate shark expedition.

WHEN TO GO: Stay away from hurricane season, but all else should be good.

CAN'T GET THERE? Several aquariums, including Tampa's, Monterey Bay's, and Maui's, offer shark diving programs on premise.

FISHING

So much water, so many fish, so little time. There are a million types of lures, poles, and techniques. There are fly-fishing loyalists, deep sea tough guys, and yahoos trolling around lakes in rowboats. We like any kind of fishing, and **the only way you'll find your favorite is by trying them all**. Regardless of where you are and what you're doing, fishing means that you are hanging with your buddies in a kick-ass location and drinking beer. Add the sport of it, and you'll set up some of the best days a guy could imagine.

During your adventures, the days will be spent knocking out some great fishing, while at night it's story time—all the while boozing it up. You will also enjoy some memorable time in the local towns before and after your days on the water. These places always provide for some of the best fish tales. From the local bar with the free foosball in Labrador to that the weird Alaskan girl who made out with your friend, local spots will add to the escapade.

FLY-FISHING

Fly-fishing generally involves wearing cool rubber waders and a sporty fishing vest. Looking like a pro, it becomes your job to spot the fish, cast your fly, and tempt the catch to take the bait. With light lures and equipment, hiking into your locations is always a good time. But when hiking in, obviously carrying twelve cases of beer isn't an option. So pack flasks of booze, or, better yet, a baggie of something they measure in ounces. The alternatives to hiking are helicopters, sea planes, and mules. **There's nothing like hiring a plane simply to fly in beer for you.** Either way, the days always end at camp, cooking up some tasty grub and recapping the day. Make sure you and the other guys stagger your fishing spots in order to hit up different areas. This window of separation definitely allows for some fish embellishments: "Dude, I had the biggest damn fish on my line, it barely got away . . ."

Expert fly-fishermen have honed masterful skills and techniques. However, for the novice, it is not difficult to get on the river and pull in some nice trout. Stores like Orvis and Cabela's can set you up with all that you need and even give you a couple of lessons. It's also worth it to hire an outfitter who can direct you to the best spots. You can fly-fish on just about any stream with fish in it, but here are some of the best:

Alaska, United States

If you live in any of the other forty-nine states, you may have a tendency to forget that Alaska exists. Their athletics are less popular than WNBA teams, they don't swing the Electoral College and Eskimos aren't hanging out in your local tavern. While the lack of attention may be understandable, once you recognize the magnificence of this place, it becomes the best state in the nation.

Bears, mountains, glaciers, and most importantly fish, are in abundance throughout this great state, especially along **the Alaskan Peninsula, Bristol Bay, Katmai National Park and the Kenai Peninsula;** these are great places to start the search for your trip. Salmon, trout, and northern pike are just the beginning of the types of fish you can go for. If you want to get wicked close to the bears and compete with them for salmon, apply to be one of the two hundred people allowed into **the McNeil River State Game Sanctuary**. It's worth it if you get in. After flying into Anchorage, the vast lands of Alaska make it difficult to hike out to the coast, so bush or float planes are solid ways to get you to your spot and will offer a glorious view of this great state.

WHEN TO GO: June through September

WARNING: Many Alaskan natives use their left or right hand in lieu of toilet paper. Thus, high fives should be performed with thoughtful consideration.

Kola Peninsula, Russia

Before you start thinking about fishing with Ivan Drago, this Russian Peninsula is very Nordic and borders on Finland. With **some of the best salmon fishing in the world**, the experience of flying into either Helsinki or Moscow and then wading in the waters of Northern Russia will be the fishing event of a lifetime. Your guide will pick you up at the Murmansk airport and take you up to the Peninsula. Before you know it, you are casting for North Atlantic salmon in freakin' Russia.

You can float in a boat or stand on the shores of both the Ponoi and the Yokanga rivers as you chase these beautiful fish. While you're definitely not in the tropics, the June-through-September angling season offers some decent weather, around fifty degrees. During the Summer Solstice you'll have the opportunity to **witness the amazing "White Nights", with twenty-four hours of sunlight**. While amongst the Russians, the preferred substance is vodka—and don't ask for any cranberry juice, just drink it. Spending a couple of days in Moscow or Helsinki is definitely required. We don't have to tell you what kind of talent is coming out of Russia these days—just don't end up with a "too-many Stoli's souvenir" from RussianBrides R Us.

WHEN TO GO: June through September

Labrador, Canada

Have you thought much about the plot of land that sits above Quebec? Well, meet Labrador. This area makes up a Canadian province that is known for its tremendous lakes and rivers. If you are a believer in going to bars with more girls because it improves your odds, then this thought process will bring you to Labrador when choosing your fishing destination. **The Woods River System and Goose Bay** are great locations, known for some of **the best brook trout in North America**, not to mention schools of northern pike, lake trout, and salmon. The brook trout are not hidden, thus the initial catch isn't overly difficult. But even for the seasoned angler, once you get them on the line, these fish can be a real battle. So, to complete the analogy, it's like being in a bar where tons of girls will come and talk to you, but getting them to your bed will require some time, perseverance, and genuine skill.

WHEN TO GO: June through September

Yucatan Peninsula, Mexico

Flying into Cancun, you may have visions of foam parties and boobies, and that is always encouraged. However, the Yucatan Peninsula also offers **saltwater fly-fishing** that is second to none. South of Cancun, you'll find the town of **Xcaret**, the island of **Cozumel**, and **Ascension Bay**. All located on the Caribbean, you are in a tropical paradise, ready to take on some of the most exciting fly-fishing you can imagine. The Grand Slam of saltwater fishing—bonefish, tarpon, and permit can all be caught in one day here. The best plan is to **get a villa on the water** and make that your home. From there, each day will be different as you hit the flats. Bonefishing involves some of the most difficult angling, but also the most addictive. The masters of the game must first locate the fish, then cast the perfect fly, not too close or too far, set the fly right, and bring that baby in. Bonefish are strong and fast, but as you build your techniques you will be hooked (pun intended).

WHEN TO GO: Fishing is possible 365 days a year.

LINK IT UP: Create more success stories by reeling in that feisty wet-T-shirt runnerup in Cancun (she's got something to prove). (See chapter 4, under "Spring Break.")

DEEP-SEA FISHING

Deep-sea fishing is a lot like hunting. You head out in search of a large beast, prepare yourself for the kill, and then wait for the target to enter your radar. The difference with fishing, however, is that once you've got the bastard, the battle has just begun. Reeling in a 250-pound marlin or tuna is the struggle of a lifetime. And the feeling of bringing that beast on board is so remarkable that Ernest Hemingway wrote an entire book about it. The best part is you will surely be fourteen beers deep while fighting the fight—making it all the more interesting.

Chartering a yacht is a must when heading out on the great waters. When picking your boat, always **ask how many and what kind of fish they expect you to catch**. Also, you'll need a place to stay. A great checks-and-balances program is to call a few accommodations and ask which charter they recommend. Then call a few charters and ask what accommodations they recommend. From there, you can see if any work together and offer "all-inclusive" packages. They may even cook your catch of the day. Anytime you're on a boat with buddies, it's a winner. Here are some of the best places to pull out incredible game:

Iztapa, Guatemala

With volcanoes twelve thousand feet high, black sand beaches, and rain forests, Guatemala is definitely a Central American gem. Not to mention, it's damn cheap and **abundant in sailfish and beautiful women**. When traveling to Central America, it's important to map out your trip and have a local contact. Flying into Guatemala City is accessible from many major U.S. cities, and the journey to Iztapa is not too far. **Each day will have you out on the Pacific Ocean**, fighting sailfish and cheering along with your fellow fishers like you're at a horse race and your five-hundred-dollar pick to win is ahead by a nose as they come flying down the homestretch. After a day like that, your entire trip has justified itself. Drinking and relaxing by your pool at night will lead to comments like, "Damn, this is awesome." While you're kicking it in Iztapa with your guides, have fun and be jackasses. If you spend a night in Guatemala City, it can be a little sketchy, just keep your head up and you'll be fine.

WHEN TO GO: November through June

"ALL-INCLUSIVE" IN GUATEMALA
Keith, 30, Los Angeles, recently married

My friends and I were in search of that perfect fishing adventure. Someone mentioned that Guatemala had some of the best sailfish in the world. So we hopped on the Internet, called around, and found an operation that seemed like a winner. With a few different packaging options, we went for the "all-inclusive" package. We weren't exactly sure what that meant, but for fifteen hundred dollars each for five days of fishing, it seemed like a great deal. When we arrived at the airport, I saw a smoking-hot chica holding a sign with my name on it. I greeted her with an, "Hola." She greeted me with a kiss. "Ok so far," I'm thinking. Annabella was her name, and she led us to a jeep outside. We each grabbed a Gallo (not the cheap California wine, the local beer) from the cooler and hopped in. After a while, we stopped and followed Annabella into a little building that turned out to be a strip club. "Holy Shit, what is going on?" We were each told to pick one. A few lap dances later, I confidently choose my girl . . . for the week. We proceeded to our house, which was complete with a deck, pool, and hot tub. After partying all night, we woke up early and cruised miles out into the Pacific. Between the four of us, we caught over twenty sailfish. So excited about our fruitful day, all we did on the way home was talk about fish. It wasn't until we arrived and went out back and found our lovely girls waiting topless by the pool that we realized the seismic magnitude of this day in our lives. That week we caught tons of fish, ate great food, and drank constantly, all in the guard of exquisite women who thought we played for the Yankees. And yes, it was truly "all-inclusive."

Montauk, New York

You're not a deep-sea fisherman until you've caught a four-hundred-pound shark, a fish that wants to and could kill you as you pull him onto the boat. Yes, **there's a reason they bring a loaded gun on board**. Only 120 miles from the mayhem of Manhattan, Montauk is the premier fishing spot on the East Coast. Some people say the fish population off this coast is the greatest in the world, not to mention some of the biggest known to man. You can easily find charters that will take you out for **mako, blue, and thresher sharks**, and some may lead you toward the mother of all sharks—the great white. Montauk is an old-school fishing town to kick back in and swap stories with genuine fishermen. As you make your way back toward New York City, **make a pit stop in the world-famous Hamptons**, also known as the Hamptonies. Dress in a white linen suit and swing by Diddy's White Party. Or get sloppy with Lindsay Lohan and Tara Reid at the Star Room in East Hampton. Your vacation began trolling for sharks and finished with a bottle of Cristal—who's better than you?

WHEN TO GO: June through October

Los Cabos, Mexico

Where the Sea of Cortez meets the Pacific Ocean, you'll find **the capital of marlin fishing**. From the nearby and fun city of Cabo San Lucas, you can easily charter out into this body of water and hunt down the big fish. **Whales, dolphins, and sea turtles will surround your boat** as you slug down dozens of Pacificos (the local beer). When you return, every local will ask if you want your marlin mounted for one thousand dollars. It's not worth it; all they do is take a picture and send it to a taxidermist. You can do the same thing yourself. Imagine an eight-foot marlin above your bed at home. Oh, the stories that fish could tell!

Downtown Cabo has great bars such as El Squid Roe and Sammy Hagar's Cabo Wabo. You'll have no problemo downing jello shots and grabbing some tail here. If your trip is more chill and you don't want to end up dancing on a bar, then just get a villa in an unruffled spot. There's also some great golf here. **Cabo del Sol**, designed by Jack Nicklaus, is worth every penny as you smash your drive along the Pacific Coast.

WHEN TO GO: Fishing is great all year round; best is March through December.

OTHER FISHING ADVENTURES RECEIVING VOTES:
- Tarpon in Costa Rica
- Muskie in Northern Wisconsin
- King Salmon in Alaska
- Conch-Diving Anywhere
- Spearfishing Anywhere
- Bass in the Everglades
- Salmon on the Alta in Norway

- Striped Bass off Massachusetts
- Fly-fishing in the U.S. and Canadian Rockies
- Trout in Patagonia, Argentina

KAYAKING, CANOEING, AND RAFTING

No traffic jams. No horns blaring. No road rage. Getting out on the water truly makes for a unique way to journey. And the great thing is there are a ton of options available for your exploration. Whether it's the rush of the rapids or the glassy smoothness of a calm lake, or a little bit of both, you can't go wrong. You'll see incredible, unspoiled wildlife, sights unreachable by land, and you'll get a workout worthy of multiple campfire beers. Your buddies may fall out. You may have to save them. Or just laugh and point. It's all a good time out on the water. Enjoy the adrenaline rush of speeding uncontrollably down an untamed river, the unique feeling of watching a sea otter play games under your watercraft, or the thrill of paddling through huge, floating ice chunks from the nearby glacier. These are just a few of the reasons to take to the water for adventure. Here are some great passages worth a trip down:

Kayaking Prince William Sound—Valdez, Alaska

Whoever said "Everything is bigger in Texas" obviously had never been to Alaska. America's last frontier brings you bigger and better everything when it comes to the outdoors and wildlife. Their waterways are no exception. From the town of Valdez, you'll kayak out into **the glacial waters of Prince William Sound**. You'll paddle amongst fat harbor seals, feisty sea otters, and maybe even pods of killer whales. **Shamu in the wild—nothing is more impressive.** You'll sleep to the thunderous sounds of ice breaking off Shoup Glacier, camp next to massive waterfalls, and trek through rain forestlike islands.

The trip is best done with a guide. They'll know where to camp and hopefully will cook up fresh halibut nightly. Make it at least a five-day journey and get near the Columbia Glacier (it's the size of L.A.) where you'll weave through magically-blue icebergs. And be prepared to poop outdoors, wear a mosquito net at times, and work up a Tony Soprano appetite. Also, **you'll have nearly twenty-four hours of sun to play with**. While in Alaska, try hiking on a glacier, reeling in a salmon, and wrestling a grizzly (that's slang for making sweet love in your sleeping bag). The minute your trip is over, you'll be plotting how the hell to get back.

WHEN TO GO: June to September

Rafting the Colorado River—Grand Canyon, Arizona

It has rocks 1.7 billion years old. The Hopi believed it to be the birthplace of human life. And it's America's most prized natural wonder. So what are you gonna do, come here, stand on the edge, smile, take some pictures and head home? Not unless you're driving an RV and wearing adjustable adult pampers. No, instead you're going to hop on a raft for an adventure that says "Yes, I have lived inside the Canyon."

You'll need to sign up with an outfitter. Private licenses take too long. **Do not go on a motorized craft or one where they row for you.** Suck it up and paddle. Or, *are* you wearing those pampers? When you're not battling the rapids of **Horn Creek, Granite, Hermit and Crystal**, you'll see Indian ruins, all kinds of wildlife, and a spectacle of naturally carved ancient rock. The entire journey is 277 miles, so pick the best put-in and take-out places for the time you have. Don't miss the rapids mentioned above, or the Lava Falls, and make room for some canyon hiking. Also, bring some horseshoes for nightly playing, beers to enjoy, and load your iPod with Indian chanting music for ambience. After this trip, you will forever look at the Grand Canyon with the highest reverence and awe.

WHEN TO GO: Anytime April to November

Rafting the Alsek/Tatshenshini—Alaska/British Columbia

Yes, another water adventure in Alaska. But screw it, they were both too good to leave one out. Anyway, this trip is different. It's rafting. It's a river. And "ey," it's closer to Canada. The Alsek and Tatshenshini (Indian for "long word that we can't pronounce so good") have been called **the last wild rivers on the planet**, because they flow unobstructed from source to sea. They've yet to be tainted by "The Man."

Pretty cool, considering **the only way to see what you'll see is via the river**. Here, you'll take in bears, moose, bald eagles, salmon (being eaten by bald eagles), goats, wolves, and other wild things. You'll dodge monster truck–size glacier debris, stare at the massive **St. Elias Mountain Range**, hike on Goatherd Mountain, and paddle furiously through the merging point of these two powerhouses—the Alsek and the Tatshenshini. Overall, your jaw will spend much of the time laying in your lap in amazement of your surroundings. And you thought only Vegas strip clubs could do that. While there, take a trip to **the old mining town of McCarthy/Kennicott**. Bike in, hike its glacier, and then head to its bar for a beer with a grizzly bear on the label.

WHEN TO GO: Summertime

Rafting/Kayaking the Futaleufu—Chile (Patagonia), South America

It's like the difference between a garden hose and a 500-psi pressure washer. Bam! This river is ready to thrash your silly ass around and then some. It's a short journey (twenty-seven miles long), but very powerful. And can be best summed up by the names of its rapids. **The Terminator, The Throne Room, Zeta, and Inferno** are a few. Beyond the unrivaled adrenaline rush you'll get from taking on this fun bastard, you'll find yourself enveloped by some of South America's most amazing scenery.

Snowcapped mountains stand high in the backdrop, canyons lead to quiet, turquoise pools, and waterfalls abound. Along this wild ride, you can add to the adventure with horseback rides, fly-fishing, rappelling, ziplining, and jumping off cliffs. If you're tired, you can always grab a six-pack and **chill Chilean-style in one of the many natural hot tubs**. Be sure to find a quality outfitter with cool lodging options along the river. While in this part of the universe, take a jaunt to **Volcan Orson** (that's volcano to you) and check off hiking on an actual volcano.

WHEN TO GO: December to April

LINK IT UP: The wild rapids of Patagonia are the perfect complement to the wild thongs of Rio and Carnival. (See chapter 1, under "Carnival.")

Rafting the Pacuare—Costa Rica

"Ooo . . . Ooo . . . Ooo . . . ah, ah, ah!" Is that the sound of you screaming uncontrollably as your raft flies down thirty-two miles of white-knuckle rapids—or is it the nearby monkeys taunting you? Chances are it's a little bit of both. The Pacuare brings you **an awesome combination of wild rapids in a wild jungle**. They're so badass that U.S. Olympic paddlers train here. But don't worry, with the right guide yelling at you to "turn left" and "get right," you'll be fine. Yeah, you'll feel like a pinball at times, but isn't that the thrill you're seeking?

While not getting soaked, you'll cruise by towering waterfalls, pass by local fisherman, and spot jaguars, monkeys, sloths, and strange birds. The rafting only lasts a couple of days—so pick a trip that offers other activities like hiking to waterfalls, exploring wildlife, and swinging from tree vines in monkeylike fashion. You'll most likely **stay at eco-lodges**, where you can sleep in a hammock, enjoy tropical drinks in a coconut, and eat breakfast with a toucan . . . Fruit Loops perhaps? It's not the lap of luxury, and, sorry, you won't have pay-per-view porn, but that's the rain forest experience. All in all, this trip is a challenge worth every drenching you receive.

WHEN TO GO: November to May is the best for good rapids.

LINK IT UP: From the jungle to the ocean, head to Belize for amazing underwater adventures. (See chapter 2, under "Diving.")

OTHER KAYAKING/RAFTING DESTINATIONS RECEIVING VOTES:
- Kayaking Baja; Baja, California
- Rafting the Middle Fork of the Salmon River; Idaho
- Kayaking Down-East Islands; Maine
- Kayaking San Juan Islands; Washington State
- Canoeing/Kayaking the Boundary Waters; Minnesota
- Rafting the Zambezi; Zimbabwe/Zambia, Africa

MOVIES NOT TO WATCH BEFORE YOU GO
Deliverance

MOVIES TO WATCH BEFORE YOU GO
Up the Creek
Without a Paddle

GOLF

Even a horrible day of golf beats the piss out of a good day at work, right? So gather up four, eight, or twelve guys and hit the links for a long weekend, a whole vacation, or whatever you feel like. Whether you're a scratch golfer or a divot-launching champion, it's really impossible to have a bad time. On top of the general golf etiquette and playing rules, there are a few others to abide by: **Make best friends with the beer cart girl**—tip her well, profess your undying love for her, and she'll be there for you. **Ramming into other carts is forbidden**—during someone's swing—all other times are totally fair game. **If one of your friends hits into you**, you are permitted to fire his ball back at him, run over it with your cart, or pee on it. Lastly, **any guy who refuses to drink** automatically adds five strokes. Be sure to promote healthy competition. You can go foursome against foursome or individually. Wager tonight's dinner, postgolf drinks, or have "loserwear" to be worn at night. Think plaid knickers and pink sweaters. There are a ton of other fun gambling games like "Monkey," "Wolf," and "Dick Out." You can always institute a scramble . . . great for the second round of thirty-six. We also read in *Golf Digest* (or one of those magazines) that anyone who can get a hand job in the woods from a female golfer wearing her glove automatically earns twenty-four hours of free drinks. Other than that, your trip is yours to execute. Here are some places you can't miss:

Myrtle Beach, South Carolina

This place was made for a guy's golf outing. Sure it gets a beating by purists for being too flashy and too cheesy, and for supplying duffers with too many strip clubs. But what's so wrong about that? Myrtle, despite the naysayers, does indeed serve up some terrific golf. **With one hundred or so courses**, it's home to more ball-whacking than a teenager with unlimited pay-per-view access. Chances are you'll swing a deal with an all-inclusive package. Just make sure you get a condo or townhouse, and stay clear of some of the sleazier hotels. You're better than that.

Course worth checking into are **The Dunes, Caledonia, True Blue Plantation, Heritage and the Barefoot Resort**. At night put on your favorite party shirt and head on out. Here, it's Cancun-lite. You'll witness "Hot Leg" contests, a little fog machine action, and some quality country line-dancing. Sound stupid? Not when you're twelve beers and six test-tube shots in. After grinding to Garth Brooks with some hot Southern belle, you'll have your pick of golfer specials at various adult establishments. In the end, **your plaid knickers will never forget this trip**.

WHEN TO GO: February through November

Scotland, United Kingdom

This is where the game all began—where man first stepped up to the tee box, stood over a little ball, and swung mightily. It was also where he would slice his ball like a mother, throw his club, and swear to bloody hell that he "would never pick up a farkin' club again." **There are a ton of great, old courses**, so pick your rounds with skilled planning. Be sure to hire caddies to give you great advice like, "Sir, put dar tree wood back in yar bag or I'll berreak it in alf." While here, play these:

- The one and only Old Course at St. Andrews
- Turnberry, where you can whack it at both Ailsa and Kintyre
- Kingsbarn—a newer, but breathtaking course
- Prestwick—the first twelve British Opens were played here
- Carnoustie—known for its punishing five-hole finish

Don't be afraid to get into the culture by sporting a kilt. When not golfing, find the oldest pub around and have a hearty day of drinking—or go castle hunting. All in all, play as much golf as you can handle. Don't forget to bring your rain gear and a little flask for "Scottish whiskey" swing oil. And remember, **the guy with the worst score eats haggis tonight**.

WHEN TO GO: For warmer temperatures, go in the summer.

San Diego, California

What you talkin' 'bout Willis? San Diego? Come on, there has to be better golf than San Diego?? Yes—if you're judging it purely on golf. However, mix together San Diego's **great courses** with its **nightlife** and a little town called **Tijuana**, and instantly you've got a supreme little white ball destination. Okay? Now come and play these:

- Torrey Pines—it's on a bluff overlooking the Pacific.
- La Costa (it'll cost ya)—has hosted The World Golf Championships.
- Steele Canyon—designed by Gary Player, it has three nines, each with a distinct feel.

- Maderas—a newer course that will take you over cliffs, creeks, and forests.

For your nineteenth hole, hit San Diego's **Gas Lamp Quarter** to find countless theme bars, pubs, and clubs. Be forewarned that you will see many really attractive blonde girls. Tell them how "your father just left you a fortune and **you can't quite figure out what to do with it all**." Also, go south to Tijuana via bus. Take in a bull fight by day and at night . . . tequila. Stay away from any donkeys, women who may have been friendly with a donkey, and bars that don't like gringos. Other than that, anything goes. Now do you see the appeal of golf in San Diego?

WHEN TO GO: Year round

Finland

Nighttime is the right time . . . to shank a drive, yell "fore," and then use your bonus, out-of-country mulligan. Here in Finland **"late-night putting"** truly means late-night putting, because during summer the sun just doesn't want to set. Your foursome will have endless tee-time options. Set a personal high of fifty-four holes in one day. It's a lot, but we know you can do it.

Nordcenter is probably the most popular course, and only an hour from Helsinki. Other courses to tee it up at are Tali Manor, Espoo Golf Club, and Hanko Golf. **You can even swing away up in the Arctic Circle** at the Artic Golf Course. This trip may not be the best golf, but probably the most unique. You'll find the Finnish enjoy many of the same activities as you—like boozing. Also, be sure to towel up for **a famous Finnish sauna**. They love their saunas here—there's even a sauna bar, where you can drink, sweat it out, and drink some more. And, yes, there's a lot of Swedish in the Finnish—so the ladies should offer a warm place between their bosoms for you to nestle your tired, golfed-out face.

WHEN TO GO: Summertime only

OTHER GOLF DESTINATIONS RECEIVING VOTES:
- Cabo del Sol; Los Cabos, Mexico
- Casa de Campo; La Romana, Dominican Republic
- North and Southwest Ireland
- Pinehurst, North Carolina
- Kohler, Wisconsin
- Atlantic City, New Jersey
- Bandon, Oregon

THINGS TO SAY DURING SOMEONE'S BACKSWING OR BEFORE THEY PUTT:
- "I've always loved you."
- "Is that (fill in blank with name of his ex-girlfriend)?"
- "Is that my ball you're hitting?"
- "Man, does my scrotum itch."
- "Look at the hooters on that grandma."
- "Watch out—grizzly bear."
- "You smell great today."
- "Anyone seen my ball gag?"
- "Hey, (name), does your mom ever talk about me?"

HIKING AND TREKKING

A hike can be a good day out on the trail, a moderate trip to where no man has gone before, or potentially months of trekking across countries and mountain ranges. Whatever it may be, your two feet are often the best way to reach the most remote areas and capture one of a kind sights. You don't want to be slobbering all over yourself as you traverse a six-inch-wide trail, so you may have to hit the gym and lay off the Twinkies for a few weeks before you head out. There are guides everywhere, ready to lead you across the best locations. However, depending on your skill level, there is no reason you and you buddies cannot map out the trip yourselves. Just talk to the right people, have the proper equipment, and don't kid yourself about your capabilities. Good shoes are a must. A GPS is not a terrible idea. And things to whip around, like Frisbees or a Nerf football, always help morale. We know you've achieved many drunken hikes from the bar back to your house. And although that definitely can be adventurous and fun, if you're looking to step it up a little, here's what we recommend:

The Inca Trail—Peru, South America

Is there anything more fun than saying "Machu Picchu?" If there is, it's hiking to this South American marvel. Before you begin your trek, you'll need to fly to Lima, Peru, and then make your way to Cusco. Once in Cusco, you can join Aunt Rose and her bridge club as they take a train directly to Machu Picchu. (Hah, we said it again!) Or you can be a man, skip over to Km. 88, and follow the Inca Trail through the ancient ruins, the peaks of the Andes, and steps created by Incan Indians themselves. Walking down these paths carved by the ancient dwellers will lead you through **the deep Urubamba Valley** and take you all the way up to the **Andean Cloud Forest**. After four days of breathtaking countryside and vegetation you will come upon Machu Picchu. The most famous of the Incan Ruins, Machu Picchu has a mysterious story with impressive construction. The hike will place your appreciation a level above the commuters who lazily sat playing gin rummy in their train car. You'll be dirty, smelly, and tough; they'll have a fanny pack and probably ask, **"Would you like an antibacterial handy wipe?"** Take it and consider it today's shower.

WHEN TO GO: May through October is dry season.

Swiss Alps, Switzerland

We agree that cheese with holes in it, exact time, and pocket knives all really exciting. But, if this is all that you know of the Swiss and Switzerland, you need to go there and see a little more. Hiking, climbing, biking, skiing, hang-gliding, and of course drinking, only begin to describe what you can get yourself into in Switzerland. So, after you land in Zurich, it truly becomes a **"choose your own adventure."** Throughout this great countryside, local trains can lug your pack and you to each daily destination. The more remote a journey, the more you'll have to carry your clothes, tent, etc. **The Matterhorn region is the most popular** and can be self-guided fairly easily. The peak of the Matterhorn mountain will guide you like the North Star and provide for impressive background pictures. A more strenuous hike for the experienced trekker is on **the Haute Route**. Here you actually start in France and make your way through the Pennine Alps and Western European glaciers. Throughout the trails there are small towns that provide shanty accommodations to the passing trailblazers. The locals will always be welcoming, unless you get caught while Ingrid the farmer's daughter churns your butter.

WHEN TO GO: Summertime

LINK IT UP: From the natural high of the Alps to a different kind of high, take the train to Amsterdam. (See chapter 5, under "Europe by Rail" and chapter 4, under "Amsterdam.")

Himalayas, Nepal

Come on, everyone's doing it. Blind people, diabetics—didn't a guy in a coma even summit Everest last year? How hard could it be? Actually, it's very hard, and realistically, you don't have an igloo's chance in hell. Plus, you'll probably die. Instead of dying, trek the surrounding Himalayan base camps and you'll still win huge bragging rights. Start your journey with a flight into Kathmandu and arrange for a pick-up. The most popular hike that doesn't require a guide and leads you through the shadows of the tallest peaks in the world, is **the Annapurna Circuit**. A three-week trek will take you from fertile green lands and lakes to desert plateaus, all in the presence of yak herds and sheep. Along the way, small stores and tea shops will keep things lively, while inns will provide you with a place to lay your head. The peaceful Buddhist communities will bestow on you so much culture and positive vibes that **next year you'll be on tour with the Beastie Boys, freeing Tibet.** There are plenty of other shorter hikes still challenging enough to declare, "I freaking hiked the Himalayas."

WHEN TO GO: December through April is best.

Appalachian Trail, United States

Here is a challenge within the United States that is completely accomplishable. Take six months and hike the **2,160 miles of the Appalachian Trail**. Starting in the Katahdin region in Maine and ending in Chattahoochee National Forest in Georgia, you will traverse fourteen states, several mountain ranges, and plenty of lakes and rivers. The trail was forged in the 1920s by people with the idealistic intention of escaping urban life and bringing it back to the wilderness. "Appalachia" might have a reputation of **cousins doing each other in the backwoods**, but this trail is designed for the modern-day adventurer. You can find places to stay throughout the trail, but a journey of this nature requires several nights on the land, so stuff your pack with a tent, stove, and a sleeping bag. This truly is a great adventure—one that will be packed with many stories of strange encounters with wildlife, eerie noises heard at night, and long days on your feet. It's one hell of an achievement. If you can't set aside six months, then map out what you can do and do it.

WHEN TO GO: May through October

OTHER HIKING DESTINATIONS RECEIVING VOTES:

- Rocky Mountain National Park, Colorado
- Patagonia Ice Cap Traverse, Argentina
- K2 Base Camp, Pakistan
- Routeburn Track, New Zealand
- Grand Canyon, Arizona
- McGonagall Pass, Alaska

TOP MOUNTAINS TO SUMMIT (REALISTICALLY):

- Mt. Kilimanjaro, Africa
- Mt. Rainer, Washington

- Mt. Aconcagua, Argentina
- Mt. Whitney, California
- Little Switzerland, Alaska

BIKING (MOUNTAIN)

Although we haven't checked the official statistics bureau, we're willing to venture that eighty percent of all mountain bikes have never seen an actual mountain. Sure, we've all hopped the curb, sped through the park, and maybe even taken a trip through the woods, but most off-terrain activity is an unusual occurrence, unless you live a geographical location conducive to it. And even if you do, there are probably better places you want to ride. Mountain biking is a feat that most guys of decent athletic shape can give a whirl. Sure you may have to walk your bike up a really steep hill, you may ride the brakes as you're descending at a forty-five-degree angle, and you may fall. But who cares, it's all a part of the adventure. It's an incredible workout, a great test of agility, and a gut check on your size of your skirt. And it's great fun, too. Bounce through trails that hardly deserve that term. Climb hills that push your legs to the limits. Fly down at speeds that could get you a speeding ticket. And do it all surrounded by some of the best natural settings on the planet. After a day of this, you'll have earned your share of cold beers and a big, juicy steak. Up to the challenge? Hell yeah, you are . . . here are some destinations ready to ride:

Moab Desert, Utah

"Holy shit, I'm on the Moon!" is exactly how you'll feel when you first gaze at this lunar landscape. Moab has become one of **the most**

popular biking destinations in the world. And it's for a good reason. From slickrock to gravel to sand, Moab brings you all kinds of interesting tracks to play on. Not to mention the arches, bowls, and other strange formations you'll experience. For the crazier, gravity-defying stretches, you should have some decent mountain biking know-how. At the very least, before you go balls out, test your skills on easier paths or practice loops.

A must ride is **Arches National Park**. With more naturally carved stone arches than anywhere else, you'll not only ride on, but you'll be surrounded by geological wonders everywhere you look. Another longer path worth looking into is **the journey from the town of Telluride to Moab**. Your scenery will magically transform from mountains to desert, and in one day you'll descend as much as 5,700 feet. Pretty sweet. When your legs are all tired out, explore dinosaur tracks, play Frisbee, while drinking beers, or go skydiving. Biking on the Moon, what could be cooler?

WHEN TO GO: April to October

North & South Islands of New Zealand

Chosen as the setting for the *Lord of the Rings* trilogy, New Zealand is a country with more types of terrain than Oscars received by the aforementioned movie. Glaciers, beaches, rain forests, volcanoes, caves—they got 'em all. Perfect for movies, even better for biking. It's also an incredibly backpacker-friendly country. **The native Kiwis are like the anti-New Yorker**, in that they'll go out of their way to guide you in the right direction. You can hitchhike without a problem. Stay in cheap backpacker hotels. And go with the flow.

On the North Island, find your way to the volcanic **Tongariro Park**, **the Waitomo Caves** for a glow worm display, and the rampaging

Huka Falls. Along the ride, enjoy bubbling mud baths, spraying gey-sers, and a hot-water beach. On the **South Island**, bike through gold mining tracks, among lush rain forests, and to other outdoor activities. Be sure to hike on the Fox Glacier, go whale-watching, and bungee-jump. As you're traveling, fall in love with at least three women—the accent alone will get to you. It's a long-ass flight, but definitely worth the seventeen bags of peanuts you'll be served.

WHEN TO GO: November to March—lots of extra sun during this period

OTHER MOUNTAIN-BIKING DESTINATIONS RECEIVING VOTES:
* Atlas Mountains, Morocco, Africa
* Canyonlands, Utah
* Copper Canyon, Mexico

"SPIDERMAN," NEW ZEALAND
Nick, 30, New Jersey, engaged

New Zealand is a long way from the States, but well worth the trip. Ki-wis thrive on adrenaline like nowhere else in the world, and every-where you turn there is an "extreme" experience to be had. The national pastime is jumping off of anything and everything. From bungy to skydiving to rapelling from buildings to canyoneering, New Zealand is jump-crazy. Personally, I signed up to rappel down a hotel in downtown Christchurch. Seemed like a unique opportunity that frankly would get me arrested just about anywhere else. Plus, I figured I might catch some chicks changing as I went by their window. I was

(continued)

quickly talked into letting go of the rope to experience a free fall, while being spotted by some guy I met on the roof five minutes earlier, on my way over the edge. That took some blind trust. It was incredible. The adrenaline rushes from all of this jumping keeps everyone in good spirits, and the girls there have accents you'll never forget—and they talk funny too.

BIKING (ROAD)

Sometimes the journey is just as important as the destination. Traveling via bicycle certainly falls into that category. A bike can help you discover sights you'd normally never see. It can offer a perspective that can only be appreciated by bike. And it can provide a sense of achievement every step of the way. Sure, you probably could drive the same route in a fraction of the time, but at the end of the day you can't say **"I pedalled my own goddamn ass here."** To accomplish some of these trips, you'll need to do some serious planning. **Be flexible about timing and rest stops.** Plan for heavy riding days and lighter, "we drank absolutely way too much beer last night" days. Map out the perfect stretch for what you want to see, bring plenty of supplies, and set your goals realistically to your condition. Your ass will get sore and chafed. Your hands will cramp up. And you'll probably eat a hundred or so bugs along the way. But screw it, you've got a lifetime ahead of you, filled with relaxing vacations that sport nice, comforting amenities. This trip it's just you, a couple of buddies, and wherever the road leads you—like to **Carla's Topless Dancing Internet Café, the World's Biggest Taco Stand, and the Dirty Disco Bar & Laundromat.**

Canada/Montana

Feeling claustrophobic in that life-sucking cubicle you work in? Then head to Big Sky Country, where you could literally run around buck naked screaming, "I want to kill somebody!" and no one would come to lock you up. Beyond the freedom to roam as you please, you'll have the majestic sights and fun adventures of **Glacier National Park** to keep you busy. The biking is endless in this wide-open space. However, you'll want to climb and conquer **"Going to the Sun Road."** Pedal yourself down **Chief Mount Highway into Canada**. (Be sure to enjoy the moment with a cold Molson). And don't forget to check off your **"I saw the Continental Divide."**

Not biking? Go white-water rafting, take a swim in a glacier-fed lake, or climb to the top of any old peak. Or **grab a fishing rod and catch tonight's dinner**. Along the way you can camp out or stay at some great lodges that will spoil you with comfort food and many beers. Between the rewarding ascents, the ridiculously fast descents, and enough scenery to make you feel like you're living inside an Ansel Adams photo, this is one freeing excursion.

WHEN TO GO: May through September

The Bavarian Alps, Germany

Just south of the beer stein capital of the planet, Munich, the Bavarian Alps are home to **breathtaking panoramas, fascinating medieval villages, and three truly spectacular castles**. You'll bike your way through tiny, authentically German towns. You'll take an excursion to Lake Schliersee, where a waterfall or a gondola ride to the Schliersbergalm peak awaits. Ride along the Isar River to the town of Garmisch-Partenkirchen, considered the top place in Germany for winter sports. And to top things off you'll make the trek to the three castles built by

crazy King Ludwig right in the middle of the Alps. Neuschwanstein (the original Disney Castle) is the highlight here. Along the way you can shack up at hostels, farmhouses, or the guest bedroom of an old German couple. While not biking, you can hike, go rafting, drink some tasty *hefeweizen*, or just figure out how to pronounce all these German names. After it's done, **motor up to Munich** for the German culinary experience of sausages, pretzels, and beer. Lastly, when hitting on a German woman with ample bosoms be sure to tell her "Yeah, I'm David Hasslehoff's nephew." You're in.

WHEN TO GO: March through October

LINK IT UP: Come in September and throw yourself into the madness of Oktoberfest. (See chapter 1, under "Oktoberfest.")

South and West Coasts of Ireland

"Ahhh, Guinness and biking, what a perfect combo," or so said the guy who just tumbled over the Cliffs of Moor. But seriously, **what a stupendous way to see the miraculous countryside of this green nation**. Pedal your way from village to village, from bike seat to pub seat, from the seaside to Molly O'McFlaherty's beside. You can go it alone or with a guide. But like a drunk old man finding his way home, you'll have a tough time deciding which path is the one for you. **The Dingle Peninsula** is a favorite: Here you'll journey along the coastal cliffs overlooking the Blasket Islands. You can stop for ancient ruins, hidden beaches, and any pub that catches your eye. County Kerry also delivers great travels: Here you can set up in Killarney and spend days tooling around **Killarney National Park** and the **Gap of Dunloe**. Add a trip to Kenmare along the Ring of Kerry. **Connemara** on the west coast is all about sweeping hills, pristine lakes, and huge-ass estates. The area is really quaint and perfect for exploring on bike. **Stay in a castle if you can**. Whatever road you take, indulge nightly in tasty seafood chowder, bottomless pints of Guinness, and Irish music. This trip is certain to be filled with stories for the ages—like the one about you, a sheep, and way too much Jameson.

WHEN TO GO: March through October—peak tourist season is June through August, and the roads will be congested.

OTHER ROAD BIKING DESTINATIONS RECEIVING VOTES:
- Highway 1, California
- Tour de France, Pyrenees Mountains and Alsace, France
- Vietnam
- Yucatan, Mexico

CHECK IT OFF
Your "forget the comforts of home" list

- ☐ Live on someone's couch for a month.
- ☐ Sleep on a beach.
- ☐ Sleep in a boat, canoe, kayak, raft, pontoon.
- ☐ Sleep in your car.
- ☐ Don't shower for a week.
- ☐ Go to Vegas or New Orleans for forty-eight hours—never check into a hotel room.
- ☐ Eat something you have caught or killed.
- ☐ Go out with no place to crash—find a girl to take you home at all costs.

(continued)

☐ Go on a road trip with no destination.

☐ Live in an unusual space—above a bar, in an old airplane hanger, sorority, etc.

☐ Live in another country for six months or more.

☐ Live in the wild for a month or more.

☐ Shit in the woods.

SNOWBOARDING AND SKIING

Dude, all the chicks are so going to want to ride the chairlift with you. No seriously, bro, they will. If not, you'll still have fun plowing through powder, bouncing down moguls, and imbibing so many microbrews that your middle name should be "Hops." Taking to the slopes for a week, month, or season, is one incredible way to spend your free time. Whether you're a knuckle-dragger or two-planker, you know what we're saying. So go. Rent a condo. Find a kick-ass resort. Gather your funniest, most uncoordinated friends. And get to a mountain. While you're there, invite the "most rad" ladies you can find back to your hot tub or local natural hot spring. Perform a ritual of jumping out of the tub, rolling around in the snow (naked), and then leaping back in the tub. Ah, good times . . . watch the shrinkage though. In most ski towns you can also discover other fun activities like snowshoeing, snowmobiling and sledding. Here are some choice places to go snowbound.

Vail, Colorado

Unless your name is spelled K-O-B-E and ends in Bryant, this place conjures up images only of greatness—like p-h-a-t powder, H-O-T ski chicks, and T-A-S-T-Y après-ski beers. Vail is notoriously glitzy and filled with more five-hundred-dollar North Face jackets per capita than anywhere else. *B-U-T*—it's still **one of the best ski mountains anywhere**. Beginners can learn quickly at ski school, while the more advanced can hit the **knee-deep-in-snow Back Bowls and the Blue Sky Basin**.

Size and diversity make a big difference. Plus, you can get a lift ticket package including places like Breckenridge, Keystone, and Beaver Creek. You can also hit Vail's **Adventure Ridge** for snowmobiling, tubing, ski-biking, and laser tag. However, if you play laser tag, please follow it by leaving immediately and going back to your parent's basement. You're beyond help. **Nightlife will be filled with options.** Typically, you'll start drinking after skiing, and end up stumbling home in your boots. People from all over the world ski here—so seek out a princess from some small country and ask if she's ever played a game of "Who's your King?" *(Naughty princess!)* Anyhow, get here before you're married . . . Now that's advice Kobe should've taken.

WHEN TO GO: November through April

Lake Tahoe, California

Ski your pants off by day. **Gamble your shirt, socks, underwear and everything else away** by night. What a great way to spend a week of your life. In Tahoe, you'll want to head to **the South Shore area**, where the action is. The north side is cool, but more laid back and rustic. The Southside's closest ski resort is Heavenly, but you can easily take trips to Kirkwood and the popular Squaw Valley. Definitely hit Kirkwood, where the snow is usually so deep you should ski with a shovel on your back.

You can stay just about anywhere on the south side, but a place with complimentary shuttle service makes the getting-around factor a nonissue. You can even shack up at a casino, like Harrah's, Caesar's, or The Horizon. Most of the nightlife centers around the gambling, so you'll be right in the thick of it. Why not? On your days off you can hit **the sports book at Caesar's**, bet on all your favorites, sit around, drink and watch your teams win huge. In Tahoe, all the goods are in place, it's just up to you to get here and exploit them.

Whistler/Blackcomb—British Columbia, Canada

Is it a ski place that parties? Or a party place that skis? Either way, these two towering mountains bring more than enough of both. With over eight thousand skiable acres, two hundred-plus trails, and more than thirty feet of annual snowfall, this behemoth stands in a league of its own. **Blackcomb is the more adventurous of the two peaks**, with its huge, half-pipes, air sending moguls, and glacier bowl skiing. Whistler is no slouch, with incredible bowls and vertical plunges certain to give you some serious windburn. Try **Harmony Chair and Bagel Bowl** here.

After a day of daffys, backscratchers, and 360s, you'll be ready for a new trick we call the **"Canadian face plant."** It's a simple trick that involves you hitting as many bars as you can doing as many shots as you can, and dancing in your long underwear with as many ladies as can—all before (yes) you plant your face into a pile of snow and need to be carried home. **Whistler has a crazy number of pubs**, look for nightly specials and contests. The Boot Pub offers a unique "ballet," worth a gander. A week here and you'll be ready to apply for Canadian citizenship.

WHEN TO GO: November to April

Ischgl, Austria

One vowel, five consonants. And so, so many reasons for you to bring your goggles and thermals to this Austrian ski resort. First, when you tell someone you're going here they'll promptly reply "Where?" That immediately catapults you into a more worldly status than them. Second, the skiing is incredible, with long, above-the-tree-line runs and powder bowls. Third, Ischgl is well known as a place that **really knows how to party**. After all, if you come all the way to Europe, you might as well go to a place that likes to have a good time.

Most hotels will be pricey, so seek out the **cheaper pensions or try renting out an apartment**. It's just a place to pass out and wake up, right? Skiingwise, there's something for all levels, and snowboarders will be happy to see **the Paradise Board Park**, with a half-pipe and over thirty-five obstacles. There's late-night sledding, sleigh rides for you and your Austrian cutie, and plenty of drinking. Don't be surprised to start out with a casual après-ski beer around four P.M. and end up dirty-dancing somewhere at four A.M.—still in your ski boots. Actually, plan on doing that—and send us the pictures please.

WHEN TO GO: December to April

OTHER SKIING DESTINATIONS RECEIVING VOTES:

- The Andes; Portillo, Chile
- Mont Tremblant; Quebec, Canada
- Banff; Lake Louise, Alberta, Canada
- Zermatt, Switzerland
- Aspen, Colorado
- Stowe, Vermont

SAFARI

It's kind of like going to the zoo, only there are no cages, no cotton candy—and, if you're not careful . . . no *you*. Chances are, you won't become lion lunch, but we've all seen that internet clip of that guy venturing out of his jeep and then, *bam!* that's it. Anyhow, there's no doubt **this will be a trip of a lifetime for you and any of your buddies who join in**. It's a huge endeavor, so you can bank on heavy-duty planning. You may need malaria or other shots. And, depending on the level of safari you take, you should get yourself in hike-worthy shape. It'll all be worth it when you stand witness to elephants stampeding across the plains, chimpanzees flinging themselves from tree to tree, and hyenas savagely ripping apart today's unlucky gazelle. It's wild out here, and that's the whole point. See a world that doesn't abide by our rules, that doesn't believe in cordial BS, and that lives according to a system of kill, hide, and run or become a snack. Also, if you're thinking that someday when you're rich and retired you'll get here, just remember **there are a lot of old dudes out there** still trying to convince their wives that a safari doesn't mean tents, bugs, heat, and hippo dung. So don't delay.

Tanzania/Kenya, Africa

As Vegas has slutty chicks and Paris has snotty jackasses, Tanzania and Kenya have wildlife; lions, elephants, rhinos, hippos—you name it, they've got it roaming somewhere. It's truly ***the* place for safaris**. Come and you'll have your pick of spots to set up camp. Well, not actually set up, there are established camps throughout the parks, offering different sights. Choose according to the animals you want to check out. **Ngorongoro Crater** is a renowned spot for quality watching. In general, watering holes (not the kind you frequent) make excellent camps. Also, seek out a reputable but smaller outfitter that won't rip your wallet apart like a lion eating a water buffalo.

While here, slip out at night for a **nocturnal viewing**. Take flight in a hot-air balloon for overhead surveillance. And venture out on a **portable tent excursion** for an even closer glimpse at this wild world. Come in the fall and see millions of wildebeest thunder across the plains. Beyond your safari, you can journey to Lake Victoria, Mount Kilimanjaro, or the islands of Zanzibar.

WHEN TO GO: Anytime—rainy season is April/May and November/December.

Elephant-back Safari in the Okavango Delta—Botswana, Africa

You know last year, when you were "really" drunk and took that "full-figured" girl back to your place? Well, consider it practice for this trip. You see, for this adventure you'll be on top of large, grunting animal that needs your help and guidance. But seriously, **talk about a cool way to see the wild lands of Africa**. Riding atop this impressive animal, you'll safari your way through fields, sand, and water. It's **the animal version of an SUV**. With a Shaq-like vantage point, you'll have a great viewing deck for all the sights around. You'll take care of and get to know your intelligent traveling buddy. Feed him a few peanuts and you've got a friend for life. Whatever elephant safari you choose, throw on some other fun excursions like a night game drive, a trip to Victoria Falls (twice the size of Niagara), and a rafting ride down the Zambezi's raging rapids. Not too many people can say they've journeyed by elephant. Just another reason to start stretching out those legs and planning a trip here.

WHEN TO GO: March through November—best times are July to October.

Gorilla Safari—Uganda, Africa

Forget Gorillas in the Mist—how about **Gorillas in your Face?** Home to half of the world's mountain gorillas, **Uganda and its Bwindi impenetrable Forest** present you with one truly unique destination. When you get here, you'll first be educated on the do's and don'ts of hanging out with gorillas. Much like being at a biker bar, you won't want to smile at, stare down, or beat your chest at any of them. After that talk, you'll penetrate the Impenetrable Forest in search of a family of gorillas. Once found, you'll stop and observe.

The gorillas may approach the group, hiss and fart, or just ignore you. Whatever happens, your heart will be pounding, your eyes will be popping and **those tiny hairs on the back of your neck will be standing up as you take in this rare encounter**. Bring an awesome camera. Be prepared to trek through some nasty stuff. And study up on the silverback gorilla before you come. No, watching Marky Mark's *Planet of the Apes* does not count. This trip won't involve more than three days, so find some add-on adventures. The Chimpanzee poo-flinging Safari, perhaps?

WHEN TO GO: September to March and June to September

OTHER SAFARI DESTINATIONS RECEIVING VOTES:
• South Africa

RACES AND RALLIES, FOR THE CHALLENGE OF YOUR LIFE

Chariots of Fire, Breaking Away and *Cannonball Run*—all solid movies about man's desire to draw a starting and a finish line, and then race like hell in between. Whether you're on foot, in dune buggies, or in grocery carts, a competitive race always brings out the best of your gung ho spirit. The training is always the most grueling and difficult. The race itself is fun, exciting, and demanding, both mentally and physically. Win or lose, **if you finish, you've triumphed**. And the adrenaline that carried you'd from the beginning evolves into testosterone. Women and libations should be in your immediate future, as you wallow in your newfound accomplishment. Each year it seems, a new adventure race arrives as the "next big thing," while the last big thing disappears. So it's important to stay tuned in to these races and decide which one is yours. Just remember, **someday your big competition will be the Memorial Day Daddy-Daughter Sack Race**. Beyond providing great memories, these feats will also be the biggest headline on your resume. The topic will consume interviews and land you a job. Here are a few of which, reading about them alone should make you think twice about what you want to do next week, next month, or next year.

The Raid, Worldwide

"The Adventure Race that picked up where *Eco-Challenge* left off" is one way to describe The Raid. This race, first held in 2004, has been a huge success, as teams compete to traverse across diverse terrains, bodies of water, and ecosystems. As a worldwide challenge, teams from different countries compete in "X-Adventures" throughout the year in order to qualify for the once-a-year main Raid race. So, you're first task is to compete in an X-Adventure. You'll have plenty of opportunities, as it takes place in locations such as Oregon, France, and Australia. **It's you and two other mates, while an assistant follows you in a vehicle** with the necessary equipment. Multisport specialists will be in heaven as they ski, surf, raft, kayak, or dive their way through the course. Finish strong and you're on the way to qualifying for the main event. The Raid World Cup involves teams of four people in a five-to-seven-day race over even more extreme conditions. This is a once-in-a-lifetime opportunity to utilize every skill and physical ability you have. **Your body will hate you, but the story of your life will thank you.**

WHEN TO GO: The main race takes place in September, but qualifiers are throughout the year.

Tecate Baja 1000, California

Two wheels or four, this **motor vehicle adventure race** will have you talking to your car like Michael Knight to K.I.T.T. When commuting to work, it's one thing to get pissed at the car in front of you, pull into another lane, speed up, and cut in front of him; it's another to do this as you're rolling through the desert on an ATV. The Tecate 1000 is a balls-out motor race across the desert, which could easily be a movie, commercial, or TV show, without doing much work. Fanatics from all over come to display their souped-up vehicles and Evil Knievelesque jumpsuits, and rev their engines like there's no tomorrow. If that's your normal crowd, then it's time for you to show your stuff. If you just want a hell of an adventure, you're welcome as well. *Yee-haw's, fuck yeah's,* and *oh shit's* will be flying out of your mouth for **two days, as you motor against a bunch of psychos in dune buggies, trucks and motocross cycles**. Lastly, Tecate is a Mexican beer. Sponsored by a beer company, this event draws a nutty crowd, and they'll all be waiting for you at the finish line.

WHEN TO GO: Third week in November

The Ironman, Worldwide

Being an Ironman Triathlete means one thing, **you are tough as shit**. "Hey, marathon runners, try swimming 2.4 miles and biking 112 miles before running your 26.2, you pussies." The triathlons are held all over the world, so you can choose which one you want to throw yourself into. Panama is great for beginners, as it's nice and flat. **Hawaii is the Super Bowl**, and you have to qualify for it. They can fill up a year in advance, so be sure and register early. You'll need about half of that time to get your body in shape, unless, of course, you've been taking bong hits and funneling beer five days a week. If that's the case, then give yourself twelve months to get your ship turned in the right direction. The training is the most important part of a triathlon. If you dedicate the time, the race itself will be more fun than painful. We know it's tough when your buddies are going for beers on Friday and you have to get up to run twelve miles on Saturday. But after you've conquered this triathlon, the beer will taste better than ever and those six months will seem like a blink.

WHEN TO GO: Hawaii is in October, others are scattered throughout the year.

Race to Mackinac, Illinois and Michigan

For years you played captain in the bathtub. Now it's time to test your skills in one of the oldest and most entertaining sailboat races in America. At 333 miles, it's also **the world's longest freshwater race**. If you have access to a thirty-five-foot schooner, then entry is only a few applications away. For everyone else, there are opportunities to work on the crew of a boat, as long as you deem yourself valuable, i.e., no one is looking for stowaways. Embarking from Chicago, there are **parties and gatherings** all designed to celebrate the upcoming regatta. Although not the ocean, Lake Michigan can stir up great swells, mighty squalls, and treacherous conditions. This is no walk in the park. As you head north towards the Upper Peninsula of Michigan, you'll feel a million miles from the metropolis of Chicago. The waters really open up as you cross into Lake Huron. The finish line is Mackinac Island, a true gem of the midwest. With no cars allowed and only five hundred residents, it's the perfect place for sailors to quote Judge Smails: **"When your ship comes in . . ."** and raise a glass to the end of their voyage. And, if you're looking for a boat name, we think "Flying Wasp" is available.

WHEN TO GO: Mid-summer

OTHER RACES RECEIVING VOTES:
* Badwater Ultramarathon; 135-Mile Race Through Death Valley
* The Iditarod; Sled-Dog Race in Alaska
* Dakar Rally; Motor Race Through Africa
* The Wild Onion; Ultimate Urban Adventure
* Any Marathon; New York, Boston, San Diego, Rock 'n' Roll

AND FOR THE NOT SO ATHLETIC:
* Big-Wheel Rally; Boulder, Colorado
* Rock-Paper-Scissors World Tournament
* Air Guitar World Championship
* Virgin Mobile Thumb Wrestling Championship

- Ultimate Staring Contest
- Hot Dog–Eating Contest; Coney Island, New York
- Bay-to-Breakers Foot Race; San Francisco, California

CHECK IT OFF
Your "other random adventures" list

☐ Fly in a fighter plane.

☐ Base-jump.

☐ Bungee-jump.

☐ Parasail.

☐ Go kiteboarding in an exotic locale.

☐ Go surfing on a wave bigger than you.

☐ Dogsled.

☐ Fire an Uzi (at a target, not at the post office).

☐ Sky-dive.

☐ Sleep in a tree.

☐ Experience weightlessness.

☐ Ice-fish.

☐ Ride a Harley.

☐ Pilot a snowmobile.

☐ Participate in a crash derby.

☐ Walk on a live volcano.

☐ Climb on a glacier.

☐ Hang-glide.

☐ Go heli-skiing.

☐ Captain a ship of any kind.

(continued)

☐ Go water-skiing barefoot.

☐ Ride a camel in the desert.

☐ Drive a race car.

☐ Zipline across a river or through a jungle.

☐ Climb so high you need an oxygen tank.

☐ Get chased by an animal that wants to kill you.

☐ Perform a stunt in a movie.

CHAPTER THREE

SPORTING EVENTS

So you've got your festivals picked out. You've ordered that
Chuck Norris workout machine to get you in shape for some kick-
ass adventures. Of course, you were drunk at the time, and you
may end up with sober-buyer's remorse, once it's delivered. Anyhow, you have several key pieces to the living-it-up puzzle, but
you're not done. It's time to move on to another important topic:
spectator sports.

From the super hype of the Super Bowl to the beer-soaked
bleachers of the one and only Wrigley Field, there are a
crapload of great, **gotta-be-there-to-experience-it** sporting events.
In fact, there are so many that if you don't get going now, you'll
never get there. So unleash your foam fingers, rinse out that
double-beer-holding hat, and start plotting your way to as many
of these incredible spectacles as you can. Some take a week,

others can be conquered in a day—all will be worth the price of admission. And do we really have to point out that your future wife will most likely (a 98.999 percent chance) be adamantly opposed to planning any vacation, even a long weekend, you bastard, around anything that involves a stadium, beer, and that oh-so-hated four-letter word: ESPN. But, hey, instead, how about a romantic B & B close to antique stores and a super outlet mall. Oh shit, just get to some of these . . . pullleasse!!! And while you're there, tailgate with ultimate passion, gamble with your fellow spectators, and make the most of each once-in-a-lifetime event.

MUST-SEE SPORTS

Super Bowl

What? Are you waiting for your team to make it here before you attend this game of all games? Well, Bob from Cleveland, Mike from Arizona, and AJ from Detroit would just like to remind you that **"You could be waiting a very, very, very long, goddamn time!"** Yeah, they may be a little bitter about the histories of their teams, but they make a good point. You can just go to the Super Bowl—with or without your favorite team.

The whole week is filled with parties, events, and total mayhem. From 50 Cent throwing a Courvoisier-sponsored bash to Hefner's girls offering hospitality in body paint to all kinds of celebrities and athletes coming to town in search of a good time, you'll have plenty of opportunity to really mix it up. Remember, you, too, are an athlete—**an Olympic bronze medalist in the luge**, that is. Hey, chicks dig lugers. Every sports agent will be laying down his corporate credit card and offering up free parties for all clients, potential clients, and hot chicks. Unfortunately, you don't fall into any of those categories, but there's no saying you're not the "best friend" of that placekicker from Boise State. Work your magic. These are the parties you'll talk about every Super Bowl hereafter.

The best advice we can give you is to plan early. Find out what the future Super Bowl sites are, pick the most fun city, and book a hotel room. Work the concierge constantly for any insider tips, tickets to events, and to get your name on party lists. In order to fully get into the spirit, bet an obscene amount of money on one of the teams. Now you have a good reason to cheer, boo, and just yell like a rabid fan in general. If you win, lap dances are on you. If you lose, well, fuck it—you're an Olympic Medalist in the luge.

WHEN TO GO: If you don't know, you don't belong here.

CAN'T GET THERE? Go to Vegas, bet on everything from the coin toss to the first player to score to the most penalties.

Final Four

Many call this tournament **the single greatest sporting event**, period. With its upsets, buzzer-beaters, and overall collegiate "I'm not a spoiled, overpaid professional yet" mentality, March Madness is truly unique. Teams like SW Mississippi A & M Tech somehow topple Syracuse. Our fifty-first state, Murray State, miraculously makes it to the sweet sixteen. The incredible seems to happen every year at this time. And after weeks of saying **"I can't believe I picked those jerk-offs in my pool!"** "Did you see Cincinnati choke?" and "God, I hate how

Duke always wins," only four teams will be left. And this is where you come in. Getting tickets for this event will be tough, but like Milwaukee Tech versus Kentucky, there's always a chance, and the harder you try the better luck you'll have.

Obviously, the destination changes from year to year. So, much like the Super Bowl, look ahead to where the Final Four is being played. Pick the best city for you. Tickets generally go on sale as much as a year in advance. Keep an eye open and get your bid in. Otherwise, scalp away. That's what eBay is for, right? When you get here, you'd better be prepared to party. If the stadium allows for tailgating, tap a keg, hire a DJ, and bring that portable fog machine. Your spot in the parking lot will soon become **the hub for all things fun**. Whatever college girls come over, you are automatically huge fans of their team. In fact, **have a T-shirt of all four schools readily available**. Beads, beer bongs, and a megaphone will add to the shenanigans. Once again, when you don't have a team to root for, betting can solve that problem for you. Yes, gambling is the answer. The games will be rowdy, tense, and full of emotion. Remember, no alcohol is served at college games—so bring a handy flask. Be careful though, you don't want to get booted out of this one.

WHEN TO GO: Late March, early April

The Masters Tournament—Augusta, Georgia

"Quiet on the first tee. . . ." the PA announcer says, as you stand there still sweating booze from last night's activities. Tiger Woods then steps up, approaches his first drive of the day, and crushes that little Nike logo 370 yards down the fairway. Your neck whiplashes to see the ball, the crowd roars, and suddenly your hangover is history. Watching a professional golfer play in person is incomparable to seeing it on TV. And if you're going to try for this experience, there is no better place than Augusta National. The Masters, founded by Bobby Jones, has become the most coveted tournament, and Augusta couldn't be a more beautiful course. As the best golfers in the world compete to put on that sporty Green Jacket, you'll have a weekend of walking the famed course, **"oooohing" drives, and "aaahing" putts**. The town of Augusta has everything you would want—local bars, nice restaurants, and thong contests.

Getting tickets to the Masters could be the biggest challenge, and will probably require you to sack up and spend a few bucks. If not, put your name on the list now and you'll at least get tickets to the practice rounds in the next year or two. The practice rounds can actually be crazy to watch, as the pro's are testing the grounds. You'll see John Daly go for the green on a four hundred-yard hole and then slam a beer, or Phil Mickelson will ace six pitch shots in a row. **With the shit these guys pull, it's like watching the Harlem Globetrotters warm up.** Getting tickets to the actual match will probably involve scalping far ahead of time. Either way, when you're down there it's always a good time. Augusta has plenty of hotels as well as houses to rent. The bars close at two A.M., so a house could be a good call for late-night parties.

The small town of Augusta actually pulls down a pretty good party scene, especially during the Masters. Before you head to Augusta, study up on the Nike Tour. This will be your story for the weekend. There are too many fanatics floating around to say you're taking a break from the PGA. For a good-times sports bar, hit up Stool Pigeons, swing by Coyotes for a little "yee-haw," and then end up at

Coconuts for contests such as bikini, hottest MILF, and naughtiest school girl. Good lord!! **If you take home the hottest MILF you've earned your silk Green Jacket.**

WHEN TO GO: First full week of April

CAN'T GET THERE? Try to get to one of the other Majors, or hit any PGA event that comes within one hundred miles of your home.

Spring Training

Before your top pitcher has gone down with a torn rotator cuff, your prized prospect has been deemed a failed experiment, and your team has officially been ruled a mathematical impossibility for the playoffs, there's a time of hope. It's called Spring Training. And it takes place every year in warm climates at small, close-to-the-action ballparks. You won't spend a hundred bucks on tickets. In fact, fifteen dollars will most likely get you a "club box." The beers won't be eight dollars apiece. And you can even get there early, have a Bloody Mary, and watch the greatest players on earth shag flies, run drills, and take BP.

You'll have two major options for spring training: **the Grapefruit League** and **the Cactus League**. Both bring a lot to the table. The Grapefruit League, in Florida, as you wisely already know, takes you to places like Vero Beach, Fort Lauderdale, and Fort Myers. **The most concentrated baseball is around Tampa**, so we highly recommend you spend the majority of your time here. The Yankees' Legends Field, Dodgertown, and Roger Dean Stadium are some of the most unique venues. Beyond baseball, Florida presents you with endless beach activities, wild bars, and if you're in Tampa, adult entertainment of the highest caliber. On the other side of the country, you've got the Cactus League. Here, you'll find yourself traveling through the desert to places like Tucson, Mesa, and Tempe. The Cubbies are a favorite, and the Giants' Scottsdale Stadium is pretty sweet with its mini-Major League ballpark look. On nonbaseball days, you can hit the little ball at many great courses, take a hike on Sedona's red rocks, or indulge in frozen margaritas by the hotel pool. Wherever you choose, most likely based upon your team, be on the lookout for special seating sections, like the Hooters VIP Dugout. **Bring a whiffle bat and ball for postgame competitions** in the parking lot. Play the "dollar-in-the-cup" game. And, overall, see as much baseball as you can, down as many cold beers and hot dogs as you can, and tell as many girls as you can "I'm slotted to start at second base this year, but I'm just taking it one ground ball at a time."

WHEN TO GO: Spring

LINK IT UP: From sitting on your ass in the stands to hoisting it into a raft, head from the Cactus League to the Grand Canyon's unrivaled rapids. (See chapter 2, under "Rafting.")

Frozen Four or Stanley Cup

While any true hockey fan should hit both, the other 99 percent of us should **bear witness to at least one of these two awesome competitions**. It's hard to recommend one event over the other, but the Frozen Four certainly has the similar "win or go home" vibe as the college basketball tourney does, which always makes for exciting, leave-it-all-out-on-the-ice battles. Of course, the seventh game of the Stanley Cup would hold its own and then some in that regard. Choose according to your personal preference, but the slight winner in our minds is the

Frozen Four. There you can watch the semifinals and finals all in one long weekend. Sure, you'll likely be cheering for teams like North Dakota and Lake Superior State, but who cares. Much the way the state of Florida has a monopoly on football talent, the northern states dominate college hockey. Fans who attend this event are not your **"oh, my company gave me the tickets so I thought I'd go"** kind. They love their hockey and have been going for years. As you'll do for the Super Bowl, we suggest betting heavily on one team, giving you a reason to root and hopefully a nice reward when it's all over. When selecting your favorite team, be certain to evaluate their goalie, as the games are usually low-scoring and a good guy in the net makes a tremendous difference.

If the Stanley Cup is your event, you'll find the skating faster, the hitting harder, and probably a whole lot more off-ice festivities. Whatever city you're heading to, immediately become their biggest fan. Find a jersey of their most obscure player, wear it, and your credibility will be instant. Before the game, look for the biggest sports bar in town, go there, slap high fives with everyone you can, and yell shit like **"We're gonna do it tonight!"** "Fuck (the other team)," and "(your new team) fucking rule!!" Let all the female fans know how nervous you are and how you could really use a hug right now. For the best cities to see a Stanley Cup game, try Boston, Detroit, Colorado, New York, and any of the Canadians. That's if any of them make it that far. Overall, hockey is a kick-ass sport to see live in person, especially when the stakes are high, and these two competitions are the cream of the crop.

WHEN TO GO: Frozen Four: early April; Stanley Cup: June

MONEY WELL SPENT

Rob, 32, Chicago, still looking for ways to tear it up

My grandfather was the longest season ticket holder in the history of Boston College hockey, until his death in 2000. My mother and my aunt went to BC games, starting when they were little girls. My grandfather took me to my first hockey game when I was five. He never saw them win a national championship.

In April 2001, I was working in financial sales and had just been sent to my first territory, in Virginia. The Frozen Four was in Albany that year and my entire family went to the games. I had just finished a meeting in Roanoke, Virginia, when my phone rang and it was my mother screaming that BC had just won their semifinal game and that they would be playing North Dakota, a perennial powerhouse, in the finals—a team that had beaten BC in the finals the year before in Providence. I really wanted to go, but . . . I was new to the business, I didn't have a lot of money, and all I could think about was the expense. Not to mention, I work in a business where I have been brainwashed to save, save, save and invest for the future. "Think long-term." "It's never too early to plan for retirement." "Pay yourself first." These are all phrases I'd heard eight million times over the last few years. And I knew a plane ticket at this juncture would be astronomical. But then I thought. "How the fuck can I pass up this?" At the last minute I cruised to the airport in Roanoke, parked my car, went to the counter, and bought a ticket to Albany, with nothing but my suit and my briefcase.

I arrived in Albany Friday night, bought clothes, and found a hotel room. I watched BC beat North Dakota in overtime to win their first National Championship in over fifty years. And, although I really couldn't

(continued)

afford that weekend, it was the best ticket I ever bought. Sure BC could've lost but . . . they didn't. The point is, sometimes you've gotta say "screw it" and make it happen. I know my grandfather would have agreed.

Kentucky Derby—Churchill Downs, Kentucky

"And they're off. . . ." Every year, on the first weekend of May, in Louisville, Kentucky, these famous three words can be heard not only at the start of the most prestigious horse race in history, but they'll be trumpeted throughout the day as the excitement of this event prompts some of the most beautiful girls in the country to say "adios" to their clothing. And you thought it was all about horses and jockeys. At the Derby, you'll be thrown into a blender mixed with the tradition of Southern blue bloods, the debauchery of Mardi Graslike revelers, and the thrill of what's been deemed the most exciting two minutes in sports. Together, it's one incredible time.

While the white hat, linen suit, and comforts of the grandstand could be a very fine time, we suggest that instead you throw on a pair of shorts, along with your I PUT OUT ON THE FIRST DATE T-shirt and head to the infield to mingle with a hundred thousand of your new best friends. The actual Derby race isn't until six P.M., but the partying begins well before noon. So be prepared for a very long haul. On the infield, you'll see that there are races throughout the day, drink and food stands a-plenty, and countless betting booths begging you to test your prophesying skills. Win, place, or show—your guess is as good as any, so definitely throw some money down.

On this day you'll need to plan your drinking prudently. Start off with a Southern-style Bloody Mary, move to Hurricane's (each comes with beads, which in turn become currency to see naked girls), and then hustle over to the mint julep vendors, where you'll momentarily be connected to the society folk sitting in the good seats. But as any skilled jockey will tell you, "pace yourself, if you want to be there at the finish line."

After the race has been run, it's time to stagger to downtown Louisville. Here you'll find everything from sports taverns to line-dancing to mechanical bulls to clubby clubs—all spilling out with the overflow of those still making the most of their day. A couple of popular post-derby destinations are **Jillian's Billiards**, which gives you entertainment up the wazoo, and **Bar Louisville**, whose Coyote Ugly approach has everyone shaking their stuff (good and bad) on the bar. For adult entertainment, Louisville is well stacked with places to get boobies in your face. **Thoroughbreds** is one that is known to never disappoint.

Louisville is a fairly inexpensive town, so this can all be done without breaking the bank. **Book your hotel early**—they can fill up by February. Churchill Downs is about a mile outside of downtown. Driving is obviously not an option, but if there are enough of you, you can arrange **a trolley** to take you to and from the Derby grounds. Put a keg on it and start your day right. Otherwise there are taxis, and it may be smart to arrange them for the day, because flagging them can be difficult, though it is possible. On this day you will truly "Run for the Roses."

WHEN TO GO: First weekend in May

LINK IT UP: From horses to horns, combine the Derby with a trip to New Orleans, where Jazz Fest is usually kicking. (See chapter 1, under "Music Fests.")

Indianapolis 500—Indianapolis, Indiana

Fast Cars and Fast Women. Ever since the first car was built, it was inevitable that some day some dude would say "I bet my fucking car could beat the shit out of your car." By 1977 guys were flying around the track at two hundred miles per hour still answering that very challenge. As the sport evolved, so did the festivities around it: tons of drinking, hard-core partying, and hot girls. Once again, the genius of bartering beads for boobs is the premise and **girls in red-white-and-blue bikinis are the target**.

The town of Indianapolis blows up at the end of May each year as it pulls together the greatest race weekend in the country. Indianapolis has plenty of places to stay, and of course will book up early. If you can stay downtown, **do stay downtown**, and hit the bars. There is no need to wander from Indianapolis unless you're going directly to the Speedway, which is about four miles away. The Indianapolis bars will be filled with hoards of out-of-town fans. Tell them your woes about "being the youngest guy ever to drive in the Indy 500 a few years ago, but after a near-fatal crash you're just taking some time off."

The other and **definitely more insane option is to drive a van or RV** directly to the Speedway and camp outside, across from Georgetown Road. The streets pretty much shut down, so race fans can park and go nuts. The afternoon before the race the Speedway hosts a free concert, which has brought in bands such as the Black Crowes and Blues Traveler. That night everyone spills onto Sixteenth Street and the mayhem begins. College kids, teenagers, rednecks, and average drunk dudes like you all enter the same arena. **There's hooting, hollering, fighting, and screwing.** The opportunities to get arrested are everywhere, but so is the opportunity for a threesome. The partying is nonstop, and at 5:00 A.M. an alarm sounds to signal the opening of the racetrack. Get your spot close to the track, park your ass on top of the car, and watch every Foyt and Andretti descendant bang out five hundred scorching miles. Within the Speedway, much of what started the night before will be present throughout the day. Don't be afraid to single out the girl who is disgusted by the forty dudes chucking beads at her naked friend. Oftentimes this girl wants to be equally as naughty, she's just a lot more subtle. As the winner of the Indy 500 celebrates with a glass of milk (this is a tradition), you could be celebrating with fifty beers, a shot of Jack Daniels, and a bunch of naked girls. Who's the real winner??

WHEN TO GO: Last Sunday of May

International Soccer Match or World Cup

No matter how crazy you think the guys who run around with their shirts off in Lambeau Field are, they don't even come close to the soccer hooligans across the world. In Cleveland, Browns fans threw crap at the refs when they were pissed. In Columbia, they shot and killed a player for scoring on the wrong goal. That's right; **these people are friggin' nuts and absolutely fanatical** about their football, soccer—whatever you want to call it. So what does that mean? People go all out for these games, and it is an incredibly good time, regardless of whether you like soccer or not. Wherever you are in the world, the city or town that is hosting the soccer game goes off like it's a holiday, because to them it truly is. Put on your jersey and **get your soccer-crazed ass to the pubs**. Cheering, drinking, singing, laughing, and cursing the other team's name will take place all day. Everyone parades to the stadium together, continuing to unify their team support. Within the game it's intense. There is not a lot of scoring in soccer, but **the excitement is so thick you need a hard nipple to cut it**. You'll no doubt become a fan and want the local team to win. Because when they do, the rest of the night will involve running up and down the streets screaming "Goala!, Goala!!"

The Superbowl of international soccer is the World Cup, and it's hosted by a different country every four years. Tickets to the World Cup are usually released a year in advance directly by FIFA. They also ration tickets to the National Teams, and they'll sell those on their Web sites. If you can make it, you'll see some of the best soccer and will no doubt be in a location that offers **plenty of debauchery and never-to-be-had-anywhere-else experiences**. As far as other soccer tournaments, second to the World Cup is the Euro Cup, which is basically the World Cup without Latin-American countries. Like the World Cup, the Euro is held every four years in a different country. The two tournaments are separated by two years, like the Summer and Winter Olympics. **As the English fans outdrink everyone and the French guys pick up the Germans' women**, the scene in the streets is one not to be missed.

If you can't make it to the World Cup or the Euro, there are plenty of teams, rivalries, and stadiums that **bring together a carnival-type event**. If you ever have the chance to see a Manchester United game or a match between Barce and Real Madrid, go! In Italy, check out AC Milan vs. Inter Milan, or if you're in Argentina don't miss Boca Junior vs. River Plate. No matter where you are, **if there is a stadium, get tickets to a football match**. It will make you appreciate the sport of soccer and understand the culture of the country you are in. You may be tempted to try to convince girls that you play soccer in the United States. This is probably not a good idea. That would be like saying you play Canadian basketball—no one cares.

WHEN TO GO: The World Cup and the Euro Cup alternate every two years during June. Otherwise, the soccer season runs about ten months a year, with two summer months off. Depending on which hemisphere and country you're visiting, the off months are generally June and July or January and February.

"I THINK I'M TURNING JAPANESE, I THINK I'M TURNING JAPANESE. . . ."
"Andy, 34, London, single

It was the summer of 2002, and I was in midtravel through the Far East. One day I got an e-mail from my old college roommate Connor who was working in Tokyo for Fidelity. The World Cup was being held in Sapporo, Japan, and Fidelity had a crazy setup for it. At the time, I was more interested in getting Fidelity to host a party for me than the soccer, but what the hell? I bought a plane ticket to Sapporo. Sure enough, there was huge tent set up for Fidelity and their clients. I had no idea what kind of clients these were or what they were saying, but I was convinced that I closed some business. Next, we were on a bus to the stadium to see England play Argentina. With a bunch of suits in the front, I was the jackass in the back of the bus pissing in a plastic bottle. Walking into the stadium, I changed my tone and soccer became the focus of my trip. These people were absolute fanatics and, like me, I don't think the Japanese anticipated just how nuts this would be. Sitting in the English section were about five wayward Argentina fans. For their own safety they had to be escorted out by Japanese guards. The guy next to me was painted head to toe in the British flag, wearing only a diaper, antagonizing the Argentineans by singing songs like "Where's your Money Gone?"

The Brits won, and then the party really began. Eighty thousand fans spilled into the streets of Sapporo. By the reaction of the town, you would

(continued)

have thought MacArthur and the U.S. Army were coming in for occupation. The bars closed, people shuttered their windows, and mothers hid their daughters. However, the local convenience stores stayed open and drinking in the streets was perfectly acceptable. After a few hours of that, we decided to head to a local club known as the Titty Suck Bar. With naked girls cruising the place, every thirty minutes the lights turned off for five minutes. The bartenders screamed *"Titty Suck, Suck Titty"* and before we knew it, we were sucking titty. I thought I fell in love with one of them, but after waiting for an hour outside, she never showed. So, at five A.M., we checked into our hotel and then checked out at nine A.M. to catch my flight. On the way to the airport I saw at least five thousand Brits passed out in the streets from a night of absolute destruction. Who knew soccer in Japan would be such an unbelievable time???

Olympics

We've all stayed up until three A.M. glued to the TV as our badminton team battled it out in hopes of achieving that bronze medal. And when they lost, you sadly put down the remote and cried yourself to sleep. Well, maybe just a small tear. Anyhow, it's amazing how the Olympics have this power to magically transform sports that we'd normally not even think about watching into some of the best competitions ever. The intensity of a swimming relay, the thin margin for error of speed-skating, and the grunting power of the shot put, all become instantaneously and incredibly important to us—all thanks to the Olympics.

The sports alone are reason to get yourself to these worldly games, but we'd be remiss not to mention the "party" factor of this event. Much like the athletes themselves, **the spectators come from all over the world**. And, like you, they're here to do more than just watch a little curling or rhythmic gymnastics. Thus, this makes for many great opportunities to utilize your high school Spanish, French, or German. You still remember the translation of: **"Would you like to come back to my hotel room and see my silver medal?"**

Now, the big question you should ask yourself is, "Winter or Summer?" Certainly, you may already have an answer, as many people fall into one camp or the other, but let's discuss it anyway. With winter, you've got hockey, skiing, the bobsled, ice-skating, and more. Pretty good stuff. You'll be staying in a mountain town. Cool. However, it'll be cold, and walking home drunk could be difficult with all the ice patches. Summer brings track and field, gymnastics, basketball, and boxing. The weather will be nice and the ladies will be less clothed. Too tough to call, **you should make the host city the tiebreaker**. For example, if Vegas is hosting the summer and Buffalo the winter, go with summer. Whatever you decide, book your lodging early. For good, cash-saving options, look for hostels or even temporary housing established solely for the Olympics. You'll also find the youngest crowd in these places. When the games are complete and the torch has been snuffed out, be sure to hand out your own medals to your group's gold, silver, and bronze medalists, for drinking, hooking up, and overall performance.

WHEN TO GO: Summer or Winter or both

Boxing Match at Caesar's Palace—Las Vegas, Nevada

The entire premise of spectator boxing is fantastic: Let's watch **a couple of guys beat the shit out of each other** with millions of dollars at stake. Your girlfriend or your wife will never want to go to a boxing match with you. And if they do, it's to keep an eye on you or to spot famous people. Regardless, it's nowhere near as much fun without your buddies. Just like the young scrapper from the streets who dreams of fighting at Caesar's Palace one day, you too should have visions of being here for a prize bout. It's a perfect excursion for bachelor parties, or an excuse to get back to Vegas for a weekend of sin. The day of the fight **you'll feel like you're Vince Vaughn** in town for a movie premiere. You'll be drinking, relaxing by the pool, and telling all the ladies "Yeah, I'm in town for the fight." Then you invite them to your VIP table at the club later. Oh, and here's a tip: **bring a huge friend and pay him to be your bodyguard** for the weekend. Everyone will think you're famous. On fight weekends, Vegas is crawling with celebrities and the freaky girls are on the prowl.

That weekend, Caesar's will be the place to be. The club Pure will surely be jumping and the pool will be packed with flotation devices (aka fake tits). Make sure you call ahead, get a cabana at the pool, and reserve a table at Pure. If you get all of that taken care of, your only concern is which girl or how many girls you will bang. But don't worry, if you can't get all of the hookups at Caesar's, you're still in Vegas and we're confident you'll make it.

"Let's Get Ready to Rumble!!!!" Yup, it's fight time. Do you remember how excited you got when you saw a fight break out at a party? Now imagine that with guys who don't just roll around on the ground like the drunk idiots they are. You will literally be jumping out of your seat as you did when the Italian Stallion dropped Clubber Lang in *Rocky III*. Leading up to the main fight, there are always a bunch of Under Fights that can be even better than the title bout, so try to see a couple of these. Unless she's Cameron Diaz or Sharon Stone, **any no-name girl at the fight is gonna be dirty**. Don't waste your time, you'll have more fun with girls at the club later. After the fight, even though you're all pumped and want to give blow-by-blow details, the ladies don't want to hear it. Just act calm and say. "Yeah, I'm glad I could make it out for the fight, it was great." Then run around the corner and high-five the guys.

WHEN TO GO: Anytime there's a fight at Caesar's

CAN'T GET THERE? Fights in Atlantic City definitely take second place but are also a very good time.

LINK IT UP: Vegas, baby, Vegas! Go hard, go strong. (See chapter 4 under, "Vegas.")

Bullfight—Spain/Mexico

Is it sport or art? That seems to be a huge debate among the bullfighting crowd. Well, we'll leave it up to you; but for now it's a sport in our book—a crazy sport indeed, but still a sport. For this endeavor, any bullfight will suffice. You just simply need to attend one. You can find them all over Spain, in cities like Valencia, Seville, Barcelona, Bilbao, and Madrid. Or in the much closer, but not as worldly country of Mexico.

The overall objective in any bullfight is for the matador to **wear the bull down to the point that he has complete domination of the beast**. They'll employ several different capes to rile up a charge. They'll use horses (bulls hate horses like Boston fans hate the Yankees). They'll even thrust barbed sticks into the bull's back. Now, that might slow him down *a bit*. After the bull has depleted every ounce of energy trying to kill everything in sight, the matador will throw his hat down and begin toying with the animal in what aficionados call an "art form" or "dance." It's **like an offensive lineman after fifteen minutes of playing one-on-one with Michael Jordan**. When the bull is whipped, a trumpet will sound and it'll be time to kill the big guy. The matador will line up the snorting creature, who will make one last charge . . . only to receive a painful dagger between the shoulder blades. And lastly, the crowd will react with either cheers or jeers, and that determines the matador's trophy fate. Cheers mean he gets to take off an ear or maybe two. Strange? Yes. It's similar to **Showtime at the Apollo, where the people in the audience decide who deserves a prize**. While you're there, enjoy some "olé's," look for cushions being hurled into the ring, and get someone to explain exactly what is going on. Also, if you can get a wave started, go for it. Plus, look out for any baby bull bullfights for you and your buddies to take a whirl at—they're smaller, but they can still knock you on your ass. At the end of the day, as you're downing sangria or tequila, you can say that you've witnessed one the world's oldest, longest-standing sports . . . or is it art?

WHEN TO GO: Anytime you can

BASEBALL PARKS

Wrigley Field, Chicago Cubs

Wrigley Field is one reason that Cubs fans have stayed so loyal to the most disappointing team in baseball history. Every summer faithful floppy-hatted fans, tank-topped Midwestern girls, and everyone else in need of a fantastically nonsober day, flocks to Wrigleyville. All are required to cheer for the Cubbies (at least for the first few innings), drink Old Style, and sing "Take Me Out to the Ball Game." Afternoon games are the staple, and **cracking your first beer at Murphy's Bleachers by 12:30 P.M.** is a must. Within Wrigley, the bleachers are the best seats, as everyone gets hammered and encourages the bikini-clad girls to lose their bikinis. When the Cubs start to lose, you can take a break from the stands and check out the patio overlooking Addison Street. From there you can spy all your postgame facilities. You can **take a few swings at the batting cages** of Sluggers, listen to live reggae at the Wild Hare, or just hit up the dozens of other bars within a bloop single of Wrigley. Keep your eyes out for Ronnie and give a "WOO-WOO!!"

LINK IT UP: Go in July and make it a double-header with the World's Largest Block Party at night. (See chapter 1 under, "Music Fests.")

Yankee Stadium, New York Yankees

Unless you're on the bandwagon or actually from New York, you hate Jeter, despise Steinbrenner, and love it when the Yankees lose. Well, there is no better place to root against them than in Yankee Stadium itself. However, you still must give your props to this place. "The House that Ruth Built" has brought us Jackie Robinson's first World Series, Lou Gehrig's unforgettable speech, and Reggie Jackson's three World Series home runs. Sitting in **famed Yankee Stadium, you are officially a part of baseball history**. Located in the Bronx, where you don't want to be unless the Pinstripes are in town, you can take the subway directly to the stadium. There are a handful of bars for pregame beverages right next to the subway station. Bill's and Stan's will serve you bottles of beer out of the big silver tins, and there's **even a bowling alley, if you want to chuck a few strikes**. After the game grab an Italian sausage, a few beers from a bodega, and take one of the many car services back to Manhattan.

WARNING: Screaming "Jeter is a homo" will get you a Bronx-style beat down from a fanatical chick wearing a Jeter jersey, two-inch fake nails, and a pencil-thick gold chain.

Fenway Park, Boston Red Sox

"Let's pawk the cah, take the T to Fenway, drink bee-ahs, get wicked hammed, and watch the Sawx knock a few over the Monstah." Translation: "Let's go to Fenway." The accents alone will make you appreciate being in Boston, except it's a little frightening hearing it from a hot girl. **Fenway is the house that Ruth was traded away from**, but they still have maintained a stadium that has tremendous history and **deserves a visit from any baseball fan**. Located in a great Boston neighborhood, Fenway is easy to get to by T (Boston's subway) or cab. Landsdowne Street has a ton of bars to tie one on at, before and after the game, and now Fenway actually has a bar right in the stadium. Cask 'n' Flagon is an old, historic bar worth having a cold one in, too. And speaking from experience, Massachusetts laws can be tight and prohibit the "overserving" of alcohol. So, each time you order another round at Fenway, put your game face on and act sober. Otherwise, like a girl you just called the wrong name, they'll cut you off.

Camden Yards, Baltimore Orioles

Since it opened in only 1992, Camden Yards doesn't exactly have a whole lot of history. In fact, places like **Wrigley, Yankee, or Fenway probably have hot dogs sitting around just as old**. However, the geniuses that constructed this place designed it to resemble something out of the 1920s. So, unlike other modern fields, you don't feel like your walking into an amusement park, Snow White isn't going hug you, and no one will want to put your picture on a T-shirt. **Camden truly captures the nostalgia of our national pastime.** What you get is an old-time park that doesn't look like a subway station on the inside. Within the stadium, make sure you check out Ruth's Bar in centerfield and chow down on Boog's BBQ. **Eutaw Street** provides plenty of outside-the-stadium fun for before and after the game. To keep the good times going in Baltimore, head to Fell's Point, the multitude of cheesy bars will be just what the doctor ordered for your drunk ass.

OTHER MLB STADIUMS RECEIVING VOTES:

- Dodger Stadium, Los Angeles
- Busch Stadium, St. Louis
- Miller Park, Milwaukee
- Coors Field, Colorado
- SBC Park, San Francisco

A WICKED AWESOME WORLD SERIES
Kevin, 30, Boston, recently taken down by marriage

My Red Sox were about to win the World Series, and I decided I'd rather have my balls in a vice than watch it on TV. I had to be there. The tough part was that it was in St. Louis. "Fuck it, I'm going." I headed to the airport and started recruiting. I got three friends to meet me at Logan. It was the first time I had ever bought a plane ticket at the airport, and six hundred dollars later I realized it wasn't that difficult. We booked our St. Louis hotel from the Boston airport, got the number from 411. We landed in St. Louis, hopped in a cab and told the driver where to go, and he thought we were kidding. When he dropped us off in the ghetto, we realized why he thought we were kidding. To best describe it, when we went to buy beer, the liquor store got robbed, no joke. We had to prove to the cops that we actually paid for the 40s that we bought (yeah, 40s, we figured when in Rome . . .)

(continued)

So now it was time to head to Busch Stadium and get some tickets. We all got tickets, only two of them together, but who cared at this point? Oddly enough, we still ran into each other at the beer stands. And yes, the fucking Red Sox won, that's right, first World Series in eighty-six years! "I'm friggin' going crazy in St. Louis tonight!!!" We hit the bars and all of us Sox fans managed to find the same places. Some of the players even joined us for the celebration. There were a few Cardinals fans, who I have to say were great sports. My buddy Pelly swapped his Red Sox jersey with a woman wearing a Cardinals jersey in the middle of the bar. I was much more excited to see her topless than Pelly. All of this excitement got us riled up for some more tits and ass, so we asked where the best nudie joints where, I'm not sure if this was their revenge, but they sent us to East St. Louis in Illinois. While the strip club was insane, we easily could have been shot. After spending all of our money on girls, we hitched a ride home on the back of a pickup truck. We jumped out of the truck by our motel, then watched the guy ditch the truck, run about a block and then get tackled by a cop. Our guess is that we rode in a stolen truck, nice. After all of this—leaving work on a whim, buying tickets on the go, and seeing the Sox win—it was the best trip I could have never planned.

NFL STADIUMS

Lambeau Field, Green Bay Packers

Ah, the frozen tundra! This NFL landmark is truly as strange and unique as it gets. Just imagine if you had never, ever heard of Green Bay, the Packers, or Cheeseheads, and you came here for a game. You'd probably freak out, wondering what's with all these fucking people wearing yellow and green, sporting wedges of cheddar on their heads, and holding a brat permanently in their nondrinking hand. Good stuff, and all the more reason to experience it. When coming here, **pick a cold November or December Sunday** for the maximum Packer ambience. Try to choose a divisional rival like da Bears, Vikings, or Lions. And you guessed it, **throw some cheese on your head** and swear allegiance to Vince Lombardi for this one day. To simplify your game day festivities, stay at one of the nearby hotels and walk to and from Lambeau. You'll be drunk, so this is a well-advised way to get home.

Soldier Field, Chicago Bears

Ditka versus seventeen tactical nuclear missiles, who wins? Ditka. Soldier Field, like Lambeau, is a place any true football fan simply has to experience. Although now modernized on the inside, Soldier Field still delivers a sense of football lore with its outside pillars, lakefront setting, and its **rabid fans who have seen the best and worst that this game has to offer**. The weather notoriously plays a huge factor here. Have you ever seen clips from the Fog Bowl of 1988? Beyond the pure madness that is a Chicago Bears football game, the Windy City also brings you plenty of fun times for the remainder of your stay. Head to Rush and Division for bars stacked on bars. Chow down on some deep-dish or go for a huge filet at Gibson's. Or **head to Ditka's very own restaurant and smoke a big, fat cigar**. Also, if you want to double your spectating pleasure, try a Hawks or Bulls game on top of "da" Bears.

Mile High Stadium, Denver Broncos

Yeah, the old Mile High is gone and the new one has some corporate name, but we're not buying it—we're still calling the Bronco's home Mile High. Anyway, if you think Colorado is home only to pot-smoking snowboarders whose only trip to a football stadium was at that Dead show back in 1990 ("Dude, you know the one where they opened with 'Sugar Magnolia?'") well, you're wrong. **Denver fans are crazy**. They paint themselves orange. They truly think John Elway is Christ's younger sibling. And they live and die by their team's triumphs and defeats. You can certainly join them in their orangeness, but we recommend that you instead **toss on a ref's uniform and throw flags at any hot buckin' bronco**. "Ten-yard penalty for taunting me with those beautiful eyes." Oh, you are so getting some referee love. After the game, Denver will serve up good times for all.

LINK IT UP: After you join the mile-high club, try the "chairlift" club at Vail. (See chapter 2, under "Skiing.")

Heinz Field, Pittsburgh Steelers

Love only begins to describe how Western Pennsylvanians feel about their Steelers. This storied franchise just reeks of good, hard-nosed football and fans. Come here and you'll hear season ticket holders still spewing tales of **Lynn Swann, Mean Joe Green, and Rocky Blier**. Not to mention their Super Bowl XL conquest and that crazy-ass reverse pass from Randle El to Hines "MVP" Ward. At Heinz Field, tailgating is performed like an art form. Forget burgers and dogs, you'll see (and taste, if you're lucky) BBQ ribs, pierogies, and game day chili. Of course, they put their namesake ketchup on top of everything. When it comes to drinking, let's just say **you'll find more kegs than cases** in these parking lots. If you really want to pimp your way into Pittsburgh, charter a boat down the river (weather permitting), invite lady friends on board, and tailgate on the water. Wear your Franco Harris or Jerome Bettis jersey, pretend you love this team and this town—and hey, you just might come away with some free beers, tasty food, and the bra of a big-boned girl wearing the same jersey as you.

The Dawg Pound, Cleveland Browns

This is not just a stadium to get yourself to, but a specific section of a stadium. Don't accomplish it any other way. **The Dawg Pound** in Cleveland is legendary. You know . . . the place chock full of maniacs with bones in one hand and beers in the other. Anyway, the Pound has survived completely losing a team to Baltimore and the closing of its original home, Municipal Stadium. And today, despite the Browns lack of success, it's flourishing. So get here, bring that **inflatable bone**, have a **pocket full of Kibbles 'n' Bits**, and be prepared to woof your head off for the Browns. Chants are not complicated ("Here we go Brownies, here we go!" is as clever as it gets), so as long as you dress the part, it's pretty easy to pass for a local. Try to see a game versus the rival Bengals, the loathed Steelers, or Satan's team itself, the "goddamn, team-stealing" Ravens. Oh, do Clevelanders hate them. After the game, head to the Flats or the Warehouse District to find some fine looking bitches—hey, we're just continuing the Dawg Pound theme.

OTHER NFL STADIUMS RECEIVING VOTES:

- Arrowhead Stadium; Kansas City, Missouri
- McAfee Coliseum; Oakland, California
- Giants Stadium; The Meadowlands, East Rutherford, New Jersey
- Lincoln Financial Field; Philadelphia, Pennsylvania

COLLEGE FOOTBALL STADIUMS

Notre Dame Stadium, University of Notre Dame

Notre Dame fans, we know you love your precious little Irish. The rest of us, well, we think you're a bunch of pansies. Regardless of how you feel, the tradition of the Fighting Irish, the history of the Stadium, and South Bend's game day experience is pretty spectacular. **Touchdown Jesus, "Win one for the Gipper"** and Rudy's **"I've been ready for this my entire life"** all epitomize Notre Dame Football. The vibe at the game will send chills up and down. "Cheer, Cheer for old Notre Dame," even if you hate them, the Chants will cause you to swing your arms a little. When heading to a game, fly into Chicago. Arrange for transport to and from South Bend that day—it's about a two-hour drive. Any spot in the parking lot is solid for tailgating. Football season is just about the only reason to go to school in South Bend, and these weekends make the rest of the year worth it . . . **almost**. Opponents that bring out the most spirited games are USC, Michigan, and Boston College. (Damn, remember that kick by David Gordon?)

Neyland Stadium, University of Tennessee

It's an Orange Nation, and towering over the Tennessee River is Neyland Stadium, home of the Volunteers. Until the Titans entered the NFL, this was *the* team in Tennessee, so the entire state is behind them. All are welcome at Neyland Stadium, so bring your drinking face, a little kick to your step as you do-si-do to the beat of country-western and strap on a beer funnel. Tailgate parties are synonymous with college football, but **tailgating on boats in the river is a trademark of the Vols**. Think of it, football games are the best, and drinking on boats is always a winner. Drinking on boats *and* a football game is an unbeatable combination. After the game, celebrate the win on Cumberland Avenue and high-five every person you see. The people are so nice here that they'll actually enjoy it.

Kyle Field, Texas A & M

Friday Night Lights and Varsity Blues are accurate on so many levels (even though Jon Voight was screwed out of an Oscar as Bud Kilmer). **Football in Texas is religion, girls in Texas are naughty, and quarterbacks in Texas are heroes.** The party starts with twenty thousand fans gathering on Friday for a Midnight Yell Practice proving that Texas A & M has spirit that is second to none. The yelling doesn't stop as eighty-six thousand plus fans enter the stadium to cheer the hell out of their Aggies and intimidate the crap out of any opponent. Make sure you bring your enthusiasm, because you will be tossed out of the game if you're caught giving less than 110 percent. The fans are officially the twelfth man busting their ass just like anyone on the team. For bonus points, hit the Texas vs. Texas A & M game, which is the pinnacle of their season. Extracurricular activities involve getting slammed in the Northgate District and stumbling from bar to bar asking **"what the fuck is an Aggie again?"**

Sanford Stadium, University of Georgia

"Georgia? What about UF, the Gators, the Swamp?" We got it, Ben Hill Griffen Stadium of the University of Florida is insane, and you should definitely go there, too. But, we opted for the southern stadium that will blow you away, versus the stadium that will literally scare the shit out of you. The people in the Swamp are animals. The University of Georgia folks get equally hammered, but there's no fear of making it out alive. Plus, Georgia girls are equally as hot. The tailgate parties are spread across the entire campus and people just simply drink their faces off. **Funnel, shotgun, beer bong, Jell-O shot, whiskey.** "Wait, when's the game?" Oh yeah, it's a sin if you miss Uga the Bulldog entering the field, so get down from that keg stand and get to the game. If and when the Bulldogs win, rush over to the ringing of Chapel Bell, and take part in the cheering and making out. As **most of the girls here could probably outdrink you**, this may be your only chance to cop a feel before you pass out.

Michigan Stadium, University of Michigan

Big Ten Football, a crisp Fall day, and the winningest team in NCAA history, all combine to make the massive Michigan Stadium an incredible football weekend experience. Ann Arbor, Michigan, exists solely because of the University, therefore, if anyone doesn't gear up for a home game they should move to East Lansing. The entire town is a tailgate party, every house is hanging their M flag, and the bars open early. Even the local high school, Pioneer, gets involved and offers its grounds as one of the top places to park your RV. Make your way to the frats and take part in some of the wacked-out activities including slip 'n' slide, dunk tanks, and mud wrestling. Remember, "Go Blue!" and "You're my boy Blue!" are totally acceptable Blue *balls* are not, and the girls of UM agree, so keep your head up. Get here for the Ohio State game and experience Michigan's intensity at its boiling point.

OTHER COLLEGE STADIUMS RECEIVING VOTES:

- Tiger Stadium; Louisiana State University
- Ohio Stadium; Ohio State University
- Folsom Field; University of Colorado
- Husky Stadium; University of Washington
- Michie Stadium; Army
- Texas Memorial Stadium; University of Texas

GREAT MATCHUPS

Duke vs. North Carolina Hoops

Da Bears vs. the Packers

Pittsburgh Steelers vs. Dallas Cowboys

Montreal Canadians vs. Toronto Maple Leafs

Islanders vs. Rangers

Colorado Avalanche vs. Detroit Red Wings

Yanks vs. Red Sox

Yanks vs. Mets

Cubs vs. Cardinals

Cubs vs. White Sox

Miami vs. Florida State (Football)

Auburn vs. 'Bama

Ohio State vs. Michigan (Football)

North Dakota vs. USC (Football)

Notre Dame

Army vs. Navy (Football)

CRAZIEST FANS TO SIT NEXT TO AND YELL AT OPPOSING PLAYERS WITH:

Red Sox

Yankees

Jets

Eagles

Raiders

Packers

Bears

Browns

Raiders

Red Wings

Islanders

Pistons

Duke

Manchester United

CHECK IT OFF
Your "additional sports fan gotta do" list

☐ Do a Big City Doubleheader, i.e. Yankees by day, Knicks by night.

☐ Rent a skybox.

☐ Sit on the floor or field at any game.

☐ Get infield tickets for a NASCAR race

☐ Throw out the 1st pitch for any baseball game, major or minor league.

☐ Drink a "beer an inning" for an entire baseball game.

☐ Eat a "hot dog an inning" for an entire baseball game.

☐ Storm a field, court, ice, whatever—just storm something.

☐ Get on TV.

☐ Dress in costume or wear body paint to a game (extra points if it's for a team not playing).

☐ Drink with a professional athlete.

☐ Attend a national championship, even if it's women's lacrosse.

☐ Hold the ultimate Fantasy Football Drafting Day with booze, strippers, and more.

☐ Go to Vegas for the NCAA Tournament opening weekend.

☐ Catch a home run ball and throw it back.

☐ Shake the pom-poms of a professional or semiprofessional cheerleader.

- [ ] Take part in a half-time show or contest.
- [ ] Bet on every NFL game on any given Sunday.
- [ ] Start the wave at a PBA, Billards, or Bassmaster event.
- [ ] Drink a beer at more than four sporting events in one week.
- [ ] Get thrown out of a stadium for heckling.
- [ ] Heckle a player so bad that he yells back or flips you off.

CHAPTER FOUR

GET YOUR PARTY *On*

Now that you've read and studied chapters 2 and 3 of this book, we can all take a deep breath, exhale a huge sigh of relief, and feel confident that you will actually engage in some physically beneficial and not all excessively lewd behavior before you bite the bullet and settle down. With that said, it's time to move forward and take your newfound lust for life to the next level. Of course, when we say that we really mean just stuff that involves booze, women, tequila, bikinis, funnels, thongs, body shots, nipples, swim-up bars, naked Swedish booty, champagne spraying, dirty-dancing in togas, mind-erasers, regretful mornings, long nights, and the best partying that the world has to offer.

The central theme of this chapter is essentially this: It's three A.M., you're drunk and running down a long, sandy stretch of beach on some island in the Caribbean; you've got a bottle of red wine in your left hand and a girl who speaks very, very little English in the right; and oh yeah, your pants are nowhere to be found. Don't worry about why this girl is with you—she just is. Maybe she's drunk. Maybe she actually believes that you're a cool guy. Maybe she's thinking "Americano husbando." Whatever it is, tomorrow you'll have one hell of a story to tell.

Think you do enough partying? Well, that could be the case, but we're here to remind you that it's not just the quantity, it's the quality. You see, the sad fact is that there will come a time when the word "party" will completely change connotations for you. Yes, someday you will hear "party" and think one of three things: It's your six-year-old-daughter's rodeo-themed **Birthday Party**, your neighbors Steve and Joanne are hosting a **Dinner Party**, or it's election time and you're either a part of the **Democratic or Republican Party**. That's right, partying will one day be very, very different. Plus, over time your hangovers will get worse. Your ability to stay up late will succumb to adult-onset narcolepsy. And (the tears are streaming down our faces as we write this) your chance to run pantless down a beach with some random, topless girl on your back will be over. Now, here are a bunch of fun places to party that certainly will blow your usual hangout to shreds. And don't forget, what happens here, stays here . . . until your friends get bombed and tell everyone.

SPRING BREAK

"Spring Break . . ." Hmm, what exactly are we taking a break from again?? For college students, it's really just changing the venue at which they absolutely destroy themselves. For those of us in the working world, we really need to get the hell away from our cube, our boss, and our commute. It's really a Spring Escape. As you break away to one of these destinations, you'll find yourself carousing with college girls who still enjoy making out with their girlfriends, going to parties that offer quite a different scene than happy hour with your coworkers, and laying on the beach saying "I'm going to do this every year . . . until everyone starts looking at me like I'm the creepy old guy at spring break."

WHEN TO GO: March every year

Lake Havasu, Arizona

Boats, booze and boobs—can you really ask for more? Located in **Western Arizona**, this body of water has become a one-of-a-kind Spring Break Destination. The concept is pretty simple. Put a bunch of half-naked people on a bevy of boats, let them drink their faces off, and see what happens.

To fully experience this American tradition, your best bet is to **rent yourself a Mac daddy houseboat**. This way, you've got your activities and accommodations all wrapped up into one. If you can't swing that, any other kind of boat will suffice. Be sure to bring supplies: beer; rum; boobie beads; a blender; cocktail mix; whipped cream; water guns; rafts; condoms; megaphone; beer bong; boom box; a monkey; whatever.

On the waters of Lake Havasu, you'll spend the majority of your time hitting on chicks and goading them to do naughty things with you, each other, or themselves. The cool thing is that many will actually do what you want. Very unusual behavior and precisely why we highly recommend that you see it firsthand. You can also enjoy a bunch of water activities such as jet skiing, waterskiing, and cliff-diving.

When the sun goes down and you're still functioning, the place to be is a club called **Kokomo's**, located at the London Bridge Resort. There you can get your dance on, your drink on, and your party on. Or you can just beach your houseboat and create your own damn club, with the appropriate cover charge . . . of course. To get to Lake Havasu, you can either drive from Phoenix or Las Vegas. Our recommendation is the latter for very obvious reasons.

LINK IT UP: Not exhausted yet? Hit the strip in Vegas (See chapter 4 under, "Bachelor Parties") or head north for different water adventures in the Grand Canyon. (See chapter 2, under "Rafting.")

CAN'T GET THERE? Try Austin Texas' Lake Travis (Fourth of July is red, white, and booby blue) where things get out of control . . . just rent a boat and find naughty girls willing to come on board.

Cancun, Mexico

Commonly known as Spring Break headquarters, Cancun is your perfect escape. Say goodbye to your daily routine and hello to foam parties, young ladies, and test tube shots. Each day will have you **covered in all-you-can-drink bracelets, all-access stamps, and the same clothes you wore last night**. Not to mention, you're in Mexico, with access to beautiful beaches and unbelievable fishing.

The parties are nonstop, and if you're not careful you'll go to all of them. Not that this is a bad thing, but it also makes sense to do a couple of adventures while you have a chance. You can book these in advance, and it's always fun to try to recruit some ladies to join you. Deep-sea fishing, snorkeling, and sky-diving are always good excursions that will also provide you some ammo on the ladies. "While you were in bed watching *Dawson's Creek* reruns, I was pulling in a 180-pound marlin." You could also organize a booze cruise. It's simple, just spend the first few days spreading the word about it, **make it the event to be at, and soon enough you'll be the Mayor of Cancun**. All of this will set you apart from the guy that just bought her a jello shot and grabbed her ass. The best place to stay in Cancun for Spring Break is hands-down The Oasis. With tons of rooms and thousands of spring breakers, this is the place where you'll make out with a random girl in the elevator, see her the next day, and wonder "Where do I know her from?" As long as you don't mind wet T-shirt contests, best blow job championships, and chugfest tournaments, you can find plenty of places to go out at night. La Boom is the club of all clubs. If you can handle more than one night of La Boom, you might have problems. **You're not going to meet your wife in Cancun, but you'll probably take home her slutty sister.**

Margarita Island, Venezuela

What a concept: an island named after a drink that usually gets you so shitfaced that you wake up with a wet bed and nacho cheese on your pillow. Well, we don't know that it's technically named after the cocktail, but it's a good way to think about this place that you might not have known even existed. MTV isn't going to be building their "Beach House" in Margarita Island anytime soon, but we like it that way. It's got everything you need to ensure a good party scene and **Venezuelan women** to go along with it.

The locals are so friendly that it'll be difficult for you to get them to be unwelcoming. Your favorite "I'm an astronaut" line will actually work, and they'll keep asking for more. It's true, they probably won't understand a word you are saying, but they'll still get a kick out of the goofy American who keeps falling down.

As you are just off the coast of Venezuela, the scene is a lot different than you would get at most other spring break locations. From other Americans adventurous enough to stray from Panama City, to boozed-up Brits, to insane Australians, **the people you'll party with will provide half of the entertainment**. Nurse yourself back to life each day at Caribe Beach over some cocktails in the sand, and then wander on down to the city of Porlamar for dancing, drinking, and tits in your face. Hey, it's pretty damn cheap, too.

Montego Bay, Jamaica

Jamaicans love to sit back, drink Red Stripe, smoke a joint, listen to reggae music, and watch girls take their panties off on stage. We think the Jamaicans might be onto something. Jamaica brings in the insane Spring Break parties that you'd expect, and also offers a relaxing Caribbean atmosphere that you can escape to when necessary. Again, party your friggin' ass off, but don't forget to make sure you enjoy Jamaica. **You, your buddies, and a handful of beautiful babies at a local shack listening to Bob Marley** over a whole bunch of Red Stripe could end up being your favorite day.

Then, at night get back to the annihilation and do the worm at the first club you go to. There are two main destinations in Jamaica for Spring Break, Montego Bay ("MoBay") and Negril. MoBay is the second-largest city in Jamaica, so it has a ton going on and a nightlife that will knock you out. Negril is more remote and exists only for tourists, so it can offer you a little more of a vacation. Both places will present you with **naked twenty-something females, conveniently packaged booze, and the Jamaican getaway** that you are looking for.

We highly advise against picking up any Jamaican women. First, there are plenty of sorority sweethearts to play "Just the tip" with. Second, the only thing that will upset a Jamaican dude is taking his woman. So just smoke his weed, not his girl.

TOP BEACHES FOR THE CLOTHING-IMPAIRED
Playa d'es Cavallet; Ibiza, Spain
Bellevue Beach; Klapenburg, Denmark
Tulum Beach; Tulum, Mexico
Montalivet, France
Paradise Beach; Mykonos, Greece
Orient Beach; St. Martin, West Indies
South Beach; Miami, Florida
Plage de Tahiti; Côte d'Azur, France
Ipanema Beach; Rio de Janeiro, Brazil

YEAR-ROUND PARTY SPOTS

Amsterdam
Home to the Van Gogh Museum, Anne Frank's house and many beautiful canals and bridges, Amsterdam has: legal pot and hookers. You can rent a bicycle, lazily pedal your way through its colorful old streets, and find your way to a hash bar to get so high you think you hear Pink Floyd singing from your buddy's eyebrows. Revel in the free-spirited and open ways of this culture as you stare up into **a red-lit window at a woman squeezing her boobs together**. Yes, Amsterdam certainly is a city of extremes. And even if you're not a huge toker or prefer not having to pay for booty, it's still worthy. Although,

we recommend at least a Bill Clinton-esque drag or a space cake. When in Amsterdam . . .

The first time you make your way through the Red-Light District, your brain will be buzzing with one thought: "Are you fucking kidding me?" **It's like window shopping for sex.** In window number one we've got a blonde with big tits in a bright yellow bikini. Behind window number two, **we've got two petite Asians in lingerie sucking on lollipops**. And through window number three, it's a large-and-in-charge black woman willing to negotiate oral sex with even the most broke schmuck on the street. It's surreal to say the least. Although we know only from hearsay, we've been told the women can be talked down in price, are very professional, and deliver just what the window indicates—though enthusiasm does vary.

The bars you'll find in Amsterdam are some of the coolest around. Many are darkly lit, lounge types with great tunes jamming. You'll have a menu of smokey treats to choose from, as well as typical cocktails. Be sure to engage in the local tradition of "happy hour." Not that you've been working all day or anything, but who gives a shit—the drinks are cheaper and the crowd is rowdy. Accommodations are plentiful, but **we suggest staying at a hostel** to save money and meet some really, really interesting people—like those two Brits who have been here for two months, just waking, baking, eating, sleeping, waking, baking, eating, sleeping, over and over. Also, hit the Heineken Brewery for a tour and tasty samples. Check out The Sex Museum . . . for porn made cultural. And be alert and careful of strange people, they're everywhere here. They may be pickpockets, perverts, or picketpocketing perverts (they grope then grab). Lastly, just remember that Amsterdam for couples is like Disney for single dudes—it just doesn't make sense. Get here now.

WHEN TO GO: Anytime, although warmer months make for optimal Red-Light-District perusing.

LINK IT UP: Moving from mellow weed to festive beers, head to Oktoberfest in Munich for a different kind of buzz. (See chapter 1, under "Oktoberfest.")

The Greek Islands

Think of your typical Saturday night of bar hopping. You head out to place number one, maybe the drinks are really cheap or there's a game on, you get a good buzz going and then you move on. You hit another place. You analyze its scene. Are there hot chicks here? Do I have dibs on the Golden Tee? Are you sure this isn't a gay lounge? It goes on and on. At some places you may stay longer because a cute drunk girl keeps rubbing up on you. Others you may flee from immediately because an ugly drunk girl keeps rubbing up on you. You just kind of feel your way through the night. Now, **take that idea and apply it to island-hopping in Greece**. It's simple. You generally don't need a day-by-day schedule, reservations, or ferry tickets. Just get there with a basic plan, a backpack, and, like a Saturday night, see what the fuck happens.

With that said, we need to point out several islands and places that must be on your radar. First, there is **Corfu and its "Eighth Wonder of the World," the Pink Palace**. Allegedly, if you don't hook up here you might as well spend the rest of your vacation at the Viking Resort (see later in this chapter), because you have absolutely zero game. This beach resort is renowned for its nightly spring break–like parties and its weekly toga bash. Whatever time you have allotted for this place, add a day, because without fail a new crop of hotties will check in and you won't be ready to check out. **Mykonos** is another island that will have you partying all day and all night. Here you'll spend your days at Paradise Beach, not Super Paradise (see the following story). And you will kill your nights in the town of Mykonos. Thus, you should stay within walking distance of either the beach or the town. A bus can then transport you back and forth. At Paradise Beach, you'll probably start each day with a still-needed nap, due to the damage from last night. Eventually you'll muster up some energy, mosey to one of the beach bars, and wind up dancing on a table with some chick from Denmark who has an aversion to bikini tops. **Give her a cold drink and watch things get even perkier.** If you don't just carry on all night at the beach, you'll head into town to discover a maze of streets. After getting lost multiple times, ask someone where the **Scandinavian bar** is and go. Do shots of ouzo, meet a lot of crazy people, and then get lost in the maze of streets when you journey home. Our last gotta-get-there island is **Santorini**. Yes, it's known as a very romantic place, and you may accidentally find yourself hugging your buddy as you behold a breathtaking sunset, but still . . . it's a fucking awesome island. You can hike a volcano, toss the Frisbee on a black sand beach, and drink tons of cheap, tasty wine. You'll want to stay in the main city of Fira, where you'll find plenty of places to get yourself into trouble. No matter where your hopping takes you, these islands guarantee to present you with tales to be told for a lifetime. And someday, when you're getting up with the sun to get a head start on "spring cleaning," you'll think: "Remember that time I saw the sunrise as I sat in the seat of an inner tube, floating in the Aegean Sea, with a girl whose name escapes me, but who's tiny toga and fetish for pampering my 'little Zeus' underwater . . . ahhhh . . . now, should I do the gutters or the garage first?" *Opa!*

WHEN TO GO: Summer, particularly June and July

SUPER TIMES IN PARADISE
Brian, 30, Chicago, married and almost totally responsible

It was the summer of 1997, Bubbles, Charlie, and I found ourselves on the tiny Greek island of Mykonos. We had followed four lovely ladies there, with aspirations of getting naked with them. However, very quickly and very unfortunately, they turned out to be more trouble than getting them naked was worth. Our original plan had been to go to Ios, where, allegedly, people partied 24/7 and anyone could get lucky. Anyway with our plan A having been altered and our plan B not happening, we moved on to plan C. We rented some scooters to tour the island and see what we could find. A local suggested that we follow the crude wooden signs to Paradise Beach. So we did.

After about a fifteen-minute scooter ride, we arrived at Paradise Beach. To our great delight there was a bar right on the beach, new lovely ladies everywhere you turned, and a DJ cranking out music. We downed some cocktails, took in the scenery of dancing bikinis and thongs, and just enjoyed a good day at the beach. Plan C was going well so far. On our way back to the hotel that evening we saw another sign for Super Paradise Beach. Wow, we thought. If Paradise Beach was this great then it would stand to reason that *Super* Paradise Beach would be even better. So, the next morning we got up early and excitedly scootered our way forty-five minutes to the even-greater-than-Paradise . . . Super Paradise. The three of us—all very white Irish Americans—strutted our way to an available spot on the beach. We applied suntan lotion to each others' backs (important note in a second), and prepared ourselves for the day's onslaught of debauchery. However, something seemed different about this Paradise. We couldn't quite put our finger on it right away. But after a while Bubbles sat up, looked up

(continued)

and down the beach, and remarked, "Do you guys notice anything odd here?" So Charlie and I took a gander around. And that's when it hit. "Yeah," I said, "there are a lot of guys here. And most of 'em are naked." Yes, it turned out that Super Paradise Beach was a *super* popular gay beach . . . nude gay beach, that is. Regardless of our mistake, it still cracks me up to think how we ended up where we did. We came to Mykonos in search of naked ladies and wound up surrounded by penis. Oops.

Ibiza, Spain

You've probably seen clips of this place on that TV show *Wild On*. You know, it's the destination with all the really hot women dressed in just enough to cover their naughty parts, they're sweating it out on the dance floor and looking all kinds of whooped up on X. Oh wait, that's just about every show of *Wild On*. Anyhow, **people from all over the world come to Ibiza** for what can best be described as a never-ending party. Literally, clubs will be bouncing around the clock. They even have what are called "carryover" parties, parties that simply carry over from one day to the next. When you take a break from it all, you can simply head to the nearest beach chair, lie down, and doze off surrounded by thongs and topless women on all sides. Yeah, this is one destination where **the objective of separating women from their bikinis has already been done for you**. Ah, the liberal ways of the European world. Be sure to offer up some complimentary tanning oil to those in need.

The clubbing scene here is out of control. However, if you don't have all of Paul Oakenfold's trance hits or **your own glow-stick carrying case**, and don't consider yourself a clubbing kind of guy, don't worry. All you need are a couple of patented dance moves (alcohol will likely inspire these), a love of being surrounded by ridiculously toned, tan women, and a positive attitude.

Plus, you can really just hang out, get your drink on, and take in the spectacle around you. And let's be honest, clubbing guys can't possibly enjoy this place in the same way you do. They'll be too busy showing each other their dance moves. Some clubs have circus acts, adjoining casinos to roll the dice at, and occasionally the always-fun foam party. Not to mention there are regular bars, strip clubs, and erotic showcases to keep you entertained. Beyond the partying, you can check out the **hippie market** for bongs, bong accessories, and other goods. You can hit **Playa d'es Cavallet**, a renowned nude beach. Try bringing along that French girl you dry-humped at the foam party last night and see if she's game for more. And you're on an island— you can charter a yacht, go snorkeling, and catch some fish. After a week of only beach chair naps, you'll sleep the whole flight home with visions of tan, bouncing boobies dancing in your head. This place is insanely free-spirited—so go, let loose and see what happens.

WHEN TO GO: Summertime

LINK IT UP: Come in late June, early July, club it up, then stampede to Pamplona. (See chapter 1 under, "Running of the Bulls.")

CHECK IT OFF
Your "hookup" list

☐ Share a hot tub with women who are topless, bottomless, or both.
☐ Become a very happy member of The Mile-High Club.
☐ Become a member of the Greyhound Bus Club.

(continued)

- ☐ Become a member of the Amtrak Train Club.
- ☐ Be the water guy at a wet T-shirt contest.
- ☐ Get some while driving a convertible.
- ☐ Have relations with someone who speaks little or no English.
- ☐ Get a stripper's phone number . . . for real.
- ☐ Take home a hot bartender.
- ☐ One word: Threesome.
- ☐ Two words: Office Sex.
- ☐ Three words: Happy-ending massage.
- ☐ Make sweet love to a woman ten years older than you, a.k.a. "bang a cougar."
- ☐ Have sex with a woman who thinks your name is Thor.
- ☐ Have sex with a woman who thinks your name is "Neon" Deion Sanders.
- ☐ Talk really dirty to a random girl and see how it goes.
- ☐ Enjoy two different women within a twenty-four-hour time period.
- ☐ Hook up with a nurse in her work attire.
- ☐ Hook up with a flight attendant in midflight.
- ☐ Hook up with a farmer's daughter—you know the joke.
- ☐ Hook up with someone from a reality show. Bonus points if it's on the show.
- ☐ Hook up with women from four or more continents.
- ☐ Hook up with a MILF.
- ☐ Hook up in the hot tub of a limo.

Reykjavik, Iceland

Why they call it "Iceland" we can't understand. This place is scalding hot. Between the natural warm springs, the party-crazy culture, and those tall, top-heavy Icelandic beauties, this country will quickly have you striving to come up with a new name. To truly take in the party atmosphere that this place serves up, you'll want to venture to **the capital, Reykjavik**. And you'll want to do so in the summertime, when the sun hardly goes away—fueling everyone's energy as they drink, dance, and grope each other way into the next day. There are a couple of prime times to make your trip here. One is **Icelandic Independence Day on June 17**. On this proud day, it's time for you to embrace your newly found Icelandic heritage, along with every lovely native girl willing to share in your celebration. Just following this huge day, you can bring in **the Summer Solstice on June 21**, as people make the most of this official longest day of the year. For those living in these far-northern latitudes, this occasion—for some reason—incites a temporary state of pure madness . . . a madness that you most definitely want to be a part of it. And to carry on with this awesome trip, you can take it to the links for **a little midnight golf at the Iceland Open**. Hell yeah, this tournament is open to players of all levels who are ready to take advantage of all that sunlight. Plus, four or five hours on the course will give you a well-deserved break from the constant onslaught of drinking and hitting on girls who don't understand your sense of humor.

If for some reason you don't sleep all day after your obliterating night, Iceland has hot natural springs to soak your booby-bruised body. **The Blue Lagoon** is probably the most famous, and it is definitely something you should experience. Don't forget your grape smuggler . . . and a sock. For a genuine escape from the insanity, Iceland has great adventures to be had. Choose from glacier-hiking, off-roading, rafting, whale-watching, and fishing. Make it a point to work off a hangover or two by engaging in some of the above. If you're not sold on this country, keep in mind that most of the country is fluent in English, making it easier to meet people. The level of openness (a.k.a., easy to get their pants off) is unusually high. And you being a record mogul from L.A. will only help this. Who wants to be the next Bjork . . . without the funny face and strange wardrobe?

WHEN TO GO: Summertime for maximum sun and fun

WHERE THE HOTTEST OF THE HOT WOMEN DWELL:
Montreal, Canada
Iceland
Buenos Aires, Argentina
Caracas, Venezuela
Los Angeles, California
Manhattan, New York
Prague, Czech Republic
Stockholm, Sweden
Hong Kong, China
Varna, Bulgaria

ALL-INCLUSIVE, ALL-EVERYTHING RESORTS

"All of my drinks are included for the entire week? Are they fucking serious?" Yes, they are. "That's fucking awesome—how do these places stay in business?" We don't know, but we recommend them as a fantastic option to really maximize your vacationing pleasure. However, there are some general rules to adhere to. **First**, you may find a really good deal on the Internet, the pictures may look fantastic, and the travel agent may say "she's heard good things about it," but if the price is so ridiculously cheap that it makes you feel weird, it's probably a cesspool. Yes, there are dumps out there. **Second**, beware of the all-inclusive, all-foreign resorts, unless you really want to spend your days at the swim-up bar with Hans the fat, drunk, neon speedo guy. **And lastly**, even if you don't have to, tip your bartender. This will guarantee speedy service for the rest of your trip—because most other cheap-asses think "Oh well, I've already paid my gratuity in the package." Don't be that person. Overall, you'll find fun people gravitate toward the all-inclusives, and you'll find an ample supply of single chicks looking for sun and anal sex. Okay, at least the first one. Anyway, here are few interesting choices in the all-inclusive arena.

Vikings Exotic Resort—Dominican Republic

Let us make it clear for all our friends, relatives, and anyone else who respects us in any way, just because we write it, doesn't mean that we consider it to be a part of our system of morals. With that said, you've gotta hear about this fucking place. It gives new meaning to the phrase "all-inclusive." On this party trip, you'll head to the sunny and beautiful Dominican Republic. You'll be picked up from the airport and taken to a wonderful villa with luxurious amenities. You'll then be invited to a cocktail party. Present at this party will be you, your four other buddies, and ten or so lovely ladies. You'll mingle. You'll drink. You'll have a lively group discussion. And then each of you will walk away with your "lady friend" for the duration of this vacation. Yes, **this trip comes with guaranteed play**. And they're not some ugly beasts either. Many are flown in from the strip club farms of Eastern Europe and Russia. So you can curb your best pickup lines, shelve that bar trick with the napkin, and you can forget about worrying if she's just being a tease. This is a sure thing. Certainly, it takes the sport out of it, but, hey, if you're looking for a challenge, **go play a round of championship golf or head out on the waters for some deep-sea fishing**.

Now, if this sounds like paradise to you, we first suggest you get a group of friends and secure the place for yourselves. Beats sharing it with some strange other dudes. Plus, the partying around the pool will be much more fun with friends. Before you pick your lady, have a **"draft order"** (much like fantasy football) so there's no fighting over Veronika with the really sweet ass. And change up your girl (unless you're in love) for maximum variety. The bylaws of the resort state that you can. Beyond enjoying the company of your new friend, this island offers up plenty of fun activities . . . that **you'll be happy to discover if you ever come back** and stay at another place. Once again, we're not here trying to encourage prostitution (if that's what people want to call it), but we would be remiss not to at least bring it up as one very interesting, thought-provoking option.

WHEN TO GO: Like most tropical locales, anytime but hurricane season

Hedonism I, II, III, and on and on

Unlike the previous all-inclusive, here you'll need to work a little harder to get some love. Not much harder, but a little. And there's actually only a Hedonism II and III. Both are located on the good-time island of Jamaica. These places, like the name says, are all about people **overindulging in everything**. Yes, there are swingers and all kinds of freaks here, but there are also plenty of horny single chicks, groups of horny single chicks, and horny recently divorced chicks. Perfect for your cause. Meeting people will be easy. Between the bars, the all-inclusive alcohol served at the bars, and the many, many activities, you'll have no problem getting to know your fellow hedonist.

Every day will offer activities like scuba diving, windsurfing, and naked versus nonnaked volleyball. Every night will bring a different themed bash, from a "pajama party" to Mardi Gras, to a seventies party. Whatever you're up to, there will always be the opportunity to wind up naked in a hot tub with two ladies who **"have always wondered what a threesome would be like."** Yeah baby. Seriously though, if there's ever a chance for doubling your pleasure, it's here. When looking into this vacation, be sure see what kind of "special" events might be happening during your stay. For example, if the "Big Boob Bikini Team" is here for a stay, that's a good thing. If the **"Hairy-Ass Nudist Dungeons & Dragons Club"** is holding their convention, that is bad. Pretty simple. Your best bet is probably to choose a nonanything week to avoid any possible strangeness. Now, before you and your friends go (and keep the number down, for competition sake) be sure to create **a master list of things to do**. Award points based on the absurdity of the task. And the winner should take home some kind of prize. To get you started, try: "Anyone who gets laid in a pool gets ten points, with a five-point bonus if you're wearing arm floaties during the act." Now, what's better than an all-inclusive hedonistic vacation?

Club Med Turkoise, Turks and Caicos

Don't freak out. This is not your family conga line kind of resort. In fact, if you're under the age of eighteen you're not welcome. This destination is for those who like to play hard and party hard all in one place. The island itself has fantastic beaches and some of the best scuba diving on the planet. The resort will allow you to enjoy both and then some. With activities up the wazoo, like sailing, deep-sea fishing, waverunners, volleyball, and more, you'll have endless daytime options at your disposal. Definitely take advantage of them: however, you should also enjoy a day or two of drinking rum slushies, playing drunken bocce ball, and enticing interested hotties into your circle of debauchery. Remember, **anytime is a good time for happy hour when you're on vacation**. (Especially when you're at a place where your drinks are included.)

At night, let the boozing begin . . . or carry on. They've got a disco and an outside bar that will be hopping. The ladies will want to dance, so the disco is a logical choice. Now here's an important thing to note, the females come to this tropical location to relax, cut loose, and get away from their normal existence. And **that includes getting away from regular, nice, boring guys—like most of us**. There's a reason that the male staff members are willing to work for near-minimum wage. They get laid constantly. (See chapter 6: Jet Ski Guy) Now, your job is to be as exotic and different as possible to fulfill these ladies' fantasies. Are you a fighter pilot? Are you a poet? Are you an Olympic medalist in the luge? (Yeah, we love that last one.) Anyway, think it through. Every night's goal should be either to go for "a walk" on the beach, take a late-night dip (who needs bathing suits?), or **get one of your buddies so drunk he passes out naked in the ping-pong room**. In order to ensure the greatest supply of single women, avoid typical holidays that might invite more couples. Also, call and ask the concierge if one time is better than another. Another great thing about all-inclusives is that, when you say you'd like to buy a girl a drink, you don't actually have to buy it. Beautiful. So get here and make us proud.

TOP CLUBS TO DO THE "ROBOT," "WORM," AND OTHER COOL DANCES:
La Boom; Cancun, Mexico
Mansion; Miami, Florida
Club B Boss; Hong Kong, China
Scorpions; Ios, Greece
Garden of Eden; Los Angeles, California

Privilege; Ibiza, Spain

Crobar; New York City, New York

Gatecrasher; Sheffield, England

Discoteca Help; Rio De Janeiro, Brazil

BACHELOR PARTY DESTINATIONS

Oh, the bachelor party. They're the beginning of marriages; they're the end of marriages. These events always make for a great time, but planning them can be a bitch, especially when there are a million guys throwing out suggestions. **"Dude, come on—midget albino hookers!"** "How about just a nice sunset cruise, Amstel Lights, and stogies!" "I got it!!! Let's go cow-tipping!" Seriously, everyone will chime in, so don't listen. A solid best man has to designate responsibilities and make all the executive decisions. Once the verdict is made, stick with it. We've highlighted some of the top locations for a bachelor party, all of which offer everything required for a successful stag and more. First, here are some general guidelines to abide by:

- **The bachelor is not in charge.** Simply get an available date from the groom, and after that just tell him where he needs to be and when. The poor guy is in the middle of planning a wedding and getting an earful from the little woman. Do you think he's in the right state of mind to advise on how many strippers to order?
- **Travel in groups.** From the first drinks in the airport bar to referring to the flight attendant as "waitress" when you order more Heinekens to inviting the cab driver to your hotel to join the party, it'll be a stupendous group effort.
- **Everyone stays at the same hotel.** Running into your friend as

you're coming home with a nineteen-year-old girl only happens if you stay at the same place. This is a must.

- **Always go.** Bachelor parties are always a goddamn ridiculously good time. If you don't have fun at a bachelor party, either you suck or your friends do. It's also the one night those of you who are sadly settled down get a glimpse of what's possible for the rest of the single dudes; so, if you're married and you say no to a bachelor party, you're dead to us.

Montreal, Canada

"Oh Canada, you get me drunk and laid." We think that's how it goes, or, at least after a weekend in Montreal, that's what you'll be belting out. But drunk and laid are just the essentials surrounded by festivities that will bring any bachelor party to Tommy Lee status. Montreal is a great destination because it sounds less intimidating when telling people where you are going for the weekend. With Vegas, people know what you're doing. In Montreal, you can be simply going to enjoy French-Canadian culture **(a culture with centuries of experience in sex and drugs)**.

Montreal has two distinct areas where you can divide your time. During the day, **Old Montreal** has great bars and pubs to lick your wounds from the night before and start your buzz again for the next day. Stop by Casino de Montreal and put down the exact amount you spent in booze the previous night on one hand of blackjack . . . win it all back. Rue Crescent and St. Catherine's Street are where to go out to find all of the trouble you'll want, discos, restaurants, bars, eighteen-year-old university girls, and of course the world-famous strip clubs. Club Super Sexe is a definite stop because of its name, and it has **the hottest girls you will ever see**, but it is not the best place to get some solid lap grinding. Go to Chez Paree, or even take a cab a lit-tle ways out of town to Bar Salon Grand Prix for some better "interac-tion." Also, hook up dinner reservations at Bar Les Princesses, where you'll be served drinks and grub by naked chicks while porn is on the tube.

These are French Canadians up here, so the opportunity to put to-gether a show-worthy performance is highly possible. Don't be afraid to draw attention to yourselves, you're in Canada, so why not? Dress the bachelor up in something really American like a hot dog outfit, or have everyone wear Elvis jumpsuits. Then, when people give you weird looks, act as if you do this every night in the States. **It'll either get you a piece of ass or a kicked out of a bar**, both memorable and required happenings for a bachelor party.

South Beach, Miami

"Bienvenido a Miami!" Yeah, it's a lame Will Smith song, but the con-cept of a hot Latino girl singing "Welcome to Miami" is a perfect image. You can think of the entire town as a **hot Latino girl asking you to ravage her**. So there is no doubt that a bachelor party in South Beach is going to be a winner. We can't believe you don't need a passport to get into Miami, because it truly feels like another country. Topless women, all-night outdoor clubs, and sexy accents were not written into our Constitution, but we're ready for an amendment.

You'll want to make sure you're treated like Cuban Royalty this weekend, so, once again, plan ahead with a few calls to restaurants and clubs. The pools at the Delano Hotel or the Shore Club are worth every penny you'll spend that weekend, so buck up and stay at one of these hotels. You and Jessica Alba can engage in meaningful chitchat over an early afternoon mimosa. People love their cars down there, so **get a kick-ass old convertible to cruise the strip during the afternoon**. You could rent one, or try to pull off that you are test-driving it for Colin Farrell. Either way, the groom will feel like a stud for the last time, and it will get you the attention of the ladies that you'll surely want to grope later in the night.

Strip clubs in South Beach are not as available as you'd think, so ordering girls to the room may be required. Unless you go to a decent place like Club Madonna, you may end up paying a Nicaraguan refugee with seven kids for a lap dance. Take your convertible to Fort Lauderdale or Hollywood for booby fun. **Dancing and getting your groove on are huge at the clubs, and participation is a must.** You could try to pull off the too-cool-to-dance-guy at the table, but not getting out there might seal your fate. Be certain to get the bachelor out there dancing, and tell everyone he's marrying Paris Hilton's cousin—he'll be swarmed. The massive clubs, where you'll run into everyone from the Puerto Rican Mafia to bachelorettes letting you suck for a buck, are Crobar and Mansion. The following week, as you drink Budweiser at your local tavern, it'll seem like a different world.

WARNING: Drinks at some of the trendier hotels and other spots can cost you a stupid amount of dough, so think flask, preboozing, or your wealthiest buddy's credit card.

Vegas

We're not sure which came first, Vegas or the bachelor party, but both were clearly designed for each other. With a small group or a shit-load of guys, Vegas can accommodate all participants. The top hotels for bachelor parties are Mandalay Bay, the Hard Rock, and

The Palms. If you really want to live it up, try **the Hugh Hefner Sky Villa in the Playboy Tower** of the Palms. This luxury suite doesn't come with seven girlfriends, but has just about everything else you'll need to get your own posse of blondes.

Vegas is an amusement park of adult entertainment, so you don't have to do too much planning to find yourself knee-deep in destruction. Some things to set up ahead of time could be a decent dinner at a steak joint, a VIP ("I'm a big shit") table at a club, and a cabana by the pool. Golf is always a great option, and of course there are the strippers. Definitely order a few of these to come up to your suite. But be ready, it can be a little awkward when they walk in and you're looking for them to dance, while they're thinking hand jobs in the closet. This is Vegas. Before you know it they'll be naked, the bachelor will be sprawled out on the floor in his boxers, and everyone will be throwing their blackjack winnings at the ladies as they embarrass your friend a little more. Chances are you'll make it a doubleheader with a trip to the nudie club later. Break it up with a little gambling, and see if you can get the "private" strippers to hit the casino with you to blow on your dice for good luck.

Other fun you'll definitely have is when the bachelor encounters a bachelorette. **They don't know if they should talk about their upcoming wedding, engage in flirtatious conversation, or just go upstairs and screw.** At the end of the weekend you'll want to kill yourself as you hazily walk through the airport. To get you through this, just imagine a video camera had been following each of your friends the entire weekend. As you sit down in your window seat, think about what it would have captured. Scary? Yes. Hilarious? Yes. Too many boobies in your face? Yes. Now, let that visual carry you home.

Tijuana, Mexico

The premise of a bachelor party is to do everything a guy is not supposed to while he's married, right? Well, **Tijuana contains just about everything you're not supposed to do at all**, so I think we have a match. Tijuana is about as sketchy as it gets, so in order to keep yourself slightly above the rest, stay at a nice hotel such as Pueblo Amigo. After a night of filth, you'll appreciate it.

Avenida Revolucion is the main road, with all that has given Tijuana the legendary status that it so deeply enjoys. **Here you'll find bars, clubs, donkeys for sale, and more importantly, women for sale.** The strip clubs are not exactly legit, and pretty much every "stripper" is a hooker. Instead of being a regular, ordinary dirtball yourself, hire a couple of girls to be your guides for the day, night, or weekend. Get two for the bachelor. From there you'll get into the better places, have immediate female companionship, and, who knows, maybe another crew of girls will get jealous.

When you walk the streets of Tijuana, you feel like Doc Holiday wandering from place to place looking to drink, gamble, shoot people (don't do this), and find women. It truly is like no other place, unless you lived 150 years ago. **By the end of the weekend, one friend will be on peyote, one will be getting tickled with feathers by six women, one will be eating breakfast with his new girlfriend's forty-seven-person family, and one will be in jail.** Most importantly, the bachelor will be ready to get married.

In order to keep your sanity and say you did something normal, play golf in San Diego while you're down there. Torrey Pines has two topnotch public courses.

MUZZY AND THE HOTDOG
Brian, 30, Philadelphia, single

The ideas for a bachelor party for our ultimate-bachelor-of-a-friend Sean were endless. Vegas, Ibiza, and Thailand were all possibilities. We also tossed around going to Chicago or New York and doing something really strange, Gorilla outfits, clown costumes—you get the idea. As it was October we decided for lederhosen, and we hit up every German bar in New York City. As there would be fifty of us dressed up, we wanted Sean to stand out, so we got him in a full-blown hot dog costume. We also hired a guy named Muzzy who had no other responsibility than to entertain us. He was dressed like a pimp, with a pink jacket, slicked-back hair, and a thin mustache; but unfortunately he was not a pimp. He really was just the weird guy hanging out with a bunch of lederhosen-clad dudes and a human hot dog. After a bunch of bratwursts, several bars, many steins, and a few "everyone tackle the fat kid in the hot dog suit" we decided it was time to hit the strip club.

Hank did the worm and Jay yelled "Who wants my hot dog," which definitely made for a strange entrance. After we convinced the manager that we weren't escapees from the loony bin, he let us put Sean, costume and all, on stage with four strippers. While the image will last forever, the hot dog garb was not quite suitable for Sean to fully enjoy his dancers. So it was time to start reeking havoc upon the rest of Manhattan.

At some point between the strip club and getting back on the bus, Sean found a Superman cape to compliment his attire. Muzzy quickly noticed this and began calling our bachelor "Super Dawg" (this was just about Muzzy's only contribution to the evening). We enjoyed it thoroughly and it got us completely riled up. We eventually parked our

(continued)

bus on Bleecker Street, alongside a ton of bars with hundreds of people in the neighborhood. With fifty guys in lederhosen, we quickly got the attention of many and began break-dancing to the sounds of car radios, bars, and cheering fans. After a solid ten minutes of dancing in the street and on top of cars, Sean gathered everyone's attention did a remarkable backflip, jumped back to his feet, and proclaimed to all. "You haven't lived until you've walked a mile in the shoes of *Super Dawg!!!*" Super Dawg won the award that weekend for the best bachelor ever.

TOP STRIP CLUBS—OR SO PEOPLE SAY:

Spearmint Rhino; Las Vegas, Nevada

Scores; New York City, New York

Mons Venus; Tampa Bay, Florida

Brandi's; Vancouver, Canada

Colibri; Hamburg, Germany

Chez Paree; Montreal, Canada

Dolls; Moscow, Russiai

Blue Rose; Ibiza, Spain

Seventh Heaven; Tokyo, Japan

CHAPTER FIVE

WANDER *The* WORLD

Are you a teacher with summers off and no need for a second job? A multistate lotto winner? Or the recipient of really good genes (aka, trust fund)? If you are, you're a lucky bastard . . . we hate you. If you're not, chances have it that **you are going to work for a long fucking time**. You won't have too many opportunities in your life to simply skip off to another part of the planet and mindlessly travel for a month or more at a time. It's true. The average job offers what? Three weeks of vacation a year? That's not enough. And even if you had four weeks, would they really let you take all of them back-to-back? The probability of that happening is about the same as having a supermodel get down on her knees and beg you to sleep with her. However, the odds of you having a "break" of a considerable length of time at this stage in your life is extremely likely—whether it's a summer during or after college, a month between old and new jobs, or the time period before you start graduate school—seize that opportunity and go travel. An opening like this won't recur until the day you retire. And, as we've said before, when you're sixty-five it just won't be the same.

This chapter is all about the experience of traveling. It's about carrying everything you need in a pack on your back. It's about arriving in a town with no map, no place to stay, and knowing just five words of the spoken language. **(And those words are "Your wife has nice nipples").** It's about flying, driving, stumbling by the seat of your pants to discover all kinds of crazy things out there waiting to be uncovered. Travel as the wind blows. Get lost in the local culture. **Discover romance in a Polish strip club.** And do it all with nothing but a money belt full of traveler's checks, a local guide book, and a bag filled with smelly, dirty clothes. Choose your traveling companions wisely, though. Make sure they're on the same page as you and are neither too high-maintenance nor too lame. Also, keep the number of travelers to a minimum, as less people make for less conflict. On these roads, the journey can be just as exciting as the destination.

EUROPE BY RAIL

Where the heck to begin? Traveling through Europe when you're young, money-challenged, and "willing to rough it," is an experience that can never be replicated. You'll see incredible sights, meet people from all walks of life, and learn a library of knowledge on subjects ranging from French swear words to Hungarian fast food to the proper operation of public pay toilets. **The train is absolutely the best way** to make the most of your time and your trip. It can take you from city to city and country to country with speed and ease. Plus, you can hop on board an **overnighter**, where the train doubles as your hotel room. This preserves your cash for more important things, like those five XL cans of Heineken you'll no doubt need for the ride.

There are several types of rail passes you can buy; check out **raileurope.com** for details on what would work best for you. On board, have games to play, your iPod loaded to its fullest, and alcohol to help you sleep peacefully. Don't be afraid to roam the train cars in search of like-minded idiots or that pack of Canadian girls on their European adventure. "Eh, we've got Molson and maple syrup back in our cabin." You will hear stories about thieves stealthily removing your passport and money on the trains. Although these tales may be embellished and **may also involve you waking up with a missing kidney.** From firsthand experience, theft does happen. So lock, hide, and otherwise protect your shit. Where you go and how you go about it is totally up to you. Europe has so much to offer that in even just a month's time you will conquer only a fraction of it. However, there are some highlights worth mentioning here.

Barcelona: beautiful women, sangria, and parties that last all night

Amsterdam: legal drugs, legal hookers, and many other things you can't experience anywhere else (See chapter 5, under "Amsterdam.")

Interlaken, Switzerland: outdoor activity mecca, stay at Balmer's

Prague, Czech Republic: Eastern-European flavor, beautiful women, and great bars

Rome, Italy: ruins, best ice cream ever, pasta-o-rama, Italian women, and wine

Munich, Germany: Beer, sausages, beer, pretzels, and beer (See chapter 1, under "Oktoberfest.") (The Bavarian Alps are also nearby and worth the trip.)

On your travels, **stay in hostels** as much as you can. You'll meet a lot of great people and the hostels are cheap as hell. Yes, most hostels (because of the bunk beds and shared spaces) are not conducive to shacking up, but, hey, just add that to your list of challenges to check off; give yourself extra points for hooking up on the top bunk while the bottom is occupied. Other ways to save your Euros are to eat at college cafeterias, shop at local grocery stores, and go to the gay bars for free drinks (hey, just trying to help). On your travels, taste every local delicacy. Sample every local beer or cocktail. And learn a phrase from each language— even if it's just "Yes, I would like your boobs in my face." Also, don't skip out on something awesome because you're trying to conserve your Euro stash. Fuck it! The opportunity will only be there once. With that said, put down this book, find a much more practical one that includes a map, and start plotting how and when you're going to accomplish this trip . . . **right now**.

WHEN TO GO: The best time is anytime, but the warmer months, March through October, are more conducive to sleeping in local parks.

LINK IT UP: If you've got a ton of time on your hands, head from Europe to Southeast Asia (See chapter 5, under "Asia.") Or, to help plan your path, see our other sections for possible European adventures, fests, parties and more.

"BARCELONA . . . BARCELONA . . ."
Michael, 30, New York, single

It was February 1999 and I was traveling through Europe. I was in the South of France for Carnival, which is pretty much Mardi Gras French style. I walked the streets, drank everything in sight, and joined every festivity I could. While marching in the parade, I suddenly I got laid out with no warning: a Lawrence Taylorlike hit put me on the ground in front of thousands of people. I looked up, and to my surprise, my college roommates Sean and Ryan happened to be stomping their feet in the parade as well, and they saw me from afar. This was a total coincidence that we happened to run into each other, but once I realized it was them, being knocked to the ground and having beer dumped all over me made absolute sense.

So we hit the streets together, did everything we could do, including getting our lives threatened by lesbians, **teaching the people of Nice, France how to play flip cup**, and sleeping on the beach. After a couple days of that, they were headed to Salamanca, Spain, and I was going on to Barcelona. At the train station we ran into a couple of girls we met the previous night. They were about to get on their train to Italy, and during our good-bye's they gave us their remaining Francs (French money pre-Euro). We figured this was payment for letting them make out with us in the street, so we were good with it. While it seemed like only change, it actually turned out to be like forty bucks. I'm pretty sure they didn't realize how much it was. Regardless, we took that money and bought a case of beer and three bottles of wine—one for each of us.

We got on our train at nine P.M., stocked and ready to get really drunk once again. The only catch was that **I had to switch trains at five A.M. to**

(continued)

go to Barcelona, while they stayed on to Salamanca. "Fuck it, I'll stay up all night" I figured. So, we snuck into a first-class train car, got our own booth, and cracked open the booze. Besides puking red wine and watching Sean piss in the corner of our first-class car, the next thing I remember is the conductor waking us up. When we gave our tickets, he gave us a nasty look, and said something weird in French. I immediately looked at my watch, it was 8:30 in the morning. **"Shit, I missed my stop, damn it."** Sean and Ryan were laughing, calling me "Americano estupido." I had to get off at the next stop and backtrack. So, as we reached the next stop. I jumped off, the train left, and I looked around: I was in the middle of the mountains, with two feet of snow all around me. "What the . . . ?" There shouldn't be mountains in between Nice and Barcelona. I had just come from seventy-degree weather.

I walked into a small train station, which was just about empty, except for a few people sleeping. After a failed attempt to communicate with the ticket lady, I started walking around to each person just saying "Barcelona . . . Barcelona . . ." I was still hammered of course. Eventually one dude woke up, walked me to the ticket booth, talked to the lady, and she gave me an itinerary of all of the stops I needed to make before Barcelona. "Where the hell am I? I'm further than I started." Sixteen hours later I got to Barcelona, **still wearing the weird hat I got in Nice** and still with no idea what the hell happened.

Four months down the road, I saw Sean and Ryan, and said "Hey, did you guys make it to Spain all right?" "Nope." They ended up in Paris. Apparently, sneaking into first class put us in the wrong car, and the trains split in the middle of the night. One to Spain, one to Paris. I got off somewhere between Nice and Paris. "Oh, so that's why everyone was speaking French . . . ?"

DOWN UNDER—AUSTRALIA

The toilets flush in the opposite direction. The moon looks like it's been flipped upside down. And many of its inhabitants have a family tree full of criminals. But, "no worries mate . . . ," you'll fit in perfectly down under. In fact, **all you really have to do is enjoy beer and adventures**, and the natives will adopt you as their own. Plus, they all take a lot of pride in their nation and will do whatever they can to show you a good time. Getting here is a long journey. It's fifteen hours direct from Los Angeles. And the country itself is the size of the United States' contiguous forty-eight states. So you'll want to allot some serious time.

Australia delivers a little something for all tastes. Beaches, wildlife, desert, rainforest, pubs, clubs, accents, scuba, bushwalking, tasty beer, fish and chips, and a whole lot more. **Your first stop will be the main city of Sydney.** This city is a great launching pad for your experience, as you'll quickly begin to pick up some customs, like the art of buying a round of beer. Yeah, in Australia, you enter into a school (that's usually three people or more), and, while in school, each member must "shout" in turn. A shout is their way of saying, "I've got this round." There's no leaving school until your shout has been shouted. It's a fun tradition that anyone can easily engage in. Two areas in Sydney that are great for going to school are **The Rocks and King's Cross**. In The Rocks, you'll find historic old pubs like the Lord Nelson Brewery Hotel—Sydney's first pub (established 1831). The other district to check out is King's Cross. Here you'll find a mini-Amsterdam, with crazy pubs, dirty strip clubs, and, yes, **Australia's version of the Red Light District**. It's legal here, too. Beyond just boozing it up, in Sydney you can hit

Bondi Beach or Coogee Beach, climb to the top of Harbour Bridge (yes, the actual top), and walk across from there. You should definitely hit an Australian football or rugby match.

After tearing it up in Sydney, you'll have a ton of directions to go. In no particular order, and certainly not mapped out in sequence (hey, we can't do everything for you), here are some areas to try and make it to:

- **Coast of Queensland:** Here you'll have the Great Barrier Reef to explore, you'll find the Whitsunday Islands, where you can charter a boat, learn how to sail, and then captain your own way around, plus the raging-fun-town of Cairns to get crazy in.

- **Red Centre:** You can't fly twenty hours and not see this. It's the home to Uluru National Park and its famous Ayers Rock. See aboriginal culture, hike, fly in a sightseeing plane, and more.

- **Victoria:** Check out Australia's other big city, Melbourne, travel along the Great Ocean Road for the sight of the Twelve Apostles rock formation, various beach activities, and whatever else catches your eye. Also, take a trip to Phillip Island for the Penguin Parade, and in the winter you can hit the slopes of the Victorian Alps.

- **Top End:** While most of the action is in the southern part of Australia, up here you'll find more "out there" activities. Take in Katherine Gorge (no it's not a prostitute or a porn star) and Kakadu National Park. This is Crocodile Dundee land, so wrestle an alligator, canoe one of the many rivers, and, when you're done, try your luck at the casino in Darwin.

Certainly there is a lot more to this huge nation. Definitely try to get to **Kangaroo Island** to see this local animal along with koalas, wallabies, and sea lions. Tasmania is just off the coast.

Who else can say they've been to Tasmania? And make a trip to Broken Hill for hiking, rappelling, and drinking at its local pubs. Whatever you do, don't order a Fosters. Australians drink XXXX, Victoria Bitter, and regional favorites. Another thing to note is that "light" beer here just means less alcohol, not less calories. So imbibe wisely. Also, eat some wild food, such as kangaroo. A month would make a fantastic amount of time to truly get to know this former penal colony. And yes, when you return you will be able to navigate a menu at any Outback Steakhouse with ease.

WHEN TO GO: The best time is their summertime—that is, November through February. But anytime is pretty much okay.

ISLAND HOPPIN'

Imagine this: You're on the beach of an exotic island where you've been dancing to the sounds of steel drums all night. Now lying in a hammock with a cold beer, you turn to the little hottie next to you and nonchalantly ask, **"Would you like to come back to my yacht?"** Hook, line, and sinker, you are getting laid—multiple times. "But *how?*" you ask. This scenario is entirely possible without being a hip-hop mogul or the star of the next James Cameron movie. If you have your captain's license, then you obviously already know the many benefits of having a boat. For the rest of us, we have to charter a yacht with a captain included. A lot of charter companies will also offer lessons, so the next time around, . . . **you are the captain**. Keep in mind, you're sleeping and eating on the boat, so the expense of hotels and meals is eliminated.

If you don't feel like standing at the helm and cruising from island to island, you can still bounce around via planes and ferries. As you island-hop, you will chow down on outstanding food, party like it's New Year's every day, and meet women at every destination. Fishing, snorkeling, surfing, scuba, and golf should also be on your activity list. If you're not already out the door and shopping for that captain's cap, keep reading for some favorite places to sail the high waters:

Greek Islands

The only thing "Big" and "Fat" about these islands is the guy serving you drinks. Other than that, the women here match the beauty of the surroundings. The Greeks are all about leisure, and as you go from place to place there is no doubt a good time will be had by all. You'll fly into Athens, where you should spend a night, then get on your way. There are literally hundreds of Greek islands, so you've got a lot of ocean to cover.

The islands are divided into six main groups: Cyclades, Northeastern Aegean, Saronic, Dodecanese, Ionian, and Sporades islands. Map your trip by these groups. For some of the most insane partying in the world, **go to Ios**. Check out the club Aftershock for a wet T-shirt contest or stop by the Dubliner for hundred shots in hundred minutes. Just think, we've all been to clubs like this, but have you ever had your yacht docked outside? Other party islands are **Mykonos and Corfu**. For a more relaxing vibe, where you can chat with local fisherman and sip ouzo rather than slamming it, try Tinos or Lesvos. These are all located in the Cyclades Islands, so consider it just the beginning of your adventure.

WHEN TO GO: Spring and Summer

St. Vincent & The Grenadines

With its own governing body and no direct affiliation with any large country, St. Vincent's and the Grenadines truly bring in **people from all over the world**. You'll probably meet more non-Americans than Americans. There are not many jamming clubs here, but plenty of beachside huts to enjoy several Caribs (a local beer) with other travelers. Many come by sailboat looking to celebrate each day the same way you are.

You can fly into St. Vincent's, St. Lucia, or Grenada. From there, you'll set sail for the incredible Grenadine Islands. Bequia has great beaches and a hotel called the Frangipani is known to be **one of Jimmy Buffet's favorite vacation spots**. The bar will be hopping every night. The best day activity will be **snorkeling in the Tobago Cays**. Also, the island of Canouan has a course where you'll want to bust out the golf clubs. One of the most famous islands is Mustique. Here you can check out the **vacation homes of Mick Jagger and David Bowie**, then get hammered like rock stars at Basil's. Wednesday nights bring a big barbecue buffet, so throw on a British accent and tell the ladies you're working with Mick on his new album. And, "Did I mention that I have a yacht?"

WHEN TO GO: Avoid the rainy season, which is May to June and September to October.

San Blas Isles, Panama

We don't think the Van Halen song has much to do with island exploring in Panama, but you'll no doubt be shouting it out as you cruise through the tremendous San Blas Isles. With a fully stocked boat, you can drink tons of Chilean wine, tie on a solid buzz, and then wander from place to place. You'll have **over 365 islands at your disposal.**

However, only forty are inhabited. Make your way to at least one non-populated island with any lady willing to join you and play **the "stranded on a deserted island" game**. Tip your captain to get lost for a few hours and convince your lady friend that it's up to the two of you to claim the tiny island in the name of whichever country she happens to be from—and you'll need her shirt to use as a flag.

At any of these islands, you can dive for lobster and starfish. Grouper makes for excellent dinner. And take in as much Panamanian culture as you can. Also, **hang out with the Kuna Indians**, who dress in full garb, speak a local dialect, and make their own goods. They're the real deal. If you want to cross the Panama Canal to the Pacific Ocean, be warned that it's not cheap and not likely to happen. However, you can and should take a day trip to see it. Wait, is that David Lee Roth we hear?

WHEN TO GO: December through April

The Bahamas

By now you know that we want you to go sailing through tropical islands, anywhere, any way possible, thus it would be wrong not to mention the Bahamas. Here you can get it all from the luxury of your boat—the warmth of the tropics, plenty of scuba-diving, snorkeling, fishing, golf, and nubile spring-breakers. The popular islands of **Nassau and Paradise Island** are perfect for partying with nineteen-year-old girls. Uh, we mean twenty-one-year-old girls. Hustling a group of bikinis (uh, we mean ladies) back to your sailboat should be the easiest part of your adventure. Have some cheap champagne on board, take the labels off and tell your female companions that it's straight from **your private vineyard**, prelabeling and all. After a couple of nights, you're free to move on if you want (but we wouldn't blame you if you didn't). Isles such as **Exuma, Eleuthera and Mayaguana** will offer plenty of activities along with a more local flavor. North Eleuthera sits on the corner of the Bermuda Triangle. Hey, just coming ashore after a trip there will give you bragging rights. Mayaguana has only three hundred residents. . . . Soak in its culture while pondering your next destination at the local bar nestled in Betsy's Bay.

WHEN TO GO: February through July

SOUTHEAST-ASIAN JOURNEY

"One Night in Bangkok . . ." Yeah, you've heard that 'eighties tune by renowned one-hit-wonder Murray Head, right? Well, after one night of your own in this Thai city, that very song will be stuck on repeat in your head for days. Especially after an evening where you were offered "anyting you waaahant" by an eighteen-going-on-sixteen-year-old girl, got smashed on bourbon cocktails, and woke up naked on the floor next to an old Australian chick you swore last night was Elle MacPherson. Amazingly, that was your most uneventful night in Southeast Asia. A trek through this great part of the world will take you through bustling cities, third-world villages, picturesque beaches, brothels, drug dens, and everything else you'd ever want (or perhaps not want) to see.

There is so much to conquer that we're not going to attempt to plan your journey for you. This will require some research on your part. Talk to those who have been here and get advice from your local massage girl. This type of trip is ideal for a break between school and work, work and work, or work and school, because you'll want to set aside a least a couple of months. And you'll feel less guilty about being served beers by a teenage girl when you know you have a job or school waiting for you at home. But be careful, you may end up **spending your student loans on a local beach shack and never coming back**.

The most popular countries for travelers in Southeast Asia are Thailand, Vietnam, Cambodia, and Laos. You can venture further to Brunei, Indonesia, Malaysia, Myanmar, and the Philippines. **It'll be a hard core effort to get to 'em all.** A flight to Tokyo will get you close, and then you'll hop another plane to Bangkok. Bangkok is a big city, so you could get caught up there, but you'd best not stay too long. Go there, have fun in the mayhem it throws at you, get a three-dollar hand job (we're kidding of course), and get out. Hanoi, Vietnam, is another city that falls into the same category. After Bangkok, you'll feel the desire to cleanse yourself on a Thai beach, which you should definitely do, but first travel to Cambodia and witness Angkor Watt and the depressing yet significant "killing fields" and the S21 Prison. After seeing some of that, nothing makes more sense than firing high-powered weapons at Phnom Phen's infamous firing range. They'll arm you with just about anything you can think of, an AK47, M16, or even a rocket launcher. And get this, **you'll take aim at a field of cows**. No joke. You'll feel like a sick bastard doing it, but it's not much different than shooting squirrels with your BB gun, right?

Southern Thailand has just about **every bit of adventure, parties, and international boobies that you could ever imagine**. By day you'll be rock-climbing, kite-surfing, scuba-diving, or just simply sleeping on the beach. Your nights will start off drinking beers with the random people you went kayaking with that day, and end up slamming Red Bull whiskies with a ninety-five-pound Thai girl on your lap. Just watch out, that ninety-five-pound girl may end up being a thirteen-year-old boy, so don't let the booze blind you, or that could really wreck a trip. The islands of Koh Samui, Koh Phangan, and Koh Tao, while touristy, are friggin' awesome. By now you'll appreciate the western influence . . . mmm . . . drunken pizza. Plan accordingly and get your ass to the island for the full moon party. (See chapter 1, under "Full Moon Party.")

A trip through Southeast Asia definitely requires some balls and motivation, but you'll never forget it. Negotiating a scooter ride across the Cambodian border, convincing Thai girls that you are **scouting for adult film stars** for your U.S. production company, and getting shitcanned with a bunch of yahoos from all over the world, will all become journal entries that you'll read hundreds of times. One day, when you're sitting with your family eating Pad Thai, you'll think "this was a lot better when it cost fifty cents, I washed it down with quarter beers, and then worked it off by going skinny dipping with fourteen hot girls tripping on mushrooms."

MANGOS AND ALI
James, 30, Philadelphia, oh so single

After being downsized from my exciting accounting job, I decided to spend a few months in Southeast Asia. I jumped from place to place as I felt the need, or when moving on just seemed like the "logical" thing to do. So, one day I found myself on an island called Koh Samui. While I was having a few tasty beverages, a gentleman asked me if I wanted a tour guide for the weekend. While he didn't seem too exciting, the five-eleven, smoking hot Thai girl with him was a gem. For ten dollars, she was my host for a few days, and my hopes were obviously for a little

(continued)

more than a host. We rode around on her red scooter, with my nose nestled in her thick, black, mango-scented hair (yeah, I paid attention). We went to beaches, bars, and even to another island, Koh Phangan, for a full moon party. Wow, this was nuts, and my girl fortunately kept me from getting myself in serious trouble. Although, I think my performance scared her enough so that anything but a tour at that point was out of the question. So, after that night of destruction, it was time for me to head back to Bangkok.

On my train back to Bangkok, I met a fifty-year-old Iranian piano dealer named Ali. We got smashed together. We couldn't smoke on the train, so we would jump in between the trains. When we got caught by the Thai police, my huge friend Ali would just grab their face and say, "You are a sexy, sexy man." Understandably frightened, the police would then leave us alone. Then Ali proceeded to peek behind the curtained sleeping quarters, cause the Thai girls to screech, and then ask if they were looking for company that night. "I like to fuck with these Thai people, you know?" is what Ali explained to me. After way too much booze and train fun, all of a sudden I found myself running to the toilet. I puked down a "squat toilet," which was basically a hole over the train tracks. Sparks were flying everywhere. It was awesome. Everyone should go to Thailand.

ROAD-TRIPPIN' NORTH AMERICA

Ah, the ole road trip. From *Easy Rider* to *The Blues Brothers*, from *Tommy Boy* to *Thelma and Louise*, (okay scratch that one), we've all been entertained for years by the simple idea of a couple of guys jumping in a car and going somewhere. We've also learned that the drive isn't always so simple, and if you play it right it can become the adventure of a lifetime. The first signs that you're on a good road trip are that you're making obscene gestures in front of the world's largest cucumber, staying in motels under moving lumberjack signs, and ordering a four A.M. breakfast of "Moons over Mihammy" from some seventy-five-year-old waitress named Flo. Take it to the next level and **imagine drinking beers at the only bar within a 120-mile radius**, getting chased out of a cornfield with the panties of the **farmer's daughter** wrapped around your head, and getting a special "rubdown" somewhere off Interstate 80. There is no better way to see this great country of ours than to grab a couple of buddies, figure out a rough idea of your destination, and hit the highway.

There are a few rules to definitely abide by. **First**, don't fuck with truck drivers. They've been on the road for days, not been laid in months, and are angry as hell. **Second**, don't make friends with anyone at the rest stops. Yes, before you know it, your new restroom friend's trouser mouse will be peeking out of his shorts as he tries to introduce himself to you in ways you're not so interested in. **And lastly**, don't fuck with truck drivers.

If you're with good friends, have good music, and are ready to laugh, just about any road trip can be a first-class time. Enjoy every moment, and when you get bored just **press your bare ass against the window** or put beef jerky in your buddy's nose while he's passed out. We've included a few basic routes to get you going. It's so very simple, just get a good group together, pick the destinations, and go. You'll figure it out. And remember, if you don't do it now, before you know it, you'll find yourself loading the wife and kids into the minivan, stopping at your wife's third cousin's pig farm in Kansas, and sneaking sips of whiskey as the kids fight over Kelly Clarkson or Ashley Simpson on the radio.

Route 66

The famed Route 66 takes you from Chicago to Los Angeles and everywhere in between. "The Mother Road" or "Will Roger's Way" is known for helping lead the migration westward and it spawned the idea for the motel and the drive-in theater. Route 66 doesn't actually exist on maps anymore, but you can definitely find directions that will take you as close as possible to the original. Starting in the Midwest, you'll be taken back to what seems like the 1960s, with old diners, gas stations, and **friendly girls in tight sweaters**. Making your way west, you'll be with the cowboys in Oklahoma and the Pueblo Indians of New Mexico. Pueblo chicks are hot.

As you drive through the desert towards California, keep in mind it's ridiculously hot, and your balls will stick to the seat. So don't go in the heart of summer. Finally, after your long drive, Los Angeles will bring you back to reality—a reality filled with **fake boobs and bleached blondes**. To keep things entertaining from start to finish, have a list of things to check off in each state that must be accomplished before crossing its border. For example, in Texas you must ride a mechanical bull for longer than five minutes, persuade a random person to yell "Yee-Ha!," and get your picture taken with a half-naked woman at the Cadillac Ranch. Beyond that, there's deep-dish to be eaten in Chicago, Budweiser to be imbibed in St. Louis, and in Oklahoma, a twister to chase down. Now get your kicks on . . . you know.

WHEN TO GO: Definitely not in the Summer; Spring or Fall would be ideal.

WAYS TO MAKE ANY ROAD TRIP MORE INTERESTING

You must pick up a shot glass from each state and then use it later.

If you see a billboard for a strip club, you must go.

If you see a billboard for a go-cart track, you must go.

Bring a camera and a list of pictures you must capture.

Keep count of every girl you can get to flash you.

See how many random passengers you can pick up. (Be discerning about this.)

For the guy who falls asleep, pull over, get out, and shake the car until he wakes up.

For the guy who falls asleep, count to three and everybody scream bloody murder at the same time . . . watch him crap his pants.

Driver must tell every female toll booth operator that he's really horny.

Pretend that your car broke down, and when people stop to assist, start barking at them.

If you see a car full of hot chicks, take your shirt off . . . see if they follow your lead.

Bring a stuffed animal to a diner and order it a chocolate milk.

Pay the toll for the car behind you.

Tell people your friend's a hitchhiker you picked up and you think he's on a prison break.

The Great Lakes

The plan here is to start all the way east in Maine's Acadia National Park, eat a huge lobster, and then head west through parts of Canada, along the Great Lakes, with your finish line on fantastic Mackinac Island. (See chapter 2, under "Races".) Beginning your journey in New England will bring you to some great little towns in Maine, Vermont, and New Hampshire, with local flavor, tasty food, and friendly townies. Crossing into Canada, you'll crash into **Montreal for some French-Canadian girls, tasty booze and friendly strippers**. Throw a "bachelor party" for the guy most likely to never get married. From Montreal, you can follow the St. Lawrence River down to Niagra Falls. With a party town on the Canadian side of the Falls, have a good time drinking Molsons, gambling, and hitting cheesy bars; then go over the Falls in a barrel and make your way further down the Great Lakes. Along your travels, make a pit stop for some quality fishing on Lake Ontario. **Whoever reels in the biggest salmon doesn't have to drive for the next twenty-four hours.** Then, time permitting, floor it to Windsor, Ontario, for more gambling, more strippers, and yes—another bachelor party. This time let "rock, paper, scissors" decide who's the lucky groom-to-be. Eventually, you'll find yourself driving north through the beautiful state of Michigan and wrapping up your expedition on the island of Mackinac. Conclude things aboard a sunset booze cruise, sipping cocktails and telling everyone on board all of the weird shit that happened since Maine. Now throw that last bachelor party . . . you can never have too many.

WHEN TO GO: Summer

TOP SONGS FOR THE ROAD

- "Eye of the Tiger"; Survivor
- "On the Road Again"; Willie Nelson
- "Radar Love"; Golden Earring
- "Highway to Hell"; AC/DC
- "Only God Knows Why"; Kid Rock
- "Born to Run"; Springsteen
- "Country Roads"; John Denver
- "Rambling Man"; Allman Brothers
- "Get Outta My Dreams, Get Into My Car"; Billy Ocean (oh, you like it!)

- "Don't Stop Believin' "; Journey
- "Fight for Your Right"; The Beastie Boys
- "I Wanna Rock"; Twisted Rock
- "When the Levee Breaks"; Led Zepplin
- "Ride the Wind"; Poison
- "Too Legit to Quit"; MC Hammer
- "Roadhouse Blues"; The Doors
- "Pink Houses"; John Mellencamp
- "Where the Streets Have No Name"; U2
- "Windfall"; Son Volt
- "Blood on Blood"; Bon Jovi
- "Folsom Prison Blues"; Johnny Cash

The Pacific Coast

From the Great Northwest to the beautiful Southern California beaches. From crunchy chicks with hairy armpits to beautiful blondes with no body hair whatsoever. Just kidding, not every girl in Seattle has hairy armpits. We've met a couple of you. Begin your journey up in this rainy town. Have some Starbucks, say hello to Big Bill Gates, eat some fresh day-boat shellfish, and **listen to any grunge bands still lingering around**. Head south, hit Portland and then stay as close as possible to the magnificent Pacific coastline. Try some charter fishing in the town of Garibaldi. Play eighteen or thirty-six at the awesome Bandon Dunes further south on the Oregon coast. And go whale-watching at some point along the way. Traveling into California on Highway One couldn't be nicer. Head inland for a day of vino in Napa . . . forget the scenery and the romance and just get plastered. After shaking off your red wine hangover, enter the city of San Francisco through its Golden Gates. Here you'll take a tour of Alcatraz, chow down in Chinatown, catch a ballgame at SBC Park, and wind up at Mitchell Brother's O'Farrell Theater—a "special" theater. Stock up on some Rice-a-Roni, keep driving south, and **play a round at Pebble Beach or Spyglass**. Stretch your legs with a hike around Big Sur, then go jump in the ocean. As you reach Southern California make a stop in Los Angeles, check out Sunset Boulevard, the Sky Bar, and **say hi to the girls of *The O.C.*** for us. But don't call it a trip yet. Either San Diego or Tijuana needs to be your end point. San Diego can be a great spot to lose the car while Tijuana is where you'll lose your friends. (See chapter 2, under "Golf," or chapter 4, under "Bachelor Parties.")

WHEN TO GO: While it's warm enough to not worry about anything else. Keep in mind, the West Coast seasons can be volatile, so check the almanac before you head out.

LET'S BE MEN AND DO WHAT'S RIGHT
John, 30, Washington, D.C., engaged

One summer, having visions of *Easy Rider* and thoughts of Jack Kerouac, some friends and I decided to cruise out from Chicago to L.A. We could get smashed in small towns and hike out through the fantastic terrain. The car was packed up and we headed off.

By day three we were somewhere in Utah. It was getting late, so we decided to start looking for an area to camp out. We spotted a sign for camping and pulled off the road. Grabbing our tents and gear, we headed down a small trail. We figured to head deeper into the woods so as to get further away from the highway and any freaky trucker who might want to fuck with us. We found a clearing and set up camp. Along the way my friend Danny picked up a woman's shoe. "Weird," he thought. As we were sitting there drinking beers and eating beef jerky, we heard gun shots. "Okay, we have some woman's shoe and now gun shots. What the hell?" The gun shots were followed by men's voices, so we got up to look around. Not far away, we found a handful of park rangers, boozing it up and firing guns for what seemed to be no other reason than they were drunk hicks with guns. Upon talking to them, we discovered that one guy had actually eaten mushrooms from the ground and was tripping balls. A few of us started to get nervous and contemplated going back to the car. "Don't be pansies," I said, "Let's have few more beers and then get some sleep."

A couple beers later we were finally relaxed. Well, that was until we heard a woman start screaming her head off. "Holy shit, the shoe, the drunk dudes with guns, now this. Seriously, let's get the fuck out of here!!" Danny said. We all stood up, walked in the direction of the screams, and found a tent surrounded by a bunch of trash. We were staring at the tent, listening to the screams. It was here where the moral dilemma began. "What should we do?" Danny was obviously out, he wanted to turn around. Rich, David, and Sean were playing both sides, and I was adamant about saving this woman's life. "You guys, I didn't come out here to die," demanded Danny as he continued to lobby for leaving. However, I knew what we had to do. I would go to hell if I ignored it. "Well, if I die and you live, tell my parents I went down doing the right thing," David piped in. So, I knew I had David with me. I declared that, "Whatever we do we should do together." So, despite Rich's wish to hold a trial by jury to decide, we all signed on, pulled out our Swiss Army knives, and moved in. "Hey, yo, hey, what's going on?" we shouted nervously as we moved toward the tent. A guy then peaked out

(continued)

the front flap. It was one of the rangers, the guy with a gun! Shit! He told us to get the hell out of there, but we held firm and told him we needed to look in his tent (for the screeching woman). Confused, he actually let us. Inside, there was nothing but more trash and a sleeping bag. Now we were baffled, and we asked him about the woman screaming bloody murder. He paused, then laughed hysterically.

"Come here fellas," he said. He took us behind the tent and pointed to a donkey. We stared at the donkey and within a few minutes, the jackass let out a shriek . . . and we heard our woman. Yup, we had convinced ourselves that it was our responsibility to risk our life and limb to save a yelping donkey in heat.

BRITISH ISLES PUB TOUR

You're not a man if you don't enjoy sitting in a pub on a Saturday afternoon drinking beers, telling stories, and watching the game. This is why a tour of the countries that originated this wonderful activity is essential. In case you flunked that geography class, Ireland, England, Scotland, and Wales make up the British Isles. You'll journey through a countryside crawling with sheep (better known by locals as easy pickings). You'll happen upon great little towns teeming with tradition. And yes, you'll plant your ass in many a great pub, where funny old men will have you singing songs and lovely local girls will have you working overtime to woo them with your American charm.

As a couple of Irish lads ourselves, we're a little partial to the Emerald Isle. So that's why we insist that you must spend some time chasing shots of Jameson with pints of Guinness, dancing like a fool to local Irish bands, and listening to old men **tell stories about telling stories**. You can start by flying into Shannon and driving up and down the West Coast. Find yourself drinking in these stops:

- **Galway:** This jumping college town brings you pub after pub in Eyre Square. Don't miss King's Head (named for the guy who cut off King Charles I's noggin) and the Quays.
- **Lahinch:** A surfer town (Yes, that's right, surfers in Ireland) filled with great nightlife, the nearby Cliffs of Moher, and some kick-ass golf.
- **Dingle Peninsula:** An amazing coastline, with beaches, and pubs. Be sure to toast a pint at Dick Mack's—it's part pub, part old shoe cobbler shop.
- **Ring of Kerry:** To drive this loop, the correct way is counter-clockwise. Stay in Killarney and down some pints at the Laurels, the Grand Hotel, and its many other great pubs. Also, try a bike ride through the Gap of Dunloe, stopping for a pint at Kate Kearney's Cottage.
- **Kinsale:** This seaside town delivers fish and chips fresh as it gets, great music at An Seanachi, and parties all summer long.

Beyond these pub havens, be prepared for countless, random "oh, we gotta have a Guinness there" stops. Play darts, get fired up for the local football match, and sing some drunken ballads. Then, continue on to the eastern coast and catch a ferry to the rest of the British Isles.

The capital city of Wales, **Cardiff**, is a pretty happening place with tons of crap to do, including hanging in a tavern and drinking heavily. Unlike the smaller towns, cities like Cardiff will have some late-night clubs to really get your groove on. Before you leave Wales for good, check out the bay, go castle hunting, and see the town of Swansea. Then stumble your way to England. If you play it right you'll be flying out of Heathrow, so for your pub tour, leave London to the end. First, motor your way to Oxford. In this historic college town you'll meet all kinds of young brainy British chicks looking for fun guys to take a break from the books and let loose with. You'll enjoy tasty brews at cool pubs like the Eagle and Child, The Bear, and The White Horse. Also, try and get into the various college-sponsored pubs for cheaper drinks. From there, drive to Liverpool, drink it up at the Cavern Club, and take in everything Beatles. After that, you can mosey on up to Scotland for some good times in Edinburgh. While in Scotland carry on with your pub crawl, but **don't miss out on the chance to play the links at St. Andrews.** (See chapter 2, under "Golf.")

With the exception of the boat ride from Ireland to England, you should do this entire trek in a rental car. The drives, especially while maneuvering on the wrong side of the road, will be some of the craziest parts. You'll find hostels in the larger cities, and the smaller towns will have bed and breakfasts. The B & Bs can be hilarious, particularly when you come home smashed and try to get the rest of the house to drink with you. The people are so friendly and accommodating that they just might trample out of bed and join you. No matter what, they'll still cook you a phat breakfast in the morning. The girls here also will blow you away by how nice they are and how much they can drink. Some are hot, and you may grope them if they let you. Others, well let's just say **they'll get you drunk and take advantage of you**. But hey, as long as you're the victim, who cares? Overall, the pubs are truly the best. You will quickly realize that these establishments are exactly what the ones at home are trying so hard to replicate. And your mission, like Indiana Jones searching for the lost ark, or that . . . *Da Vinci Code* guy looking for the holy grail, is to **track down the "perfect" pub.** It's here where you'll quickly realize that, yes, there is heaven on earth, and yes it's time for another round of Boddington.

GOIN' SOUTH AMERICA

Other than Asia, it's probably the only continent left where your money will take you a long, long way. And where it'll take you is to a land of beautiful women, fantastic beaches, jungles, mountains, big cities, tiny fishing villages, parties, ruins, rivers, great wine, incredible adventures, and more. You'll be able to spend each day doing something completely different. From lounging on the thong-happy sands of Brazil (hey, this is where they invented "the Brazilian," don't forget) to playing with penguins in Punta Arenas to experiencing **the healing powers of an Amazon medicine man** as he tries to help with that "problem" you picked up in Buenos Aires. This is not a trip for those who think the Holiday Inn constitutes roughing it. To fully conquer this continent, you're going to have to get sweaty, filthy, and exhausted—and we're not talking just about that strip club in Rio.

No matter what your timeframe allows you, and whatever activities hold special interest, plan on designating **Rio de Janeiro** either as your beginning point or your finish line. This good-time city works both as a fantastic way to wrap up the trip or the perfect place to get it started. Would you like your butt floss as a dessert or appetizer? While here, stay near the ocean, go to the beach (Ipanema or Copacabana), play some volleyball, hike the Hunchback, boogie-board, have afternoon cocktails, and search for the bikini with the absolute least amount of material. (When you find it, take a picture and send it our way.) At night the parties are endless and full throttle. So head out; but be careful with the shadier people, it can get ugly. Beyond Rio, there's an unreal amount of things to do, but here are some definite "you gotta look into these" adventures:

- **The Amazon:** Come on, it's the Amazon! Paddle, hike, boat—just explore this magical and bizarre land of piranhas, monkeys, birds, and lots more. Most excursions start in the town of Manaus.

- **Peru's Machu Picchu:** Find this lost city after a long, memorable hike down the Inca Trail. (See chapter 2, under "Hiking".)

- **Iguazu Falls:** Hike through the jungle to these massive falls—more than 275 of them pouring into the Iguazu River with a force on a par with that time you had to pee so bad, but found yourself stuck in a traffic jam for an hour.

- **Skiing in Portillo, Chile:** Yeah it's August and you're on the slopes . . . pretty cool. No doubt, the après-ski beers will be mighty tasty.

- **Punta del Este, Uruguay:** In December all the cool kids come here to party it up on the beach—why not join them? Just remember, you are a fashion photographer for *Elle* . . . no, *Vanity Fair.* "Strike a pose, por favor."

- **Lake District, Chile:** Choose your own adventure here. Hike, bike, raft, get drunk on Chilean wine. It's up to you. Truly a great place for any of the above.

- **Lake Titicaca, Peru:** Funny name, great place to jump in for a swim. Yeah, it's very, very cold, and it's the highest navigable lake in the world. Bring a towel.

Your journey should take you through Brazil, don't-cry-for-me Argentina, Uruguay, perhaps Paraguay, Chile, Peru, but not Columbia (hey, we like you alive). Along the way, be sure to check out a football match, with bonus points if there's a riot. Try some ceviche, asada (bbq beef), and many great, cheap wines. Stay with a family, if you can, for the ultimate dip into the culture. Or try hostels in the big cities and eco-lodges out in the wild. On your way home, don't offer to transport any religious statues or swallow thirty-two balloons of cocaine for that new buddy you met. Seriously, those cocaine balloons can give you some really nasty gas, and your prison roommate won't appreciate it.

FROM RUSSIA WITH LOVE . . . AND VODKA

Nobody says "comrade" anymore. BK, KFC, and McDs are here now. And the KGB can only be found in a museum. But hey, as you wander about, especially at night, **you will still feel like a double agent** on the lookout for the mole who's got the secret info about that secret thing that nobody knows about. Plus, after years of communist oppression, the Ruskies are finally letting loose and having fun. The bundled-up babushkas have taken a backseat to the Anna Kournikova's and Maria Sharapova's of the world. And their love for getting wacky on vodka has only grown stronger.

Plus, they drink all kinds of beers now, too. This relatively new-found capitalism certainly makes for interesting times and travels. So, get here and explore the strange sights, tastes, smells, and culture that is Russia.

You'll definitely want to hit the two main cites of **Moscow and St. Petersburg** for some good urban insanity. Both have hostels for cheap sleeping. In Moscow, by day you'll ramble your way through the Kremlin, Red Square, Gorky Park, and the Arbat (a street of souvenir stands). At night, you'll feel the need to venture into the madness of the pubs, clubs, and other drinking establishments. The clubs are picky here. Many have face-control policies, special cards for "special" people, and high cover charges. Try the Hungry Duck, where the ladies have been known to get wild, get naked, and get more than just their dance on. Or head to one of the ex-pat bars for simple, safer drinking with others like you. St. Petersburg, your other big city to hit, is better known for its arts and culture—so take some of that in if you want, then bring your vodka-soaked self to one of its **famous bomb shelter bars** for live music. If you're here in June, you can experience the White Nights and the nonstop, retarded partying that accompanies it. The adventures you'll have in both cities will be directly related to the people you meet. If you can buddy up with a local, do it. With his guidance, you can safely hit casinos, tremendous strip clubs, and other cool, but potentially scary places. Also, sweat out your worst hangover at a big, old Russian *banya* (bath-house)—just don't drop the soap.

After days of knocking back vodka, eating caviar, and receiving lap dances from Russian strippers you swore you met in Vegas, it's time for you to board the **Trans-Siberian Rail**. It crosses seven time zones, links eighty-seven cities, and takes you through a tunnel two kilometers long, over a bridge two thousand and six hundred meters above the Amur River, and is the longest, continuous rail line on earth. Pretty sweet way to see a land not seen by many. However, before you jump on, get ahold of a flexible ticket, so that you can **hop on and off as you feel like**. The only way to get one of these is through a travel agency. And for semi-comfortable amenities, make it a second-class ticket. On the train, you'll mix it up with your fellow riders. Drinking, playing games, and hopefully some late-night "what's that noise from up top?" bunk sex with a Russian nurse should make the time fly by. At many stops, you can restock your food and drink supply by buying Pirozskis, sausage, and beer from the pushy babushkas at the station. The trains have food, but this is a cheaper avenue. If you have the time, cruise all the way to Vladivostok, which is on the edge of China. From there, go to Japan or China and then fly home. Why not? Along the way, make stops at:

- **Novosibirsk**—the biggest city in Siberia, with nearby hiking and rafting around the Altai Mountains
- **Irkutsk or Listvyanka**—either makes a great stop to get to Lake Baikal, the largest freshwater lake in the world. Come, find a fishing charter, and reel in a fat sturgeon as a bear sits on the shore watching.
- **Vladivostok**—end of the line, and an historic, strategically well-positioned city for Russia and its military. Along with your train friends, toast chilled vodka, accompanied by caviar, to a great journey. Then head to Asia.

Russia is a very different land, and its people are a very different breed. They'll be offended if you shake hands while in a doorway, but will have no issues with a double smooch on the cheek. So, study up on some of the customs and try not to offend. Also, if you have some extra dough to spend, **take a wild flight in a MIG**. Yes, probably due to a defense cut, these bad-ass planes have become Russia's answer to the rollercoaster. Open to tourists, anyone can go for a ride. Just try not to puke, you wussy.

As you journey through this massive country, eat the borscht (it's their favorite), learn to love caviar, and drink Baltika beer. Remember, just because the age of espionage is over doesn't mean you can't be a man of mystery. So, bring or buy a suit and go out one night like you are on a hush-hush mission. Tell the ladies **you are here on an "unofficial official visit."** They'll be confused, intrigued, and really drawn to you. Order a bottle of champagne, woo them with stories about encountering silver-back gorillas in Uganda and diving with sharks in Nassau (see chapter 2). They'll think you're worldly, and most importantly, rich. Of course, when you take them back to your hostel with bunk beds you may have some 'splaining to do. Have an excuse ready for that.

WAYS TO SAVE ON TRAVEL

Ask if your hotel has a "film" rate.

Claim it as a business expense.

Shop at local supermarkets.

Go off peak season.

Forget the Ritz, stay at a hostel, pension, brothel—whatever.

Use the Internet.

Use your credit card internationally for the best exchange rate.

Negotiate.

Find happy hours—they're everywhere.

Take the red-eye flight.

If you're young enough or you still have your college ID, take advantage of student travel discounts.

Sleep in airports, train stations, or just stay out all night.

Bring goods that may be worth bartering.

Go to notoriously cheaper destinations.

Travel with your wealthiest friend.

CHAPTER SIX

GREAT JOBS BEFORE YOUR REAL JOB

Okay, maybe you've got a serious job, maybe you don't. Maybe you have a serious job, but would really, really love to get the fuck out of your cubicle and do something different. Maybe you think it's important to quickly and immediately establish the building blocks to a long, fulfilling career . . . because that's what the brochure at the college career center suggested. Whatever your situation may be, there's a certain reality that you at least need to consider. And that is the simple, kick-me-in-the-nut-sack fact that you're going to spend your entire life working hard, trying to make enough money to pay off the mortgage, provide for your little ones, keep your wife smiling, and have just enough left over for some beer for you. Most likely, this job will involve you waking up early, battling nightmarish traffic jams, downing many cups of coffee to stay alert, dealing with jackasses all day long,

and then getting stuck in bad traffic on your way home. So, before you go and jump into your career job, **why not spend a year
working somewhere for fun?** What's one year when you're fac-
ing a fifty- or sixty-year sentence in career-building hell? Nothing.
It's a blip on the radar. So, go nuts. Be a Jet Ski rental guy. Be a
DJ. Be a blackjack dealer in the Mediterranean. Be free from the
routine you will someday be a slave to. Hey, you might even
learn something from one of these jobs. If not, who cares?

Now, it's important to pick your **"temporary vocation"** with
some thought and planning. Do it according to the things that
most appeal to you. Do you want to work outside? Do you wish
to live in an exotic place? Do you care if your bedroom is a tent
or the cabin of a boat? Are your job requirements directly pro-
portional to the number of times they'll help get you laid? All important questions to ask. Also, unlike some of the other chapters,
where the experiences take at most a month, these jobs will consume a good three months to as much as a year of your life—
maybe more if you're smart and/or you get addicted to life as a
river-rafting guide. With your health, happiness, and the fact that
we're pretty sure you're an idiot just like we are, we've done our
best to list jobs that take little or no skill to qualify for. After all,
it'd be really cool to design golf courses or fly the space shuttle,
but being a caddy in high school or watching the discovery
channel a lot doesn't quite cut it . . . sorry. With that said, if you
want a reference for any of these jobs, we'd be happy to vouch
for your workmanship, your ability to get along with others, and
the way you always step up to the plate when needed. Hey,
we're here to help.

Jet Ski Rental Guy

Your office is a hut on the beach. Your clients are people on vacation having a blast. And your biggest responsibility is making sure they come back to shore on time. **So, if you know how to read a clock you meet all the necessary requirements.** And just think about the places where it's possible to rent a Jet Ski every single day. The Virgin Islands would be the perfect place to begin your new career. St. John's, St. Thomas—basically **any island that starts with "St."—will be just fine.** And the funniest thing is the people who will be renting these "big, complicated water vehicles" will think you're the coolest and most talented person in the world as you effortlessly show off your stuff. Plus, all ladies love the Jet Ski guy. He's fun. He's probably tan. And he's adventurous. So, it's especially important to "make sure the Jet Ski is operating properly" by doing your most impressive stunts when a group of lovely young ladies come along. After that, you simply help them into their life jackets, give them a push out to sea, and after their thirty minutes of water sports fun is over, you invite your new friends out for daiquiris or piña coladas later—after your long, hard day is over. It's almost unfair how easy it is. Some great places to be the Jet Ski guy are Club Meds, Sandals, and other resorts where the ladies come specifically looking to cut loose and have a good time. The key word there is loose. You know what we mean..

EMBELLISHMENT FOR YOUR RESUME: Operational Water Craft Manager

Chairlift Operator, Ski Instructor, or Anyone at a Ski Resort

We don't like to stereotype. It's wrong. It's extremely judgmental. And there's always a situation where the stereotype is proven false. However—is it us, or does every chairlift operator position come with the requirement that **you must take a pull from a big water bong before**

arriving for work? Like a restaurant reminding workers to wash their hands, there's probably a sign that reads: "All employees must be high as the mountain you work on before returning to the slopes." Okay, maybe it's stereotyping. Anyhow—what an awesome job! Whatever resort you work at, you're in a beautiful location. You get to ski all the friggin' time—for free. And you'll get to hang out with a lot of cool, laid-back, fun people for the duration of your stay. If you go beyond the chairlift guy and actually instruct, you'll be on every woman's "to bang" list. Yeah, we believe ski instructor is right in between "pro athlete" and "fighter pilot." Add an unusual accent while you're teaching them how to snowplow and you'll move up the list. If you can't get either of those positions, try anything else—especially **valet car parker.** Hey, you get tips doing that job. Your time there will be spent skiing, snowboarding, and playing foosball at your favorite bar each night. Talk about a fun way to spend a winter. Not to mention, you'll meet a lot of cute, crunchy chicks who are free-spirited and horny.

EMBELLISHMENT FOR YOUR RESUME: Mountain Activities Ambassador

Cruise Ship Bartender

Remember Isaac from the Love Boat? Come on, Ted Lange, **the cool black dude with the mustache** for all the ladies to go for a ride on? Yeah, it was always the dorky doctor who supposedly got the hotties on that show; but trust us, the stuff Isaac was doing with the drunk, freaky women was way too rated R for ABC to show on prime time. If only it was an HBO show, then we would've seen Isaac's many escapades. But seriously, like the jet ski guy, everyone loves your friendly vacation booze server. And all you need to do is know how to work a blender and throw cherries on top of everything. Yeah, you might have to wear a silly tie and vest, or a fun, party Hawaiian shirt, but **you're still everyone's best friend**. And on your time off you can take to the islands, lay on white sand beaches, and hit the local bars to talk shop.

There may be rules about commingling with passengers, but that only applies to those who get caught or commingle with someone's fiancée. We have faith you'll be smart enough and sly enough to enjoy the kind of triumphs that would make Isaac proud. Now, before you run off, get your bartending certificate, and start applying, be sure to **choose your cruise judiciously**. Stay away from Alaskan cruises (unless you want to run into your grandma on board) or any kind of river cruise. Pick one that's in the Caribbean, Bahamas, or Mexico. There are plenty of Web sites specializing in cruise jobs. If you know another language, Mediterranean ships are definitely a possibility. And, if for some reason you can't find a position, just head to the islands, start passing your resume around, and work it like Tom Cruise in *Cocktail*.

EMBELLISHMENT FOR YOUR RESUME: Hospitality and Beverages Supervisor

Casino Dealer

Watch a guy lose a fully-loaded Mercedes on one hand of blackjack. Bear witness to a hooker triple last night's earnings while wooing today's paying customer. Get a **five-hundred-dollar tip from a pro athlete** who had to cut the gambling short due to an already-scheduled threesome with some lady friends from a nearby strip club. All this will be "all in a day's work." Your new job will show you **a side of life you've never seen before**. You'll work strange hours. You'll meet strange people. And all you gotta do is deal the cards. Ideally, you'll want to go to Vegas for the ultimate glimpse into the gambling world and all the crazy shit that happens here. Sure, you could work in Atlantic City, on a cruise ship, on a river boat (lame), or in the islands, but Vegas just has so much more going for it. You will need to get a dealer's license, which is not that hard, especially if you already know cards and don't have serious crap on your record. For example, if you got busted in college running a bookie business, you aren't getting a job here. Otherwise, get to Vegas, **find an apartment in a complex full of strippers** (make sure it has a pool), and have some fun. Obviously, the better hotels have the better casinos. Choose with caution. Hard Rock, Mandalay, Caesar's, MGM, and the Palms are all good. We're not sure if dealers get laid much (most of them do wear bow ties, after all), but we're thinking, if you're smooth, the cocktail waitresses are yours for the taking. The burnout factor has to be huge at a job like this, which is perfect because after a year you can change directions, or go back to what you used to be doing. Only, now you can do it knowing you have experienced some crazy good times, like the party your neighbor Misty Giant Tits threw on Halloween.

EMBELLISHMENT FOR YOUR RESUME: High-stakes Casino Dealer

GREAT "DRINK ON THE JOB" JOBS:
Bartender (duh!)
Brewery taste tester
Fisherman
Clown
Postal worker
DJ
Wedding videographer
Drummer in a band
Event planner
Bar/restaurant critic
Stay-at-home mom (just kidding)

Adventure Tour Guide

Steer screaming clients down a class IV river. **Climb up thirteen thousand feet of jagged mountain** with them. Camp out each night under more stars than most city dwellers see in a lifetime. If you're an outdoor adventure-loving kind of person, why not spend a year or two taking people through, across, and over some of the most awesome sights on the planet? By summer you can work in Alaska, escorting people out onto the waters of Prince William Sound, or hiking through bear country. By winter, head to Baja to paddle from beach to beach in kayaks with five or six customers rowing behind you. **The options for being an outdoor guide are endless.** Hell, there are a lot of people out there who love the wilderness but couldn't put up a tent to save their lives. You won't make a lot of money—just enough to cover your food and gear, but cash is not what this is about anyway, right?

The skills you'll need for this job are totally dependent upon how advanced is the activity. If it's just daily river-rafting jaunts in Jackson Hole, you won't need much. If you're taking people to the top of Kilimanjaro, you'll need a bit more. **There are many great schools**, like BOSS or NOLS, which specialize in training for the many different activities. Some great Web sites to look at for jobs are coolworks.com and backdoorjobs.com. Also, peruse the last few pages of any *Men's Journal* or *Outside* Magazine to look for outfitters that spark your interest. Great adventures are waiting. While most people pay huge bucks to have such adventures, you're enjoying them for free. Well done.

EMBELLISHMENT FOR YOUR RESUME: Adventure Entrepreneur

Actor or Extra

It's simple. You move to L.A. or New York. Rent a one-bedroom condo. Share it with a buddy, aspiring super model, or whomever. Take turns sleeping on the couch. Stock up on Ramen noodles. And yeah, **audition for roles by day and play bartender, waiter, or telemarketer by night**. You'll work just enough to get by, that way you don't cramp your style too much. And you'll hope to get that one big break. Why not? Even if it's a TV commercial, you could make forty thousand dollars from just one of those. Or maybe you're perfect for the role in that new Alyssa Milano made-for-late-night Showtime movie, where she seduces you just to the point where you get to touch her boobies—and then her alien, lesbian stalker devours you with one fatal chomp. Hey, **you're dead and it only paid seven hundred and fifty bucks**, but you fondled Alyssa's boobs. Be sure to screw up the scene right before you get eaten to ensure that you hear the beautiful words, "Take two!!"

It's not an easy life going from audition to audition, but if you don't take it too seriously and just have fun it's not so bad. All you need are three appearances in any commercially viable production and you get your SAG card. The membership does cost money, unfortunately. Whether you get it or not really doesn't matter, unless you're looking for a career. **If you're offered an extra role, take it.** You'll get free food all day, sit around doing nothing, and then have to walk anonymously by in one scene and, *bam,* you're done. And you get paid something like eight hundred dollars, and you'll probably meet a hot wannabe actress. To become an extra, just register with the many casting agencies in town and they'll give you a call when you fit the criteria for an extra they need. Not bad.

EMBELLISHMENT FOR YOUR RESUME: Actor (Beats the shit out of "waiter.")

Travel Writer

Fly in an F-16 over Death Valley. **Write about it.** Eat a turkey sandwich in Turkey. **Write about it.** Spend a night in Hanoi's happy-ending district. **Write about it** . . . under an alias. Being a travel writer (especially for the short term) does not require you to be Hemingway. Nor do you need to be well-versed in cultures, cuisine, or foreign currencies. In fact, you could even be shitty at reading a map and still do your job. All you need is a sense of adventure, decent research skills, and a willingness to subject yourself to whatever the story needs. There are many ways to get such a job, but **the key is getting one that pays for 99 percent of your travels**.

You can write for **magazines, Web sites, or guidebooks**. If it's a guidebook, your travels will be purely about obtaining the latest scoop on accommodations, restaurants, sights, and so on. It's more investigatory work, but it allows for many great stories to be had . . . just not written about in the book. You can also freelance for various magazines, from Frommer's *Budget Traveler* to *National Geographic Traveler* to *Playboy*. If doing this, our suggestion would be to **create a niche for yourself**. Are you "a nonadventurer doing the adventurous?" Or a "traveler getting by on as little money as possible?" Or how about the traveling writer who "gets drunk globally?" You can also target various periodicals like *Golf* Magazine for an idea about a golf article you have. Or a cigar magazine about your plans to smoke a Cuban with Mark Cuban. And there's always the *Maxim* and *FHM* category that could have you scribing a story about a group of nymphomaniacs from Norway who know how to spend those twenty dark hours in the winter. All you need is a fun idea. And, along the way, maybe you'll come up with a good book idea . . . just send it to our editor Ben Sevier. If he accepts, you just owe us a fair, nominal commission of 15 percent.

EMBELLISHMENT FOR YOUR RESUME: Global Journalist

CAN I WRITE ABOUT THIS?
Dutch, 30, New York, married

"Travel Writer . . . yeah, I could do that," is the sentiment that basically got me to apply for a freelance travel writing position in Mexico. And, to my shock, they gave me the gig. I knew very little Spanish, had no insurance, and the pay was basically nothing. I figured I'd travel around, eat some good Mexican food, recommend hotels and sites, and that would be about it. Either way, it was better than New York in the winter.

Starting in Durango, I spent a solid two hours working on the book, got a couple of churches and museums under my belt, and made my way to a local establishment for a few cervezas. I met up with a couple of gringos who were also visiting, we got ridiculously drunk together, and, before I knew it, I was several miles outside of town, drinking more beer, and listening to a local band jam in a random backyard. I was convincing myself that this was the best way to get material to write about in the book. Before I knew it, I woke up to a guy named Hector telling us that we were going to "sweat off last night." We ended up chanting in a weird hut that was like 150 degrees inside. I was kind of freaked out, but it knocked the hangover right out of me. Next, they asked me to go to Cabo with them, about a thousand miles away, I said no, and we parted ways. I rationalized that I had to focus on writing the travel guide.

But—after about thirty minutes—I thought, "that was stupid," so I went to the airport and flew to Cabo. In no time, the band was back together and we were slamming beers at Cabo Wabo. Throughout the night most of the guys left with some chicks. Kneils and I were too drunk to talk to ladies, so at about four A.M., we headed back to his hotel. Because I wasn't there when they checked in, the hotel manager gave me a hard time. Brilliantly, Kneils and I went outside, changed shirts and then tried to enter the hotel again. This time, the hotel manager was the least of our problems. The Mexican federales (police) were on us and tossed us into the back of a cop car.

We were freaking out. Kneils was shaking. I was thinking of my family and racking my brain for any congressmen that I might know. I didn't know what to do. But I knew these fuckers must have wanted money, so I mustered out "¿Cuánto usted quiere?" Kneils whispered under his breath "Are you bribing the Mexican police? Are you insane?" The car took off and within three minutes we were outside a bank machine. I took out the equivalent of two hundred dollars and gave it to the federales. They drove for another five minutes, pulled over, and literally pushed us out of the car. We both stood silently, hugged, then walked for a half an hour to get back to Cabo. We then, of course, started drinking again.

"How to bribe the Mexican police" didn't make it into the guide book, and I can only imagine what the travel guide company would do if they knew what I was up to, beyond deciding whether to give a restaurant three or four forks and a hotel two or three dollar signs.

CHECK IT OFF
Your "yeah, I drank that" list

☐ Drink absinthe.

☐ Drink something with Tabasco in it.

☐ Drink a Cement Mixer (lime juice and Bailey's)

☐ Join The Century Club—a shot of beer every minute for a hundred minutes.

(continued)

- ☐ Drink a Guinness in Ireland.
- ☐ Drink vodka in Russia.
- ☐ Drink tequila in Tijuana.
- ☐ Drink ouzo in Greece.
- ☐ Drink a Johnny Walker Blue.
- ☐ Down a Sex on the Beach while engaging in that very activity.
- ☐ Hit the same brewery tour three times in a row (and enjoy the free beer three times over).
- ☐ Drink a Redheaded Slut, then go home with one.
- ☐ Buy a girl a Blow-Job shot; have her return the favor later.
- ☐ Enjoy a White Russian with a woman named Ivana.
- ☐ Do a Jell-O shot off a beautiful woman's belly.
- ☐ Do a Jell-O shot off a fat, hairy dude's belly (just kidding).
- ☐ Drink the most expensive after-dinner drink on the menu.
- ☐ Buy the entire bar a round; tell them you just won on "Wheel of Fortune."
- ☐ Drink a full yard of beer. (Be sure to bring along a second shirt.)
- ☐ A beer an inning.
- ☐ Drink something on fire.
- ☐ Drink from one of those beer-holder hats.
- ☐ Crack your first beer at eight A.M. and your last at the same time the next day.

Lifeguard

If a guy like David Hasselhoff can get laid as a lifeguard, so can you. Perched on your stand, towering above the beachgoers, walking the beach with your weird orange rescue thing, or cruising up and down in your ATV, will all make you look cool as shit. The beach is the place for ladies to see and be seen in their little bikinis and newfound tan. And you've got a license to leer, since **you're just there "doing your job,"** ready to rescue any helpless victim at any moment. However, you may occasionally (or frequently) find yourself mingling with the crowd and **assisting with appropriate sun tan lotion application**, specifically for those ladies with very little coverage. If being in shape and tan doesn't give you a leg up on the other guys, then the fact that girls can feel safe around you should.

Off duty, you're living in a beach town where you can partake of the usual beach town drinks, house parties, and debauchery. Great places for this would be **anywhere along the East Coast**, like the Jersey Shore and Virginia Beach. Try the other coast and its many **Southern California gems**. Otherwise, any lake in between will suffice. You'll have to be certified, but generally, this isn't difficult as long as you are in shape. Each summer the beach will have lifeguard orientation in which you'll have to undergo a few runs, swims, and rescue tests. Just don't show up drunk or too hungover and you should be fine. Also, being certified in CPR before you apply definitely helps. You're not going to retire early as a lifeguard, but you will have enough to live on—that is, enough to eat, drink and sleep. To sum it all up, this is your day as a lifeguard: "Come closer to shore; slow down on the beach; hey ladies, got enough sunblock?"

EMBELLISHMENT FOR YOUR RESUME: Aquatic Rescue Engineer

Cab Driver

No, don't change your name to Apu and pick up a taxi medallion. What you do want to do is head to a vacation town or island and get a job shuttling vacationers to and from wherever they're headed. You'll be the first guy they see as they get off the ferry or train, and their last driver each night, as you take them to an after-hours party. Shuttling around a bunch of drunk chicks (even dudes) can be entertaining and will provide you with laughs, stories, and material to use on them the next day at the beach. Hot women will jump in your car and say things like "Hey, Mr. Cab guy, what should we do now?" Your options at this point are endless. "I've got the place for you . . ." should become your standard response—set up a quid pro quo arrangement with a local bar and exchange your cabful of hotties for a tip, or at least a few free drinks the next time you're off duty.

A job as a cab driver has many other perks as well. **First**, you make your own hours. Had a good night of tips? It's beach time tomorrow. **Second**, it's all cash. This can be dangerous, because you often could have a few hundred dollars burning a hole in your pocket. However, on a positive note, Uncle Sam doesn't need to know jack shit. (Just kidding, you should always pay your taxes, and the IRS is a wonderful agency staffed by honest, hardworking American patriots). **Lastly**, this is one leisure job that can actually earn you some spending money. Your friends will be waiting tables six nights a week at a crappy restaurant as you're fraternizing with the rest of the town and **quickly becoming their favorite chaperone**. To land one of these gigs, the first thing to do is to start calling the local cab operators and ask if they are looking for drivers. Generally, you'll have to pay them a fee to operate under their license. You'll most likely need your own car, but this is a good thing. Get a kick-ass jeep with a booming sound system, chicks will dig you. Plus, we've heard that many ladies who are short on fare or just lonely from being away from their boyfriend will often give you the **ultimate gratuity**. Before you know it, you may have your own business, leasing out cabs to other guys and raking in the cashola. Could be a pretty good deal, so check it out.

EMBELLISHMENT FOR YOUR RESUME: Transportation and Logistics Manager.

"GET LUCKY ON THE JOB" JOBS:
Strip club pole repairman
College professor (Who wants extra credit?)
Lead guitarist in a band
Lead guitarist in a wedding band
Pizza delivery guy (You want extra sausage with that?)
Poet
Porn star (Hey, it's guaranteed.)
Personal trainer
Massage therapist at an all-inclusive resort
UPS deliveryman (Yes, Ma'am, I've got a package for you.)
I.T. help desk (Just kidding.)

OKAY, IF THAT'S WHAT THE JOB CALLS FOR . . .
Aaron, 32, St. Louis, married with kids

I was working as an art director for an ad agency in Chicago. My project at the time was to create a commercial for a major beer company. After endless samplings of the product—for inspiration—we finally had a campaign and were preparing for the shoot. And, oh yeah, the

(continued)

commercials were going to need a massive supply of smokin'-hot ladies. Hey, our target was young guys. We were simply playing to the interests of our demographic. Anyway, the search would not be easy. We weren't talking about semiattractive, "I'd bang you if I was drunk" types of women. We were talking about the "holy crap, I'd give my left arm just for you to say my name in a naughty voice" caliber of female. So the question was "How exactly do we find these women?" A plane trip and a cab ride later, my fellow coworker and I found ourselves in one of L.A.'s finest cabarets. We were drinking. We were getting dances. We were "just doing our job." Yes, believe it our not, this was an initial casting session for the commercial—and we were expensing lap dances. The ladies would ask "Would you like a dance?" We would respond "Have you ever done any acting?" I can't believe we were the first paying customers to say they were casting agents in search of talent—but holy crap, we actually were. Some would think we were full of shit, others saw us as their ticket out of the daily "grind." After many drinks, many "auditions," and many repetitions of "I can't believe this is work," we got some numbers and said we'd call them for further casting sessions. We also attended a *Maxim* Super Bowl party for more drinking and "casting." The party itself was like the magazine come to life: lingerie, massage booths, boobs, and other good stuff. At one point I was interviewing a woman who looked like Pamela Anderson, spoke like Arnold Schwarzenegger, and wore nothing but bodypaint on top. Fantastic. While conducting a purely professional acting/casting meeting, I couldn't help but notice how her nipples were amazingly sticking out like antennas the entire time. And it wasn't cold in here at all. Picking up on my observation, she told me "I get dem hard and den da paint keeps dem pointing out." Wow, you truly do learn something new every day. All in all, we found some fantastic "actresses." However, I have to say that there were a few winners from the night before (who seemed perfect after ten beers in a dark club) that in the light of day—Holy Jesus, did they look different. But fuck it—sure beats working in a cube crunching numbers, right?

Dude Rancher

If you've seen the movie *City Slickers*, you're familiar with the idea of middle-aged men paying money to become "dude ranchers" for a week. If you've reached a point in your life that you're **actually paying money to work another job**, then you've missed out on something. So, do this now before you're living in a Billy Crystal movie. The best places for a roundup are **Jackson Hole, Wyoming or Bozeman, Montana**. Working at a dude ranch does include some crap work—literally crap work—but you'll also be wrangling cattle, crossing killer terrain on horses, and slamming booze with other cowboys. You'll be **smoking Marlboro Reds and drinking Coors Original**, as urban cowgirls travel to your ranch to be impressed by what a western stud you are. Take them on the trail, show off your lasso skills, or be a badass and brand a calf. You'll get paid to live in the mountains, walk around like John Wayne, and have access to so much more than cows. Fishing, hiking, and rafting are just the beginning of what this "job" will bring you. And, without a doubt, you will become tough as nails as the months progress. And when you return to civilization your friends will refer to you as "Cowboy," while the ladies will deem you "dangerous." And that, as we know, is a great, great thing. Some day, when you're stuck in your four-by-six cubicle, you'll think of the open plains you once roamed and not feel quite as bad about the padded walls packed with pushpins and PowerPoint charts that now surround you.

EMBELLISHMENT FOR YOUR RESUME: Ranch Facility Manager, or just the classic: "Cowboy"

Golf Course Marshall, Pro Shop Manager

Ah, I think today I'll sell a few drivers, make sure those foursomes get out on time, and then I'll go play a round myself. Tonight, I'll hit the **nineteenth hole bar**, where my favorite waitress Tina will supply me with free drinks 'til closing time, followed by a naked driving contest on the back nine. Seriously though, just think how great it would be to work on a golf course for a year or even a summer. With a kick-ass track at your free disposal, pros to help improve your game, and good weather, it's hard to beat. The big question is where to get such a job? Definitely steer clear of your typical country club, where you'll find way too many old, snobby, boring people. Instead, search out resorts and destination golf courses. And if you want your job to last more than the summer, head someplace with sunshine year-round.

A few recommendations would be **the Bahamas Paradise Island, Hawaii** and **Myrtle Beach**. They're warm. They're fun places. And they have great golf. You could also try the many courses of Arizona, Bandon Dunes in Oregon, and North Carolina's Pinehurst. Stay away from Florida. Sorry, just too many old birds. You can also **take your search abroad** to Ireland, Scotland, and Spain. Visas will be in order, and you'll probably have some trouble getting in, but if you land a gig you'll be golden. Check it out though, and after you're finished take a month off and travel all over Europe. (See chapter 5, under "Europe by Rail.") Hell, there are millions of dudes out there who count the days every week until they get out and smack around the little white ball. With a job on a golf course, you'll get to do it every single, goddamn day. Glorious!

EMBELLISHMENT FOR YOUR RESUME: Manager of Golf Course Operations

Video Game Tester

When researching the qualifications required for such a skilled position as this, we read several articles commenting on how the "right" person will need to be **"tenacious," "innovative,"** and **"a solid communicator."** Yeah, we laughed, too. Hell, you just need to be able to conquer many levels, kick ass along the way, and then describe to someone exactly how you felt about annihilating a pack of mutant aliens that looked a lot like Cher, if she had seven arms and a boob on her forehead. With that said, **you must really, really, really, really love video games to consider such a job**. Your task will be to test every dimension of a particular game, like a secret service agent sweeping the president's hotel room for potential dangers. Yes, it will be your responsibility to ensure that the quarterback from Fresno State in the latest NCAA football game truly has the cannon of an arm he's supposed to have. And that he can pass like mad, all over the allegedly piss-poor secondary of Notre Dame. You'll be in search of any bugs, hiccups, or fuck ups. And they will pay you decently for sitting on your ass all day interfacing with a machine. How's it different from your average cubical job, you ask? Because you actually get paid to annihilate your coworkers with a submachine gun, rather than just fantasizing about it. You won't want to do it for the rest of your life, but six months . . . why not? Also, in order to pass the interview please do not shower or shave, make sure to bring your cousin's Trekkie membership card, and say things like "I often have nightmares when a certain facet of a game just doesn't work right." Now, **get your Neosporin out, because your thumbs will be blistered**—from the game playing and the lack of female companionship, due to the game playing. Sorry, only a very select few ladies will be turned on by this job—but if you find them, they're likely to be pretty dirty—in all senses of the word.

EMBELLISHMENT FOR YOUR RESUME: Electronic Recreation Consultant

Reality Show Contestant

What will your fifteen minutes of fame be for? Will it be for **asking the Bachelorette if you could touch her boobs?** Will it be for eating pig anus washed down by elephant sperm? Or will it be for winning a bunch of cash for somehow not getting kicked off an island, winning a race, or proving to the world that a dork can get a super hot chick? Or will you just be one of those instantly forgettable reality faces? Hey, in many ways that isn't so bad. The fact of the matter is, the odds of you gaining any substantial fame, glory, or money from reality television are as slim as Lara Flynn Boyle on the South Beach Diet. If you go in with the right attitude, the chance that you'll have a hilarious and awesome time is quite good. Finding a show for you is not the problem. There's *The Amazing Race, Road Rules, The Bachelor, Real World, The Apprentice, American Idol,* and so on. If it's semilasting fame you want, definitely shoot for the bigger networks and names. **If it's on the WB and called "MILF-orette,"** you won't become famous, but you will have great stories . . . which we'd like to hear. The better-known shows will guarantee you a good six months more of perks, ranging from parties at the Playboy Mansion to Super Bowl tickets to reality star bonus sex. Yes, there are plenty of ladies out there who's closest thing to celebrity shagging is a reality show schmuck. Hey, **that schmuck could be you**. If you don't want to be recognized but want to test the reality waters, you can try a show like *Blind Date,* where you'll spend only a night with some crazy chick whose fake boobs you'll no doubt witness up close at that random hot tub all the daters always seem to go to. You're young; it's all good fun. Just remember, don't end up like some of the serial reality folks. Oh, you know 'em, the Miz, Theo, Rob, and Amber, that slutty chick from *Real World Vegas* with the boobs—need we go on?

EMBELLISHMENT FOR YOUR RESUME: Just leave it off and hope your new boss listens to the radio.

Band Member or Roadie

You've got two choices here: You can either play in a band—most likely an average one that performs cover songs in bars—or you can travel along with a bigger name and help set up the stage for the show each night. The choice will depend heavily on whether you can play an instrument or sing. If you can, and you have some buddies willing to join you, start a kick-ass band and play for a year. Call yourselves something funny, like **Mr. Potato Head's Missing Package**. Or be a jam band that plays lots of trippy Dead songs. Or make yourselves a tribute band to a certain decade. **Play all the party bars** where the patrons are perpetually drunk and never notice a missed lyric or a horribly bad chord. Travel to college campuses and play their pubs, frats, and sororities. If you're an eighties band, don't be afraid of fog machines, doing the moonwalk, or that song "I Wear My Sunglasses at Night."

Now, if the bongo is the only instrument you can play, **how about being a roadie?** A roadie is basically anyone on the traveling crew for a stage production. You could be a stage technician, lighting guy, sound guy, laser guy, stagehand, or in general management.

For any technical position you will need some experience. And, most likely, getting started out will have you touring with some little punk rock band, rather than the Stones, but, hey, that could be more interesting. In one summer alone, you'll most likely be surrounded by more out-of-control partying than you'll see for the rest of your life. **You'll meet groupies looking to give it up in every new city.** And of course there will be the token overdosing of a drummer—save his life and maybe his girlfriend will be really grateful. The work itself will be demanding, but the experience—pretty sweet. Bouncing from venue to venue, city to city, it's like a road trip with a job at each stop.

EMBELLISHMENT FOR YOUR RESUME: Musical Genius, or Recording Industry Operations Manager

AH . . . THE LIFE OF A ROCK STAR—SORT OF
Brent, 34, Chicago, recently married

Recording companies weren't knocking on our door. U2 hadn't asked us to open for them yet. *But* that didn't stop us from rocking the shit out of this Bowling Green college town bar, where we played on an approximately 4' × 4' stage to a crowd of some five hundred underaged students who were silly hammered. Foxy Boxing (hot girls battling with huge, oversized gloves that they eventually take off, along with their shirts, and just wrestle naked) was playing on the projection screen TV behind us. We were cranking out some quality "Blister in the Sun," and "99 Red Balloons." This night was ripe for craziness. By the end of the show, and absolutely by closing time, everything became a total blur and everyone in the band went their separate ways. I was escorted by some cutie (I think) back . . . um . . . to her . . . um . . . dorm room where we made out on the top bunk while her roommate was there listening, below in the bottom bunk. "Oh, Oh, Oh, Brent—you're the best, you're the best ever!" I think that's what the roommate probably heard. No one knew where the drummer was, and he was the one with the car—our only way home. The lead singer found some hot chick as always, and the bass player (whose mom still packed his lunch and who still lived at home) didn't hook up, lost his wallet, and had to stay at the hosting band's apartment, which wasn't fit for bums to sleep in—and their pets were rats. We were truly all over the place. And this was before everyone had a cell phone or pager, so tracking each other down was far from a simple "Hey, where you at?" Somehow, the next morning we all kind of wandered back to the crap apartment. There we found the drummer's car parked in the middle of a lawn, the bass player scared and shaking from his traumatic sleepover, and the lead singer smiling from another conquered, naughty college chick. How we all managed to find each other at the same time the next morning is still a mystery. *Band members! Band members! Unite!* (Sound of a seashell horn.) I wish I could play another college bar gig, but, unfortunately, I think I'd just be the creepy old guy covering eighties tunes.

Teach English Abroad

"Repeat after me, 'I want to vote in an election.'" "I want to hold your erection." "Very good." If you like to travel and have thought about living abroad for a year, **teaching English to foreigners makes for an ideal setup**. And it's simple. First, you'll most likely have to get certified to teach English. How hard could that be? You already know the friggin' language. You can start by looking through the many different programs that hire teachers to place throughout the world. Look at the programs and start thinking about where you want to live. Japan? The Czech Republic? Costa Rica? The majority of jobs you'll discover are in Asia, Latin America, and Eastern Europe. **Choose your job based on what country you'd like to experience most.** If it's geishas, sushi, and karaoke, try Tokyo. If it's outdoor adventures, go to Nepal. If you plan ahead, you should be able to get to where you want to go. Sorry, the Red Light District in Amsterdam is not on too many lists.

As a teacher, your program will most likely afford you just enough to pay the rent and eat cheap food. Some may set you up with established housing, which won't be great, but may be better than finding your own pad. Save up a little cash before you take off. You'll need it. Your hours will be similar to those of a normal teacher, which will give you freedom for weekend excursions and help you make the most of your time overseas. Plus, unlike the Jet Ski operator, this is a fun job that will actually impress people. When they see your resume, they'll think **"What a fine young man."** If they only knew how you spent that night in Bangkok. Let's recap: "Where am I? Who are you? Why are you holding my Rolex, and could you please give me back my underwear?"

EMBELLISHMENT FOR YOUR RESUME: Foreign Relations Ambassador

"IT'S ALL ABOUT THE PERKS" JOBS
Member of a celebrity's entourage
Production assistant for a XXX movie company
Usher at a ballpark (only if you have a good team)
Roadie for a kick-ass band
Pool boy in Beverly Hills

Event planner for a beer company

The guy who carries the boom box for strippers

Spray-tan operator

Gynecologist—in Hollywood

Water spray guy for bikini shoot

Towel guy at a topless pool in Vegas

CHAPTER SEVEN

LOST WEEKENDS

You heard it in *Old School,* from Will Ferrell:

> Oh well, um, actually pretty nice little Saturday. We're uh, gonna
> go to Home Depot. Yeah, buy some wallpaper, maybe get some
> flooring, stuff like that. Maybe Bed Bath & Beyond, I don't know.
> I don't know if we'll have enough time.

If you think this is cinematic exaggeration, you are very, very wrong. There will be a day when responsibilities (a.k.a. errands and chores) will become an extremely important part of your life. How this happens we can't say for sure. You buy a house and you're instantly in charge of every weed, every chipped-off piece of paint, and everything else your wife doesn't want to handle. You'll spend full days shopping for holiday gifts, when it used to take you a lunch break at work. You'll wake up one Saturday to your wife asking **"Can you do me a favor?"** Seventeen favors later, it's Sunday night and you're wondering *where the hell did my weekend go?* That's what happens. So, enjoy your duty-free weekends by making the most of them. Make them interesting. **Make them story worthy.** Make them something that'll help bring a smile to your face one day, as you're standing in Old Navy while your second-grade daughter tries on every outfit the store has to offer. That's a big fucking store. This chapter is a hodge-podge of ways to spend your two days of freedom. We highly recommend that you improvise and add to any of them with your own special twist. Be creative. Start annual events, monthly outings, and weekly endeavors. Certainly, any average night at the bar can turn into the event of the century, but more likely it's gonna be just another night at the bar where you almost talked to that chick, but she left before you could, so you got wicked drunk and woke up on your couch at five A.M. with late-night pick up food stuck to your shirt. Mix it up and try some of *these* lost weekends. Many will leave your head cloudy, your body exhausted, and, certainly, your work will suffer on Monday—but that's **nothing, compared to what Bed Bath & Beyond can do to you**.

MUST-CRAWL PUB CRAWLS

Why spend your time pounding beers in one measly establishment when you can do it in many? The almighty pub crawl transforms drinking into something so much more. A pub crawl **promotes exercise** (hey, there could be several blocks to walk between each bar). **It encourages camaraderie** and teamwork—you may need help getting from bar to bar. **It can be a challenge,** complete with tasks, dares, and other achievements to be had. Plus, the ladies love to join in on the fun—just be careful who you invite to tag along. Don't be afraid to fine-tune these crawls to your own tastes. However, based on experience and expertise, **the more full-blown you go, the better**. Have official sign-in sheets. Have cameras to capture all the moronic behavior. And most importantly, have a good group of pub crawlers. There are plenty of people out there who suck for pub crawling. Such characteristics as "always having an opinion," "always need-ing things their way," and "being generally anal retentive," can be signs of an unworthy crawler. Instead, look for instigators, those who are good followers, and **people who could have fun waiting in line at the airport**. They will make your pub crawl a success. Of course, impromptu pub crawls are encouraged, too. Along the way, spread the love by giving cute girls "pub crawl hugs," invite them all to the last bar on your list, and be ready to buy all of them a drink when they show up. Here are some great crawls that can be set up in any town and always produce a good time.

Costume Pub Crawl

Just picture it: twenty-five Santa Clauses, each with a full white beard, pants, coat, and black belt, parading from bar to bar, chugging down beers, convincing nice and naughty girls to sit on their laps and whisper what they want this year for Christmas. Or how about fifty leprechauns? Or seventy-five sumo wrestlers? Or a bunch of idiots in Elvis jumpsuits? Whatever the costume may be, you'll no doubt gar-ner a crapload of attention. **"Did I just see . . ."** will certainly be heard from down the street. Costume pub crawls are a guaranteed good time. However, it's important to **have complete costumes, where**

everyone looks the same, and no one (absolutely no one) wusses out. If you don't have Santa's red pants, you don't come. Be sure to lay down the law. You can always accessorize as needed to become a ghetto pirate with a huge afro. Bring additional items for groupies to wear, too. Also, add a charity element by charging other bar patrons to take a picture with you, then give the proceeds to a worthy cause. As Mom always said, **"Chicks dig guys willing to dress stupidly for charity."** If the bars are far apart, procure a bus or trolley to take you around. Be sure to save room for those lustful groupies who will want to jump on board. Make it an annual event, or monthly—whatever you feel like. Please, just take your costume to a dry cleaners after you're finished.

ALL I WANT FOR CHRISTMAS IS A BUZZ AND A FEW NAUGHTY ELVES

Denis, 33, Austin, Texas, single

In 2003 we started what has now become The Annual New York City Santa Crawl. The idea was to make a true event with no half-ass costumes or annoying Mrs. Clauses. So, the goal was to get at least thirty guys (again, just guys, no elves) in full Santa suits (not just hats) and wreak havoc on Manhattan. We were not sure what to expect—if we would be well received, if bars would kick us out, if girls would think we were freaks, etc. After the first bar, I realized quickly that walking into an establishment dressed as Santa is just about the only time you'll feel like Mick Jagger. You are automatically a stud, people flock to you, and girls—well, let's just say it's not so difficult to get one to sit on your lap. Plus, we raised money for charity, so the "good cause" intentions only helped our case. As we crawled from bar to bar, people cheered, took pictures, and asked if they could join up. Hot girls are always a good addition, but they usually only last for a bar or so; it's too easy to get distracted by other hot girls. The stories are endless, but here is a list of shenanigans that ensued after just the first year:

- **Lone Santa** passed out at the Grand Hyatt, security was booed when he got kicked out
- **Camo Claus** (even with the camouflage pants, we found you)
- The old-timer at McSorley's who wanted to join up
- Six Santas and a bachelorette party in the back of a UPS truck
- Santa dry-humping the window of restaurants where people were eating dinner
- The bartender from Coyote Ugly **making out with a Santa Bozo Claus**
- Santa buying a **sixty-dollar Christmas tree** and carrying it into the bar
- Santa waking up to a random elf and asking her, "What's your name?"
- Lone Santa II at The Sound Factory
- Santa getting checked through the plexi-glass
- New Jersey Claus (sleeveless santa suit)
- "What the fuck, Santa never pays a cover."
- Cowboy Claus
- To the sushi waitress: "What do you want for Christmas?" Her response: "A sugar daddy."
- Claus asks "Have you ever been tied up by Santa?" . . . "No, but I like what you're thinking."
- "Which one of you naughty Hohoho's wants to sit on Santa's lap?"
- Puking Claus
- Lone Santa III strolling through Scores at three A.M.

Polaroid Pub Crawl

Remember Matty Davis's birthday party in fourth grade? You know, the one where you went on a **scavenger hunt** in search of things like an unsharpened pencil, a frozen lima bean, and a pair of grandma panties (yeah, Matty was always into weird things). Anyway, this pub crawl is kind of like that. Only, instead of finding and acquiring items, you have to capture them on film. **We highly recommend the Polaroid over the digital camera for several reasons.** One, it adds to the uniqueness of this event. Two, the fun of watching the picture fade into visibility creates extra drama. And third, women are more likely to perform for a Polaroid than a digital camera. It's something about digital cameras and their easy linkup to the Internet, we think. You can always bring both—but make the official camera a Polaroid.

Now, this hunt can work one of two ways: you can **split the crawl into two camps**, sending each group to a different set of bars, to compete over who gets the largest number and the most interesting photos checked off their list (quality counts just as much as quantity); or you can just have one group with one list. Two teams definitely adds the always-fun element of competition. So, go with that. Now, about that list . . . we suggest a nice range of scavenger items, from the simple picture of someone doing a shot of tequila to the more difficult picture of some girl doing a shot of tequila with her boobs hanging out. **Some other pictures to take would be:** someone without pants standing on the bar; two girls kissing; the girl with the least amount of clothing; a girl's hand down the pants of someone in your group; someone giving a cop a high five; a guy drinking a wine spritzer; a guy with a DD bra on his head; a guy doing deep knee bends in the middle of the bar; someone getting a "massage" by an Asian woman—you get the idea. Eventually, the two teams should **meet up, exchange photos, and declare a winner**. The loser then has to buy a round of drinks, steak dinners, or a trip to Vegas. To help obtain photos, tell the ladies, or anyone else, that your winnings will be donated to a worthy cause. "Come on, it's for dying puppies!"

Big Wheel Pub Crawl

Anyone can transport themselves from bar to bar by foot, but it takes someone special to do it via the almighty Big Wheel. This pub crawl is likely to be unlike anything you've ever seen or done, which is why you need to make it happen. The first step in organizing this "pedal-a-thon" is gathering **a sweet collection of Big Wheels**. You remember that thing you used to motor around your driveway in, crashing into garbage cans and chasing around that fat kid who lived next door? Well, you can find modern ones at your local Wal-Mart, Toys "R" Us, and other stores. Hit eBay or your folk's garage for some more old school rides. Also, make sure several outcasts of the group are equipped with **Huffy Green Machines**. Yeah, there were always a couple of kids who had to have those. And to really kick things into gear, buy one **adult version of the Big Wheel** and make the rider of this vehicle the leader of the pack. You can find them online. Also, don't be afraid to pimp your ride with flashing lights, stickers, and racing sound effects. Now for the crawl itself, let the bars know beforehand that you'll be coming and ask about parking for your "wheels." Don't go to any place that thinks it's too classy for Big Wheel riders. If you can, park your rides all in a row, just like the Hells Angels would. Ask every hot lady to join your gang. Have a portable Breathalyzer test to make sure everyone is drunk enough to ride. And set up wheelie contests in between stops. For huge bonus points, do the crawl sporting a full-blown Evil Knievel racing suit. **Drinking and driving has never been authorized like this before.**

Around-the-World Crawl

Don't worry, this is not some, "Hey let's try and experience the many cultures and customs that make up this great planet we live on." No, it's more like: **"Hey, instead of just drinking Budweiser today, let's drink a lot of other stuff from all over the globe."** You can easily set up this endeavor with some basic planning. First, get out a map. Create a list spanning many nations: Mexico, Canada, England, Ireland, Spain, Germany, Russia, Japan, Italy, Greece, and on and on. Now think of their favorite drinks. Create a nice range of lighter beverages like beer and some heavier ones like a shot of ouzo. Go to each bar, tell them about your "global effort," and see which drink they want to give you at a "special" price. Go all out and set up assorted entertainment at each venue. For example, **have a bagpiper at the pub**, where everyone must down an Irish car bomb and **a limbo dancer** at the piña colada bar. Create a theme of **"Think Global, Drink Local,"** and make this crawl **a for-profit event**. Collect money by selling T-shirts, cups, and French kisses from the most bombed girl on the crawl. Watch drunk people part with their money and wake up the next day with enough crinkled-up cash for that new HDTV you've been rubbing up against at Best Buy.

Random City Pub Crawl

When traveling to a new city, you certainly can hop on board the trolley, the Duck Boat, or other touristy transports, and let some guy with a microphone take you to all the great sights. Or, you could try to have fun. Yes, we think **a much better way to explore any new place is through its watering holes**. From its finest dives to its swankiest lounges to its most expansive outdoor beer gardens, there's truly no better way to soak in the vibe of a town than to drink with its locals. And hey, in between beers you can stop and observe some historic monuments, architectural wonders, and other things in your guidebook. Unlike your normal pub crawl, this one needs no planned out path. On this crawl you're totally winging it. However, this doesn't mean you can't have some dares, challenges, and general goals to achieve. For example, at one bar **you and your buddies are from Germany and speak zero English**. At the next bar you're part of a minor league hockey team. At another place you all just got fired from the same company. (Hey, it'll get you a free round.) Ask other patrons which bar to go to next, and whatever they say you must obey. Whether it's darts, foosball, or just hitting on women, hold contests where the losers always must buy. All in all, utilize your "I'm-a-stranger to this town" status to meet local girls, get free drinks, and learn about more must-do activities. **Great cities for pub crawls** are New York (you'll need free drinks there), Boston, Chicago, Milwaukee, Memphis, Miami, Seattle, San Diego, Philadelphia, Washington, D.C., and, of course, big college towns are always good bets.

OTHER WORTHY PASTIMES

Poker Tournament

Has poker ever been as popular as it is now? Everyone from teenagers to the little old ladies at The ShadyTree Retirement Home seem to jumping on the bandwagon and wagering a small fortune on a little No-Limit Texas Hold 'Em. Well, the craze is fun, and so is the sport of bluffing with nothing but a Jack high, going "all in" with a potential flush, and wearing sunglasses at two A.M. With such exploding popularity, **locating a game is about as easy as finding porn on the Internet**. You can join in at a buddy's house. Head to one of the many casinos that offer up various poker tournaments. Be sure to put in some training time online. Setting up or being a part of a high-stakes game between friends and friends of friends probably offers you the best odds, because there's no doubt that several totally clueless guys will show up. For such an event you can rent out a hall or the back room at a bar. Settle up all the money ahead of time and deal only with chips. Gambling is still illegal, and, with no dollar bills lying around, you can tell the authorities, should they show up, that it's "just for shits and giggles, not cash." Creating a No-Limit Texas Hold 'Em game is a rather simple endeavor. Set up tables with four to five guys at each. The winner from each table then moves to another table. Finally there's one table remaining, and the guy on top wins the pot or a portion of the pot, depending on how you want it. Allot a good twelve hours for the tourney, especially if you've got a good crowd. Create decent blinds to keep the games moving. **Have entertainment** (strippers perhaps?) **for all the schmucks who went all in on the first hand and lost**. If you want to go big and be the next Chris Moneymaker, try some of the on-line games, where the winner gets a shot at a real tournament, like the World Series of Poker or the World Poker Tour. We've all seen how a no-name can wind up with a million-dollar payout. If there's a point in your life when you can afford to lose a grand or two, or three, or four, to gambling, it's now. Unless you don't mind your kids asking "Dad, why are we having Ramen noodles for dinner again?"

THIS AIN'T NO RIVERBOAT
Rich, 30, New York, married

It was a Saturday night in New York City, and we started out drinking in a large group. After several hours, my friend Wells and I were the last of the Mohicans. In the past we had made some late night runs to Atlantic

City, when we felt the drunken need to gamble—although neither of us were in any shape to drive and a bus ride seemed miserable. Then I thought "There's gambling in New York City right now, somewhere, I know it." I had to find it, but the trick is *where*. After asking around and being sent from place to place, someone at this bar with red walls gave us the final directions and proper instructions. We threw down a certain knock on some door and, sure enough, it worked! Well, sort of . . . There was a massive front man who stopped us and began the interrogation. He was positive that we were cops. "No, just looking for a game," we said. After some time, he granted us access to an elevator, where another bouncer asked us if we were cops. "No, of course not." They believed me, but kept eyeing and questioning Wells.

The elevator opened into a giant hall where there was a dimly lit bar and a regular party going on inside. Twenty, maybe thirty guys and girls were inside, freshly gelled and ready for some sort of action. With no poker tables in sight, we saddled up to the bar, bought two five-dollar Budweisers, and asked ourselves "What the hell happens now? Are we sure this is a casino?" After a few more "Are you cops?" and several beers, two sets of doors opened into another large room. That's when we saw it. There were about five tables offering up games of blackjack and poker. Jackpot! Most of the dealers and clientele were of foreign descent. Neither of us could really believe it, but we went up to a table, each plunked down two hundred bucks, got our chips, and we were on our way. Now, however, we were looking at each other suspiciously. We were convinced that we were about to be taken for a ride. And, as we each lost the first few hands, I was now certain we were fucked. But wait . . . we then won a few hands. Maybe we were going to destroy this place, not the other way around. Ah . . . nope: Five minutes later Wells was totally out. His two

(continued)

hundred bucks vanished like a martini in an alcoholic's hand. And after five more minutes, I, too, was history. I stood, thanked the dealer, and we walked back to the bar. We enjoyed another beer, didn't say much, and concluded that losing two hundred dollars really wasn't so bad—that we didn't belong there, and that things could've been a whole lot worse.

The next day, as I awoke in my apartment, I thought "What the fuck was I doing last night?" My guess is that the bar with the red walls gets a cut of every sucker they send to that place. But hey, I still gambled in an illegal casino.

Play Grunk Dolf (Sorry, That's "Drunk Golf.")

Sure, we've all thrown in a few beers in our bag or hit up the beer cart girl for some cold ones, but have you ever played in a tournament where **intoxication was all a part of your handicap**. The key to this weekend event is to secure a golf course that is not very good. And, if you can, do it off-season. Set things up so that you and the five or six other foursomes can all play back-to-back without worries of other golfers wanting to throw clubs at you. **The tournament will commence at a nearby bar.** Have some Bloody Marys, a breakfast sandwich, and play a little Golden Tee to get you in the right frame of mind. After a solid two hours of drinking, hop on the little bus you've rented and head to the course. Now, the tournament can work in a number of ways, but we recommend you play **two-player best ball**. That's taking the best score from either golfer on each hole, and the lowest total for eighteen holes wins. Now—about that drinking. In this tournament you can **earn mulligans, extra putts, and even a free throw-out from the trap, by drinking**. For example, if you're buried in the trap you can get free relief by doing a shot of tequila. If you chug a beer, you lose one stroke on the hole. If you puke, add a four-stroke penalty. The other twosome in the group obviously needs to bear witness for verification. You certainly can make up your own rules, based on the drinking ability of the group. The big question at the end of the day will be "Did the winner play well or just drink a shitload?"

Engage in Paintball Warfare

The easiest way to figure out just what kind of a pussy you'd be during an actual war is paintball. Yeah, as you sit in a foxhole, scared shitless to move because paintballs are whizzing over your head at a rate of fifty per second, you'll no doubt think **"What if these things we're real?"** Well, that's the beauty of it. They're not; and they only sting a little when they nail you. Now, with paintball you'll probably have a couple options in your area. **There will be indoor paintball**, which is usually played in a dark space with lots of walls, barriers, and obstacles to hide behind. Although very fun, this venue guarantees that you will get blown away by friendly fire from a teammate who didn't realize you were fighting for the same cause. You'll also get pummeled at close range by the enemy, because indoor courses are just smaller. That's why, if possible, **we suggest the outdoor fields for the optimal experience**. Plus, outside paintball parks bring you a ton of courses to wage war on. From the field with smashed-up old cars to the one with haystacks and fake cows to an actual mock town, with buildings and all, every game will have a different look. The key to any game of paintball is to fight the fight with your buddies and only your buddies. **Do not play against the "regulars."** One more time: do *not*, under any circumstances, play with the regulars. Easily recognizable, these are the guys in full-out camouflage, headsets for communicating, and that "I like to torture helpless puppies" look in their eyes. Get the right number of guys, so that you'll compete only with each other. Have team captains who pick their men. And of course, **place a serious wager** on this conflict. Drinking beforehand is not advisable (this could be a first for this book). You'll have enough trouble not tripping over shit and maneuvering for cover. There are several types of games you can play. The best time seems to be good old Capture the Flag game. Special tactics and strategy for playing this game are probably out there. We just say fuck it, go nuts and storm toward your enemy, or just find a quality spot and have a good time picking off the idiots storming toward you. Please wear a cup (you want kids someday, right?). And afterwards, throw a party for everyone to recap their battles and show off their Rambo-like wounds.

PARTIES WORTH THROWING

At some point in your life kegstands, funneling, sucking Jell-O shots off random girls' bellies, break-dancing on someone's coffee table, staying up until all the beer is gone, doing naked beer slides, and playing drinking games with skill and passion, will all go *poof,* and you'll be left sipping wine (can you say: "Gosh, this pinot noir is so smooth?"), popping funny-looking appetizers, and talking about work, gas prices, and that new restaurant that opened up at the mall. **"I hear they serve a fantastic chocolate mousse there."** In general, it's probably a good thing that keggers fall to the wayside, because, frankly, our internal organs would all begin failing us if we kept this lifestyle up for too long. However, while it's still a part of your life and still a solid option for any Friday or Saturday night, you need to capitalize on this option and not just throw a party, but throw a party that causes people either to beg you to repeat it again next weekend or to **"please, please do not have another one like that for at least a year,"** due to the regretful next morning they endured.

The fundamentals of a good party are booze, women, and ridiculous behavior. The more you can take people out of their element and into a world of craziness the better. **A good party incites people to do dumb things,** like drink too much, make out with people they normally wouldn't even talk to, and break out dance moves they didn't even know they had. The following day should be spent with their friends trying to piece together exactly all that transpired. "Wait a second, we went to a bar after the party?" "Holy shit, I think I took a shower with that chick?" "Shut up! I did *not* try to pee in the closet!" Now, that's the kind of stuff you want to hear the day after your party. We've put together some easy-to-assemble bashes that you should seriously think about throwing next Saturday.

Black Light

It's dark. Music is blasting. And some random girl just asked you to write on her white panties. **Quick, get yourself a highlighter.** A black light party remains a fantastic way to get all participants to mix it up in ways they'd normally not. And the fantastic thing is just how simple one of these soirees is to pull off. All you need are a bunch of black garbage bags, a keg, multicolored highlighters, some booze, white backup T-shirts (extra-small for the ladies), and a black light or two. That's it. You put all the garbage bags on the walls and ceiling. Hook up the black light in a good spot. Tell everyone to wear an expendable white shirt. And, *bam,* you've got the setting for one incredible time. The party itself will consist of **a bunch of people with white shirts scribbling dirty things on each other**. You'll have to get to work early to be the guy who gets to highlight the nipples of some cute chick. And if you're looking for a little extra fun, throw on white boxers and let the ladies draw on your ass and outline your balls. Just try not to pop a tent. The next day you'll wake up wearing three different white T-shirts, a pair of white boxers over your pants, and a lot of comments about having a small penis. Good stuff.

Toga

"Was it over when the Germans bombed Pearl Harbor?" Ever since *Animal House,* fraternities across our great nation have been turning to the ancient garb of the toga for the ultimate in party attire. Why is it that, from the second you put on one of those things, you instantly feel like chugging Everclear-spiked punch, having a hot girl feed you grapes, and declaring the empire under your rule? When it comes to parties, the toga party couldn't be easier. All you need is a bedsheet and your costume is complete. Sure, you could add a festive laurel leaf for your head, but that's about it. We recommend that you **wear your costume "Roman-style,"** without any shorts or underwear. The breeze is fantastic. The ladies, however, have many different ways to sport their togas. Our personal favorite is the bikini toga, where part of the bedsheet works as a bikini top and the rest hangs like a normal toga. Encourage that. Beyond just getting shitfaced, lifting up every hot girl's toga, and whatever else you're going to do, be sure to **get everyone singing along to "Shout,"** and a little slow dancing to "Shama Lama Ding Dong." For extra credit points, create a special room entitled the **"Orgy Room."** Hey, it's only in keeping with what the ancients did. Tonight, if you do happen to get laid, make sure she calls you Caesar, Pompey, or our favorite, Apollo.

'80s, '70s, '20s—Pick a Decade

In the last century, **three decades have risen to the forefront for good times**. They may not be the most memorable decades politically or economically, but when it comes to fashion, music, and general vibe, they stand out like no others—maybe not for all good reasons, but, nonetheless, they do stand out. And today they make for the best friggin' parties. In the '70s you had girls in tight bell-bottoms, platform shoes, and smooth polyester shirts, looking to get their disco on, do some designer drugs, and make love to the voice of Barry White. In the '80s there was huge hair, miniskirts, and one-hit wonders. And the '20s brought us speakeasies, gangsters, and women dressing like hookers. Whatever decade you choose, a quality onslaught of drinking, dancing, and debauchery will ensue to celebrate it.

Now, for a '70s party, we recommend you fill your stereo with all the disco tunes you can find. Get or grow an afro. Get or grow a mustache. Get really tight pants and stick a John Holmes–size cucumber in there (not that you're not *already* packing . . .). Get a disco ball for the ceiling. Put some retro porn on the TV. You could also **turn one room into a more hippie-themed space**, with lava lamps, bongs, a free love couch, and Donovan playing on the 8-track. For the '80s, we're talking mullets, acid-washed jeans, Richard Simmons outfits, zipper pants, *Miami Vice* on the TV, and a nice, solid mix of one-hit wonders and glam rock. Also, for either the '70s or '80s, you could up the ante and **make it a prom theme** as well. Hey, didn't every girl give it up on prom night? Now, for the '20s, or your Great Gatsby bash, you'll either dress like **Al Capone** or an **old-school golfer**. You may need to rent a space for this one, and book a kick-ass swing band. Bring your flask to go with the Prohibition theme. The ladies at this party will flat-out look awesome in their flapper dresses, as they naughtily taunt you with their boas. No matter which decade you take a trip back to, make it an annual event with prizes for the sluttiest costume, the person most likely to have lived in that decade, and the drunkest individual.

40s Party—the Drink, Not the Decade

Load up your fridge with forty-ounce bottles of St. Ide's, Old English, or Colt 45, set up some lawn chairs (even if they're inside), spin some old-school Snoop (we're talking Doggystyle), and have yourself a good ole 40s party. The concept is genius on many levels. First, **did we just say malt liquor, lawn chairs, and Snoop?** Yes, that's not just a Tuesday night we're talking about, that's a good party right there. Second, everyone gets absolutely smashed, because for those of us accustomed to drinking twelve-ounce beers, we don't like it when the beer gets warm. Therefore you drink really fast. We're telling you now, slugging down two bottles of St. Ide's will bang you out. Third, have you ever seen a really hot girl drink out of a big, glass bottle with a twist-off cap? It's a sight to be seen, and you're just about guaranteed to want to make out with her. It's even cuter when she pours some out for the brothers who are no longer with us.

There are definitely **a few guidelines for 40s parties** though. People will get a bit crazy, because, as we've said, most of us are not used to to drinking malt liquor at this pace. Have a few Grateful Dead, Dave Matthews or Coldplay CDs handy to calm people down when necessary. After spending a few hours feeling like Ice Cube from Boyz 'N the Hood, guys might forget who they really are and start throwing 'bows around. A little "Ants Marching" will bring them back to reality. Anyone with blonde hair (except Eminem of course) cannot say "dawg," "brother," or "dank." And the only fights that are permitted are between girls, but they have to be topless and lubed up. These parties will take you to where no Budweiser can, and will have you praising Billy Dee Williams for inventing Colt 45.

Mustache Party—No Mushachio, No Entrancio

Unlike some other parties, this one requires planning several weeks in advance (or months, if you're still getting your first whiskers), as you'll need time to grow that beautiful mustache. We advise first letting your full beard grow out. Then shave everything but the mustache part on the day of the party. **Require that every guy wishing to enter your party has a furry lip.** Thus, you should give plenty of notice for all participants. Goatees do not count. State trooper, redneck, Goose Gossage, handlebar, porn star—these types of mustaches are all endorsed. Those guys who are "too cool to grow a mustache" should be beaten and then forced to draw one with a permanent brown marker. For a twist, **don't tell the ladies what the theme of the party is**. Just let them arrive to discover a bunch of guys with mustaches. It'll freak them out at first, and then they'll be turned on. Do you remember how many women loved Magnum, P.I.? So, wear your white shorts and Hawaiian shirt. Chicks dig this shit. Standing around with your buddies, all with 'stashes, is absolutely hysterical. Serve mustache-worthy beverages like Miller High Life, Red, White & Brew, and Jack Daniels. Rate the mustaches, take pictures of them, and **hand out mini-brushes** for all partakers. As you make your way through the party, your line is: "Hey, have you ever made out with a guy with a mustache?" As long as it doesn't remind them of their creepy uncle, you're in.

Drinking Games Party

If there is one thing that college taught us, it's how to play drinking games. So there is no reason we shouldn't carry those lessons with us for eternity. After all, it was a great teacher of ours who once said **"You should learn for a lifetime."** Regardless, your shirt is soaked with beer, the floor is sticky, liquid is dripping from the ceiling, and you're screaming "Drink, you big pussy!!!" Every guy should be able to bounce a quarter three feet in the air, hide cards in his crotch, and drink sixteen ounces of beer in less than eight seconds without using his hands. If you can't, you should be embarrassed and should start practicing right away. **Drinking games liven up any party**—taking it to the next level and giving meathead guys something to compete over, other than just girls and stories about the glory days of high school athletics. Any drinking game can be complemented with a stripping element. "It's up to you: you can drink the whole pitcher, which will cause you to puke all over that very nice sweater of yours, or you can just remove the sweater. Your choice."

Cover the furniture in plastic, order a crazy amount of sixteen-ounce Solo Cups, and equip your place with a solid wood table and at least a keg of beer. Create some sort of tournament, flip cup, Beirut, beer pong, speed quarters, case race, or whatever you can conceive. Have a NCAA-style bracket leader board on the wall, and let the battle begin. Come up with team names, like "The Barking Clams" or "The One-legged Whores." Make rules as you go, like the losing team plays the next round with their pants down. And have war paint to intimidate the competition. (Okay, that may be a bit much.) Girls need to be forewarned, but their participation is definitely sanctioned. Again, it's pretty easy to have some bras flying around as the competition gets fierce. The cleaning lady should be on call for the next day, and there should be a trophy for the winners. **The losers have to host the party next year.**

Pimps and Hos

Although we find this party, particularly its name, to be a slap in the face of the entire women's movement, we have to say what an awesome time you'll have at one of these. It's your chance to throw on a purple fur coat, a lime green suit, and gold chains with spinning rim medallions. **Carry around a fluorescent pink cane**, and say shit like "Yo, beeyotch, you hit your quota today—fizzizzle fazalla." However, say that to the wrong chick and you may find yourself on the floor being beat silly with your own pink cane. Say it to the right lady and she may respond "Fizzizzle zazzle zoo, don't worry, Pimpee, I'll make up my quota with you." Just for the record, if "fizzizzle" actually means anything, we have no idea what it is. At this party you'll be surrounded by leopard-print lingerie, furry miniskirts, and more cleavage than a Victoria's Secret Wonderbra commercial. Good stuff. To make the party legit, have the appropriate cocktails. Courvoisier, Mad Dog 20/20, cheap champagne, Colt 45, Old English, and of course gin and juice. Hand out fake bling-bling jewelry that says shit like, "Playa," "Pimp4Life," and "PHD." **That's short for Pimpin' Ho Degree.** At this party, be certain to include games like Pin the Tail on the Ho, Soul Train Dance-Off, and the Pimp of the Party award. Also, give yourself a pimp name and have people only refer to you by that. For example, Michael Burke's pimp name is **Treacherous M.B.**

ABC Party

We're not sure who came up with this party idea, but whoever it was deserves one giant high five. Short for **Anything But Clothing**, an ABC party is a bash that requires all attendees to arrive wearing anything (you guessed it) except what is deemed as normal clothing. Certainly, this party offers up a premium excuse for you to look and act like a total jackass. It also presents the perfect occasion to satisfy that fetish of yours to **observe women in saran wrap or other household items**. Seriously though, what's a better way to force women into something that may have difficulty staying on their bodies? "Oops, your aluminum foil T-shirt just fell again." Plus, after wearing something that most likely will be uncomfortable and a little annoying, they'll be dying to just let you take it off. Now, the key to the success of such a party is stringent obedience to the rules. When drafting the invitation, **explicitly spell out the guidelines** that partiers must follow. Let it be known that "any form of clothing in any state" is forbidden. Or, be generous and only allow underwear. Give them examples of items that are acceptable, like foam, the cardboard from a beer case, wrapping paper, foil, duct tape, BEWARE OF DOG **signs**, fruit, toilet paper, and so on. Have a lawyer friend notarize the invite to make it official. If for some reason someone arrives with clothing, have backup supplies available to them so that they may make amends. Have awards for the best nonclothing clothing, the most creative ensemble, etc. Also, buy the cheapest tape possible—for your guests having difficulties with their outfit. This will guarantee "wardrobe malfunctions" of Janet Jackson–like proportions.

Impersonation Weekend

Don't get us wrong, this is not to say that who you are and what you do is lame. We're sure you're a "tremendous" slouch. Instead, **we offer up a challenge** to see what you can pull off and how good you can do it. It's not only a test, but it's a fantastic way to break up the boring, cat-and-mouse-game, blah-blah-blah BS that typically happens when mixing it up at a bar. You know it. You meet a girl. You try to be funny and charming, to impress her with how cool you are. She plays along and then ditches you for the moron with the fake tan and shirt with its collar up. Well, for one weekend forget about this charade. Try a totally different approach. This tactic is not so much about impressing the ladies you meet as it is about convincing them that you are someone you're absolutely not. And the more unique that someone is, the bigger pat on the back you will earn. There are three different categories to pick from. There's your **fake accent, your bogus job, or your mental or physical limitations**.

Beginning with the phony accent, you've got your Irish, Scottish, Australian, and South African. Forget British, unless you add that you're royalty of some kind. **Chicks dig Irish and Australian in particular.** Have some token phrases from each place. Australians love to say, "No worries," and the Irish have a penchant for the word "shit," only they pronounce it *shite*. Know your hometown, and have a good reason for being in America. Either give the ladies hope that you'll be around for a while, or tell them you're taking a plane back in two days. To prepare for your role, watch movies like *Angela's Ashes* and *Crocodile Dundee*. Your next category to give a try is **faking a certain profession**. And we're not talking about, "Oh, I'm a lawyer." You're going out as a smoke jumper, a foot model, a women's thong designer, an Olympic luger, the Ambassador to St. Bart's, a stunt plane pilot, a movie pyrotechnician, a hip-hop artist—and that's just a start. Have your buddies decide who exactly you'll be, just for the sport of it. Always know a little about what you do. And when in doubt, use the line **"Hey, I don't like to talk about work; let's talk about *you*."** And after mastering 124 different professions and three accents, try going out as someone with an abnormality of some kind. As your group of friends converse with a couple ladies, suddenly you pass out. "Oh my god, what happened?" "Don't worry, he'll wake up in a second . . . (whisper) **he's narcoleptic**." Or, as you shout out, "Bwoop! Lick my big balls," your buddy apologizes because you suffer from Tourette's Syndrome. He continues to explain how he'd leave you at home, but feels you deserve a night out, too. "Oh you're so sweet . . . ," she responds. Take turns being "the screwed-up guy." Much like a designated driver, tonight you'll be taking one for the team. "Bwoop! Fucking fuck! It's just one night."

THE SENATOR'S TRIP TO NEW ORLEANS
BK, 30 small town in Indiana, not married or responsible quite yet

In September 2002, my brother-in-law had his bachelor party in New Orleans. I did my very best to completely defile myself. On Saturday afternoon, after several hours of drinking, I decided that it was time to attend the local French Ballet, across from our hotel. So a bunch of us headed there for some entertainment and more refreshments. As a gesture of my fondness for my soon-to-be brother-in-law, I enlisted the help of two attractive ladies for dueling lap dances. During the course of this activity, my dancer asked me where I was from and what I did. So, of course, I told her that I was a State Senator from the 23rd District in Illinois. Not a U.S. Senator, mind you, because that would have been too obviously untrue. She was very impressed, of course. Naturally, as I had about fifteen beers under my belt, I fell in love with her. As far as I was concerned at that point, she was the cutest thing I had ever seen, and I was determined to save her from this life she was leading.

She told me that she was a student at LSU and that she only danced part-time. As we were talking she mentioned that she was about to get off of work, so naturally I offered to take her to dinner. She said that she would love to, but she had to get a ride home to Baton Rouge from her roommate, so she didn't think she could. Well, as it turned out, her roommate also happened to be an entertainer at the French Ballet. So, immediately advancing the situation to its logical conclusion, I said that I would take both of them out to dinner. She seemed pretty delighted by this, discussed it with her friend, and they agreed. So I sat in the VIP, lounge while I waited for them to change into their public attire. The three of us went to dinner at the venue of their choice—some seafood place. We had a great conversation that involved stories about girls making out with each other and other sexual deviations. I was certain that this night was going to be the crowning achievement in my young life and that I would become a legend among my friends. As the dinner wound down, I was devising my plan to get them back to the enormous suite we had at the Royal Sonesta. I suggested that we all should meet up with the rest of our group. They responded: "Why don't you come to Baton Rouge with us?" Baton Rouge? This seemed like an interesting idea, but the more I thought about it, the more I realized that only bad things could happen. First, it was forty-five minutes away and I had an eight A.M. flight the next day. Secondly, I started envisioning myself getting smacked over the head with a brick and being violated on a pommel horse in some backwater basement in the bayou. So, common sense prevailed and I had to give up the dream that seemed so close just moments before. I'll always wonder what might have been, but at least I still can say that this "state senator" had dinner with two strippers.

Rent a Porsche and Just Drive

Ah shit, it's only Wednesday and the forecast is already calling for a pitifully lame weekend ahead. Yeah, there are a couple of college football games to watch, a *Road Rules* marathon on MTV, and possibly a keg party at some chick's place—but nothing too terribly exciting. This scenario (which happens approximately 16.5 times a year) presents the perfect opportunity for you to make something happen. And that something just might be you and **the power of a Porsche**. Invite a buddy if you want, and split the rental cost. Start out by cruising through all the local hot spots where you might run into an ex-girlfriend or some chick who gave you a fake number two weekends ago, grab a Starbucks, hit that bagel place, sit outside your Porsche talking on your phone. Yell shit like **"Yeah, I would like to own** a baseball team," and "five million—shit, that's a bargain. Take it." After a little parading around, it's time to take the little bitch out for a drive. Hit the highway, **find some long, old country roads**, and see how fast this fine piece of machinery can go. Enjoy the thrill that is a Porsche. Drive until it gets dark. Crash at the nearest hotel. Ask every local girl if they've ever given road head in a Porsche. And the next day, drive home, romp around the town again, then sadly hand over the keys to the sales guy at the luxury rental car place and cry the whole way home in your friend's Kia.

Destination Unknown

This is the ultimate leap of faith for friends. The way this idea works is that, once or twice a year a group of you and your buddies will venture off somewhere for a long weekend. The twist is that **only one guy will know where the hell you're actually going**. Yes, each time a different guy is in charge of planning absolutely everything. He merely tells you what to bring and when to be at the airport, at the train station, or what time he'll be picking you up. Whether it's Vegas, Miami, or just a road trip to a party one hundred miles away, thrown by that girl you met on the Internet, no one knows what's up until the day you leave. The hilarious part is not only the surprise factor, but **the competition that no doubt will take place to outdo each other**. "Okay, last time we hit Memphis, saw Graceland, got lap dances from a female Elvis impersonator . . . this time we're going to Vancouver, flying in a seaplane, going rafting, and getting lap dances from someone without fake chops." You should set up price limits for each trip and push the guy in charge to work for the best deals possible. It's pressure, no doubt. But just remember—as long as at some point you and your buddies are getting drunk with hot women you've done okay. Certainly, **refer to our other chapters for inspiration**. Golf always is a winner. Sporting venues certainly make for good times. And of course there's Vegas, Atlantic City, New Orleans, or Amsterdam. The decision will be tough; take into account accommodations, side ventures, and everything else. As the cruise director, you'll need to make the others on board happy.

Crash a Wedding

By now we've all seen the movie *Wedding Crashers* (or, at least, should have). And, unquestionably, thoughts of **taking advantage of vulnerable bridesmaids** and every other single female, as they wallow in their "I want to be married" and "that should be me up there" frame of mind, is most likely on your radar. So, yes, you should absolutely go to a random wedding where you don't know a soul. Be a torso model, a matador, or the inventor of The Clapper. Make out with the hot aunt, the desperate maid of honor, or the barely legal cousin. Your best bet for locking down a random wedding is by checking out the engagement announcements in the local paper or the upcoming wedding dates at churches and temples. Verify the ages of the couple, the younger they are the more "available" guests there will be. Also, although it won't count as much, you could crash a wedding that a friend is attending, as long as nobody else knows you. Cocktail parties and dancing are ripe for making your entrance. However, **the dinner can be tough**, particularly if there's assigned seating. If it's a buffet, you're golden. Otherwise, just duck out for a couple of hours and slam some beers with the valet guys, then sneak back during the daddy-daughter dance. Make it a goal to get invited to another wedding with someone you met at the one you crashed.

For a twist on things, **you can also try crashing a wedding to which you've actually been invited**. Yes, at some point in time, some girl that you hardly know is going to ask you to her second cousin's wedding, where you'll know exactly zero other attendees. In this instance, we highly encourage you to **crash it by becoming "that guy."** "That guy" is the guy shotgunning a beer on top of a table, behind the bar making martinis, dirty dancing with the bride, mooning the videographer, performing the "robot" to a slow song, and wearing only his T-shirt by the end of the night. "Who is that guy?" people will ask. Give a toast about how you and the groom picked up Russian chicks or flew in Vietnam together. Your date will be appalled or may love you. Either way, you barely knew her, you definitely didn't know anyone else, and you will be all that anyone remembers about that couple's wedding. Oh, please, please be that guy. Every good wedding needs that guy. **We love that guy.**

CHECK IT OFF
Your "continued weekend freedom" list

- [ ] Play PlayStation for an entire weekend.
- [ ] Smoke dope and play PlayStation for an entire weekend.
- [ ] Smoke dope, drink beers, and play PlayStation for an entire weekend.
- [ ] Play seventy-two holes of golf in one weekend.
- [ ] Get a keg, get some friends, and see how long it takes to kill it.
- [ ] Attend or compete in a women's Jell-O or mud wrestling match.
- [ ] Win a karaoke contest singing "Born to be my Baby" by Bon Jovi.
- [ ] Host a party with a topless waitress.
- [ ] Host a bachelor party for someone who's not getting married.
- [ ] Road trip to the nearest big city to your south.

☐ Road trip to the nearest big city to your north.

☐ Tailgate at the nearest sporting event—who cares what it is.

☐ Bloody Mary's at ten A.M., beers at noon, martinis at three P.M.

☐ Hold a party with midgets or monkeys serving drinks.

☐ Throw a backyard party with a blow-up boxing ring and giant gloves or sumo wrestling.

☐ Throw a normal Friday bash, only tell one of your buddies that it's a seventies costume party.

☐ Throw a normal Friday bash, only tell one of your buddies that it's a diaper party.

☐ Declare any weekend "The Weekend of (Insert your name here)."

CHAPTER EIGHT

DON'T WAIT. PLAN IT. DO IT.

This is the official **"get off your ass"** section. Yeah, it's kind of stupid, but the reality of the situation is that the only way in hell you're going to truly live out this period of your life **the way you should** is by planning, plotting, and motivating. You need to be an instigator and you need to be proactive. Otherwise, you're going to miss out on some incredible experiences, unbelievable opportunities, and unforgettable moments in time. On the following pages you can list your top places to travel, top fests, sporting events, and so on. You can then attempt to plug those into your annual "Check It Off" Log. And start planning what you are going to do while you still can. Then, keep track of your achievements as you progress. While you examine your list, pull out a calendar and look at all the months ahead of you. Then think about when you can best get this stuff done.

As a crazy, drunk man wearing a bright orange hat and hailing from Northern Minnesota once said **"Be a predator, not a scavenger . . . the kill is always better."** We're not sure if he was just talking about shooting deer, but, when it comes to living your life, it's a pretty damn good metaphor. You can't sit back and wait for things to happen. So get going now, because all too soon this period of freedom will go bye-bye. Do it all now, so that when it's gone you won't be left wondering "Why the hell did I pass up on that trip to Montreal for Dave's bachelor party?" We've also thrown in some scare tactics with lists about what life will someday become. Hey, fear is a great motivational technique, and we're willing to do whatever it takes to get through to you. Anyway, have fun with this, and some day when your boss comes by, drops a turd on your desk, and asks you to work the weekend, at least you'll know that in fifteen days you'll be scuba diving with sharks by day, engaging in a Caribbean-style pub crawl at night, and waking up naked on the beach with Jennifer Love Hewitt's younger, larger-breasted sister. Or something like that.

THE OFFICIAL "CHECK IT OFF" QUESTIONNAIRE

- How old are you?
- Roughly (and realistically) how many years do you have before marriage?

That's it. Just think about how old you are and precisely how **few** years you really have left until you're standing scared shitless at the altar. Okay, now subtract 1.5 years off your estimate, because, between dating your future wife, the engagement process, and the fact that everyone gets married and responsible sooner than they think, you're probably wrong. Now, how many years do you really have? Or is it months? Holy shit—don't tell us weeks. Fuck. Get to Rio quick. Or hit Hedonism! Or screw it—drop this book, run to the airport, call your best friend, and fly on the first plane to Vegas! Otherwise, start putting your plan together.

SOMEDAY YOU WILL:

- Wake up early to get a head start on chores, errands, and other household duties.
- Cut yourself off at three beers, due to your fear of a hangover.
- Vacation at Disney World.
- Spend Friday night shopping at Target.
- Kill a Saturday at the petting zoo.
- Have a discussion about diaper-changing techniques.
- Deliberate over what kind of comforter cover you'd like for your bed.
- Referee an eight-year-old girl's soccer game.
- Drive a minivan because you "find it very practical."
- Hang out with guys who also drive minivans.
- Feel wrong about attending a wet T-shirt contest.
- Feel wrong about yelling "show me your tits!"
- Look at the guys on *Sports Center* and not know who they are.
- Turn on Nickelodeon and know exactly who everybody is.
- Scroll through the message boards of some baby Web site, looking for crib information.
- Frequent Chucky Cheese.
- Take a vacation that involves waterslides, ice-cream sundaes, and tour buses.

- Look at the brochure for a romantic B & B and think "how quaint and nice."
- Spend multiple weekends just on lawn maintenance.
- Consider a Blockbuster Night a "fun" evening.
- Look forward to work for no other reason than it gets you out of the house.
- Be responsible for cooking dinner on Tuesdays and Thursday. (Ordering pizza doesn't cut it.)
- Buy clothes only because they're wrinkle-free.
- Have more breast milk than beer in your fridge.
- Pay ten dollars an hour for a babysitter.
- Get caught inappropriately checking out the babysitter.
- Host a housewarming party, a baby shower, and a princess-themed birthday party.
- Get in trouble for coming home smelling like a stripper.
- Get in trouble for coming home thirty minutes later than you said you would.
- Not remember the last time you did a shot.
- Not recall the last time you got shitfaced with your buddies.
- Totally forget what your life right now was like.

WARNING SIGNS THAT YOUR DAYS ARE NUMBERED

- You joined a running club.
- You read the paper every Sunday.
- You bought a dog.
- You find yourself cleaning your apartment a lot.
- You choose "getting sleep" over "getting it on" with some chick.
- You stop eating late-night food.
- You find yourself watching the news instead of Comedy Central.

- You look at a girl and "How do I get her pants off?" doesn't cross your mind.
- Your roommates want to start charging your girlfriend rent.
- Your girlfriend is dieting in preparation of her first wedding dress fitting.
- Your girlfriend cried at the last wedding you were at.
- Your girlfriend and you have a list of "great date places."
- Your girlfriend's friends have a nickname for you.
- You say "we" a shitload more than "I."
- Your girlfriend is changing the way you dress, the decorations in your bedroom, and the food in your fridge.
- You passed up "free beer" at last Friday's happy hour.
- You choose a less crowded bar, not because it'd be easier to get a drink, but because you want a less chaotic atmosphere.
- The bartender called "last call" fifteen minutes early and you didn't get pissed off.
- You refused to drink from a used cup at a keg party, leaving behind free beer and many hot chicks.
- Your fridge is covered in wedding invites and baby announcements.
- You pay attention to financial planning commercials.
- You frequently say things like "synergize," "out-of-the-box thinking," and "whiteboard."
- You complain about a neighbor's loud party.
- Your best friends are couples, not just guys.
- You have more than ten ties.
- You've thought about who your groomsmen are going to be.

DURING THE WRITING OF THIS BOOK, WE'VE COME TO REALIZE:

- Booze invariably plays a leading role in most hilarious stories.
- In fact, if you're in search of a good story just get smashed in a different town and that should lead you to one.
- Thinking and writing about all the stupid things our friends (and we) have done is both great fun and scary.
- If you get drunk on an average of just two times a week for ten years, then you will have been smashed 1,040 times (and this is probably being a little conservative.)
- How many of those approximately 1,040 times have good stories to go with them?
- Although funny, these three stories had no place in our book (or anywhere really):
  1. Our buddy who had a Thai massage girl stay with him for three days in New York, during which she wore only his Real Madrid jersey and ate orange sherbet. Yes, that story had several happy endings.
  2. The guy who was so drunk that, while engaging in the act with his girlfriend, he started screwing the couch cushion instead of her. And she called him on it.
  3. The story about a guy peeing in a bar, losing his balance, and falling into a promotional Camel cigarette stand with his dick still out.
- Discovering cool places to go is exciting.
- Thinking about never getting to all the cool places is a downer.
- People love to tell great stories because it's proof that they've truly lived.
- If you don't have any good stories, you'd better start trying.
- Using "I'm writing a book" as a pick-up line in a bar is a total hit or a big miss.

- Using "I'm a silver medalist in the luge" as a pick up line is always a hit.
- The thought of publishing a book about doing fun shit and being a jackass is a little weird.
- There are way too many books about how to "better" yourself with good habits and hard work, and not nearly enough about how to "better" yourself by having a good old time.
- We love the words, "shitload," "debauchery," and "boobs."
- If you follow the advice in this book, you will often find yourself surrounded by a shitload of debauchery and boobs.
- If we could have bought stock in Vegas, Mardi Gras beads, or the phrase "show me your tits," we would have—and we'd be very rich.
- The more things you do that cause you to say "I can now die happy," the better.
- We're not sure if our parents will laugh or cry when they read this.

TIM'S TOP TEN "OH CRAP, I SHOULD'VE DONE THAT" LIST

1. Sailed a yacht into Jost Van Dyke for New Year's Eve
2. Spent a year as a ski resort bum, or any bum for that matter
3. Gone scuba diving in Phuket, Thailand
4. Thrown a bogus bachelor party every year for any friend
5. Gone rafting in Patagonia, followed by Carnival in Rio
6. Cannonballs at the Playboy mansion pool
7. Kentucky Derby (damn, I even passed on an invite)
8. Road trip from Whistler, Canada, to Tijuana, Mexico
9. Pedalled in a Big Wheel Pub Crawl
10. Traveled to the Far East for an indefinite amount of time

MICHAEL'S TOP TEN "I STILL GOT TIME TO DO" LIST

1. Fish the Kona Peninsula.
2. Organize a "Win a Trip to Rio" flip cup tournament.
3. Drink a Budweiser in the Sistine Chapel.
4. Throw a New Year's party at the Hefner suite of the Playboy Hotel.
5. Road trip in John Madden–like cruiser.
6. Run the Dublin marathon, finish with a pint of Guinness.
7. Do the worm at Oktoberfest in Munich.
8. Ride an elephant (the animal, for clarification).
9. Sleep in a tepee anywhere.
10. Be a pirate for Halloween, meet a girl, and make her say "Argggg!"

TOP TEN "THINGS YOU SHOULD NEVER TELL A GIRLFRIEND, MENTION AT A FAMILY REUNION, OR UTTER AT A JOB INTERVIEW" LIST

1. The Viking "all-inclusive" resort
2. Amsterdam
3. Hedonism
4. Exotic Erotic Ball
5. Lake Havasu
6. Fantasy Fest
7. Tijuana
8. Anything between midnight and eight A.M. in Thailand
9. Nudes-a-Poppin' Pageant
10. That one time in Vegas

TOP TEN "YOU ARE OUR HERO" LIST

1. There's a girl out there who thinks you are a prize-winning matador.
2. You've golfed three or more of the infamous courses of Scotland.

3. You've tailgated at five or more of the college football stadiums listed.

4. You have been to a bachelor party in Vegas, Montreal, and Tijuana.

5. You've drank a beer at Oktoberfest, Milwaukee Summerfest, and après ski in Whistler.

6. You've gotten a lap dance in more than three countries.

7. You've celebrated St. Patty's Day in Dublin, Chicago, and New York.

8. You've hooked up at a Halloween party with a nurse, a devil, and a Catholic schoolgirl.

9. You've caught a 150-pound fish and swam with a shark.

10. You've spent a year or more doing one of the jobs listed.

TOP TEN "STORY LINES THAT YOU MIGHT WANT TO KEEP TO YOURSELF" LIST:

1. "So we ended up snuggling."

2. "And now I'm not allowed in the Spearmint Rhino in Vegas anymore."

3. "I still can't figure out why it burns when I pee."

4. "I had tickets to the Super Bowl, but I got too drunk to go."

5. "If you pay for it, it's not cheating, right?"

6. "Yeah, I caught a foul ball at Game six of the 2004 Cubs playoff game!"

7. "She wasn't that old, and she had all of her teeth, I think."

8. "Bangkok is awesome, I was there for like three weeks, not including that other week."

9. "I got fired from my job—which was chipping icicles in Vail."

10. "We were hiking in Appalachia and met these local guys. . . ."

YOUR TOP TWENTY-FIVE LIST

Think wisely about this. Which activities will procure the best stories; which are absolutely something you'll not be able to do after you walk down the aisle; which ones need more planning; and which ones can you try to check off this weekend.

1.
2.
3.
4.
5.
6.
7.
8.
9.
10.
11.
12.
13.
14.
15.
16.
17.
18.
19.
20.
21.
22.
23.
24.
25.

CHECK IT OFF
Year 1

(Include a minimum of two fests, one sporting event, one adventure or party or world wandering, and three lost weekends.)

- [ ]
- [ ]
- [ ]
- [ ]
- [ ]
- [ ]
- [ ]
- [ ]
- [ ]
- [ ]
- [ ]
- [ ]

CHECK IT OFF
Year 2

(Include a minimum of two fests, one sporting event, one adventure or party or world wandering, and three lost weekends.)

- [ ]
- [ ]
- [ ]

(continued)

- ☐
- ☐
- ☐
- ☐
- ☐
- ☐
- ☐
- ☐

CHECK IT OFF
Year 3

(Include a minimum of two fests, one sporting event, one adventure or party or world wandering, and three lost weekends.)

- ☐
- ☐
- ☐
- ☐
- ☐
- ☐
- ☐
- ☐
- ☐
- ☐
- ☐
- ☐

CHECK IT OFF
Year 4

(Include a minimum of two fests, one sporting event, one adventure or party or world wandering and three lost weekends.)

- ☐
- ☐
- ☐
- ☐
- ☐
- ☐
- ☐
- ☐
- ☐
- ☐
- ☐

YES, I HAVE CHECKED THIS OFF:

- ☐
- ☐
- ☐
- ☐
- ☐
- ☐

(continued)